The Holocaust
in University Teaching

HOLOCAUST SERIES

The Holocaust Series will publish original, interdisciplinary research centering on Jewish life and the Holocaust. Drawing on history, theology, art, philosophy, psychology and many other fields of the social sciences, the series will cover hitherto unexplored areas of Holocaust Studies shedding light on the human and social conditions of the period.

The International Center for University Teaching of Jewish Civilization

Academic Chairman   Moshe Davis

Director of Publications   Priscilla Fishman

Continuing Workshop on University Teaching of Jewish Civilization

Director   Gideon Shimoni

Workshop Coordinator   Matelle Godfrey

Advisory Committee   Haim Avni, Israel
Michael Brown, Canada
Deborah Dash Moore, U.S.A.
Sally Frankental, South Africa
Paula Hyman, U.S.A.
Judit Liwerant, Mexico
Dalia Ofer, Israel
Mervin F. Verbit, U.S.A.

The continuing workshop is made possible with the assistance of the Joint Program for Jewish Education (State of Israel Ministry of Education and Culture — The Jewish Agency for Israel — World Zionist Organization) and the Memorial Foundation for Jewish Culture.

The Holocaust in University Teaching

Edited by

GIDEON SHIMONI

This volume has been prepared
in association with the International Center for
University Teaching of Jewish Civilization, Jerusalem

PERGAMON PRESS

Member of Maxwell Macmillan Pergamon Publishing Corporation

OXFORD · NEW YORK · BEIJING · FRANKFURT
SEOUL · SYDNEY · TOKYO

U.K.	Pergamon Press plc, Headington Hill Hall, Oxford OX3 0BW, England
U.S.A.	Pergamon Press, Inc, Maxwell House, Fairview Park, Elmsford, New York 10523, USA
PEOPLE'S REPUBLIC OF CHINA	Maxwell Pergamon China, Beijing Exhibition Centre, Xizhimenwai Dajie, Beijing 100044, People's Republic of China
GERMANY	Pergamon Press GmbH, Hammerweg 6, D-6242 Kronberg, Germany
KOREA	Pergamon Press Korea, KPO Box 315, Seoul 110-603, Korea
AUSTRALIA	Maxwell Macmillan Pergamon Publishing Australia Pty Ltd, Lakes Business Park, 2 Lord Street, Botany, NSW 2019, Australia
JAPAN	Pergamon Press, 8th Floor, Matsuoka Central Building, 1-7-1 Nishi-Shinjuku, Shinjuku-ku, Tokyo 160, Japan

First edition 1991

Library of Congress Cataloging-in-Publication Data
The Holocaust in university teaching/edited by
Gideon Shimoni. – 1st ed.
p. cm.
"Prepared in association with the International Center for University Teaching of Jewish Civilization, Jerusalem."
Includes bibliographical references.
1. Holocaust, Jewish (1939–1945) — Study and teaching (Higher) — Outlines, syllabi, etc.
I. Shimoni, Gideon. II. International Center for University Teaching of Jewish Civilization.
D804.3.H647 1991 940.53'18'0711–dc20 90–28617

British Library Cataloguing in Publication Data
The Holocaust in university teaching. — (Holocaust series).
1. Jews. Genocide
I. Shimoni, Gideon II. International Center for University Teaching of Jewish Civilization
940.5318
ISBN 0–08–040798–6

Printed in Great Britain by BPCC Wheatons Ltd, Exeter

Dedicated to

SAMUEL AND ESTHER BROCHSTEIN

Models of a learning Jewish family

CONTENTS

EDITOR'S PREFACE

This publication is the second of its kind to result from the Workshop on the Teaching of Contemporary Jewish Civilization which forms part of the International Center for University Teaching of Jewish Civilization established in Jerusalem by Professor Moshe Davis in 1980. Following the lines of its predecessor, which presented syllabi on Contemporary Jewish Civilization,* the present volume focuses specifically on the Holocaust, a subject on which courses proliferate at universities in the United States, Israel and a number of other countries.

The syllabi are here presented in a standardized format that provides the reader not only with a course outline and readings, but also with an explanation of the considerations, conceptual frameworks and objectives that inform each syllabus. At the same time, the autonomy and individuality of each contributor has been respected, allowing for varying degrees of detail in the presentation as well as for differences in course structure, methodology and prescribed readings. In some cases, the contributors have included examples of examination questions and essay topics that further illuminate the process of study that the course means to stimulate.

The publication as a whole is a cooperative product of participants in the seventh session of the Contemporary Jewish Civilization Workshop. Entitled "University Teaching about the Holocaust; Concepts and Resources," it was held in Jerusalem in July 1988 with the participation of twenty-five university teachers in a variety of academic disciplines and from various countries. The syllabi included in this book reflect the mutual exchange of teaching experiences, concepts and bibliographies within the workshop. In addition, a number of colleagues who were unable to accept the invitation to join the workshop nevertheless agreed to contribute their syllabi for publication.

---

* G. Shimoni, ed., **Contemporary Jewish Civilization: Selected Syllabi** (New York: Markus Wiener Publishing, Inc., 1985).

At the workshop session it became evident that there are considerable differences of approach among academics who teach on this particularly sensitive and emotion-laden subject. Some of these differences arise from the varied teaching contexts in which professors function; for example, small, selective, private universities in contrast with large colleges, or Israeli students in contrast with mixed Jewish and Gentile student attendance at courses in other countries. Other differences of approach were of a more fundamental nature, arising from the often precarious balance between passionate involvement in the awesome human issues evoked by exposure to knowledge of the Holocaust on the one hand, and the academic ideal of detached objectivity, on the other. The differences in approach aired at the workshop are reflected in some of the syllabi presentations in this volume.

The workshop also considered the possibilities of multi-disciplinary teaching about the Holocaust, the place of theological and philosophical reflection in the wake of the Holocaust, and the use of art and film in teaching the subject. These issues and ideas find expression in the short essays that constitute Section I of this volume.

In the interests of multi-disciplinary enrichment, and in conformity with the approach used in the workshop itself, the syllabi have not been arranged according to academic discipline. The wide interest on the part of both scholars and students evoked by this painful but enormously important subject is reflected in the broad range of the syllabi and the wide geographical dispersion of the courses given - from the United States and Israel through to Brazil and Australia. Although history courses form the major cluster, the range of courses offered is strikingly diversified. It includes courses as different as Isidoro Blikstein's highly specific "Semiology of Nazism" and David Roskies' broad historical canvas of "Jewish Responses to Catastrophe" or Colin Tatz's "The Politics of Genocide"; it ranges over literature courses, such as those of Anita Norich and Sidra Ezrahi, the theological vantage points of James Moore and Jocelyn Hellig, and the sociological foci of William Helmreich and Nechama Tec.

The syllabi are here presented essentially as offered in practice. They purport neither to be models of excellence for universal emulation nor to be representative of every variant in the field. Rather, they are offered to stimulate mutual exchange of ideas and experience, to indicate to a broader academic public what kinds of courses are being offered in various countries and university contexts and, in so doing, hopefully to stimulate the development of enhanced course options on this important subject. For the greater convenience of teachers and interested readers alike, a bibliography is provided. It lists all the works cited in the essays and syllabi included in this volume. To these items we have added two important reference works that have appeared very recently and that will undoubtedly be indispensable to all those teaching in this field:

M. Gilbert, **Atlas of the Holocaust** (Oxford: Pergamon Press, 1988).

Y. Gutman (ed. in chief), **Encyclopedia of the Holocaust** (Jerusalem: Yad Vashem, 1990).

I wish to thank the workshop participants for their collegial cooperation; Priscilla Fishman, the International Center's publications editor, for her untiring help in preparing the typescript; Jane Vogel-Fischman for her generous assistance in proof-reading; Glenda Kershaw, Desk Editor for the Social Sciences at Pergamon Press, Oxford, for her initiative in preparing the bibliography; and Hana Abels for her valuable aid in completing the entries in Jerusalem.

Gideon Shimoni
Jerusalem

I. TEACHING APPROACHES AND RESOURCES

THE VISUAL ARTS AS AN AID FOR TEACHING ABOUT THE HOLOCAUST

Ziva Amishai-Maisels
Department of Art, The Hebrew University of Jerusalem

The visual arts are among the most underused resources in teaching about the Holocaust. This may be attributed to the teachers' lack of art or art history training, and the even greater lack of adequate texts, collections of photographs, and slides. However, the many advantages that can be derived from the inclusion of visual arts resources within the structure of a course make the investment of the necessary time and effort worthwhile.

A well-worn but true adage holds that "a picture is worth a thousand words". Many students indeed respond more strongly to visual materials than to oral discussions or written texts, and are not being adequately reached by a course which is solely oral or textual. Some teachers recognize this and add photographs and films to their curriculum, both in order to reach these students and to impress all the others. However, the visual arts offer several advantages over photographic material, and can be used to supplement it.

For instance, documentary drawings by camp inmates or liberators often record scenes not otherwise available. This is especially true with regard to depictions of all phases of daily life in the camps. Such material has the added force of a primary document, since most camp art was created for this specific purpose. This category of material has been amply published;[1] books such as Blatter and Milton's **Art of the Holocaust** and Green's **Artists of Terezin** should be placed on all Holocaust course reading lists, and can be used in various class contexts.

Non-inmate art also has a documentary value. For example, it is important to note through contemporary works of art, particularly those of left-wing artists, just how early the basic facts on the Holocaust were known and depicted. Artistic expressions of the fight against the Nazis date from the early 1920s, with well-known German artists such as Otto Dix, George Grosz, and John Heartfield in the forefront of this battle. The struggle continued in Germany and abroad after Hitler's rise to power and even during the war itself, forming an artistic resistance which has been studied in depth.[2]

Camp inmate art also provides us with important insights into the psychological responses of the prisoners to various situations. This can be seen through an analysis of their selection and arrangement of scenes, their choice of style, and the expressive factors which they consciously or unconsciously display in depicting their life. For instance, the need to impose control on a life in which they were powerless led to restrained, orderly depictions of camp activities, occasionally so calm and commonplace that it is hard to believe that they took place in a camp. On the other hand, the negative feelings engendered by life in the camps - hatred of the situation, horror at atrocities, etc. - found an outlet in expressionistic renderings of camp life. Interestingly, both responses can be found within the works of one and the same artist who reacted to different aspects of camp life in extremely different ways.[3]

These psychological reactions can also be found in non-inmate art which can be used to explain underlying ideas about the Holocaust and the public's reaction to it, in the same manner that one utilizes non-inmate literature. Art and literature are complementary modes of cultural expression and response, and much can be learned both from the manner in which text and picture complement each other in presenting a more comprehensive view of the Holocaust, and from the ways they differ from each other in responding to a particular event or presenting a specific idea. The artistic problems of depicting the Holocaust are not only esthetic; they reflect the problematics of the public's ability to confront the Holocaust and to understand its details. For instance, the tendency to deny the Holocaust can be seen in the withdrawal of a whole generation of West German artists into abstraction, and their refusal to deal with the war period. At the same time, many artists and critics in Europe and America were unable to admit publicly that specific works of art dealt with images taken from the Holocaust or were in any way influenced by it. A combination of denial with a tendency to universalize the Holocaust has even led to a recent attempt to take a major work which specifically deals with the Holocaust, Pablo Picasso's **Charnel House** (1945), and interpret it as a general anti-war statement.[4]

Finally, the artistic approach to the moral lessons drawn from the Holocaust, and the attempts made to interpret it in symbolic terms, reveal a good deal about our own - and the students' - attempts to cope with and understand the meaning of that event. For instance, the need to put the Holocaust into a historic or religious framework, in order to be able to comprehend its significance, can be found in art in the development of the prototypical biblical or mythological hero and martyr as symbols of the Resistance fighter or the Holocaust victim respectively.[5] In like manner, the problems faced by artists in portraying the Nazi, and the various solutions they created to depict and to stress the contrast between the normality of his appearance and the monstrous way he behaved, can be well utilized in any discussion on the "banality of evil" or in a consideration of the problems raised by the Eichmann trial. Art has also confronted the need to curb man's inherently destructive nature, as seen in the Holocaust, in a manner which strongly highlights society's lack of concern and inability to learn the lessons of the Holocaust. A discussion of the work of Zoran Music, a survivor of Dachau who returned in the 1970s to his camp drawings to create a series entitled "We Are Not the Last," could be very rewarding in a class dealing with the moral dilemmas of the post-Holocaust world.[6]

To explain the possible uses of the visual arts in teaching about the Holocaust, I have chosen a few examples which fit into some of the different contexts in which the subject is taught.

In the framework of courses on general and Jewish history, inmate drawings are invaluable primary documents for aspects of camp life not covered by photographs. They depict both what it looked like and what it felt like to be in situations such as cattle-cars, gas chambers, death marches, etc. The force of these human documents cannot be exaggerated, and since they were for the most part based on personal experience and told in the simplest and most straightforward terms and naturalistic styles, their impact is increased sevenfold. Moreover, if the historian wishes to examine with his students the nature of the witness-report documentation and all its problems, a great deal can be learned by comparing these drawings with each other, with photographs, and with witness-report texts describing the same or similar situations. Such comparisons will clarify in a striking manner not only the existence of different approaches to reality, but the extent to which a change of emphasis in supposedly similar impartial reports can convey an entirely different impression of the facts. It will then be possible to analyze the reasons underlying these differences: the character of the witness, the conditions under which he or she produced the report, and the goals the artist wished to attain, including the message to be conveyed to the spectator.

Another example: the Stroop Report, the main photographic document on the Warsaw Ghetto revolt, offers a very one-sided view of that event. Although there were seemingly no surviving artist-witness reports, artists who later wished to tell the whole story often compressed it into a single scene, conveying their meaning with accepted, and thus easily readable, images. For instance, most artists stress that the ghetto resistance fighters were Jewish by including an older bearded man in some form of

Jewish garment among the fighters.   Many artists also stress both the heroic stand of the ghetto and its inevitable fall by showing the heroes overwhelmed by Nazi forces or falling over even as they urge their comrades to deeds of greater courage.[7] In such works, a response is being evoked which is not only narratively more clear than the Stroop Report photographs, but may actually make us more aware of the elements of courage and revolt, even in submission, as apparent in the faces and stances of the conquered ghetto fighters in the photographs, men and women alike.   Comparison of the works of art to the documentary photographs on the one hand, and to later film and literary reconstructions of the revolt on the other, can be illuminating for the students both in examining the actual history of the revolt and in comparing the facts to contemporary and to later perceptions of the event.

In literature classes dealing with the Holocaust, an examination of the visual arts will help to define more clearly many of the problems of witness-reports and memoirs with their inherent play between art and reality (as discussed above), and of pre-Holocaust warnings and post-Holocaust interpretations.   Art contains all the categories of response found in literature and projects many of the same esthetic problems even more strongly and clearly.   For instance, both art and literature deal with questions of how one can express horror and atrocity in art forms which have rules of beauty and decorum, to what extent these elements are open to an interplay with eroticism, and the values and dangers posed by the injection of either beauty or eroticism into this context.   In like manner, both fields deal with such problems as the possibility of creating poetry and/or painting *after* Auschwitz and *about* Auschwitz, the validity of personal interpretations of historical events, and the problem of style, i.e., the distortion of syntax and form in order to convey expression.

There are, however, several important differences between literature and art dealing with the Holocaust, and they reveal interesting facets of the possibilities and limitations of each medium.   For instance, the widespread prevalence of the Sacrifice of Isaac as a primary Holocaust symbol in literature is not apparent in art, where it is replaced by the image of the crucified Jew.   The reasons for this difference lie in the traditions inherent in each medium.   Literature has long used the Sacrifice of Isaac as an archetype for Jewish martyrdom (often ignoring the fact that Isaac was spared at the last moment), contrasting his salvation with the death of more modern martyrs, or hinting at an alternate tradition that told of Isaac's death and resurrection.[8] The writers thus had behind them not only a tradition, but a wide gamut of responses on which they could enlarge.

In art, however, the traditional approach to the Sacrifice of Isaac was much more limited; the moment chosen for depiction was constantly that in which the angel appears and stops the sacrifice. Artists such as Mordechai Ardon, Frederick Terna, and George Segal, who wished to apply this theme to the Holocaust, had to take great liberties with the visual tradition and, in fact, often relied on literary texts in portraying Isaac dead on the altar, Abraham committing suicide rather than kill his son, or Abraham and Isaac slaughtered together, side by side.[9] On the other hand, Christian art had always seen the Sacrifice as a prefiguration of the Crucifixion. The tradition of painting Christ as a Jew had been firmly established by Rembrandt in the seventeenth century and had been revived by major Jewish artists in the 1870s as part of their dialogue with the Christian world. It was thus much easier for artists such as Chagall to adopt the Crucifixion - a theme in which the victim is clearly and visibly killed - to a Holocaust context, in the process continuing the dialogue with Christians in general and with the Church in particular, and using their own major symbol to take them to task for their part in the Holocaust.[10] An analysis of these differences, as well as of the different messages which devolve from the particular symbol chosen to represent the Holocaust can greatly enhance the student's understanding of the specific subject under analysis and of the problematics of symbolism in this context in general.

The use in art of Crucifixion symbolism could also be fully analyzed in Christian theology or general religion classes dealing with the Holocaust and its implications. This visual image, the various ways it was applied in art and the images with which it was combined throw a great deal of light on all phases of Christian involvement in antisemitism, the problematic reactions of the Church to the Holocaust, and Jewish and Christian responses to these reactions. Jewish artists used this symbolism as a way of both beseeching Christians to stop the Holocaust and blaming them for their deeds. The fact that Christian artists, such as Graham Sutherland, also used this symbolism, and that photographs of Holocaust victims served as the model for his Crucifixion in St. Matthew's Church, Northampton (England) should make the student think deeply about the many implications of the Holocaust for the Christian, not only in terms of history, but in terms of life in a post-Holocaust world.[11] In a class on Christian theology, such visual imagery is unexpected, and it can thus be highly effective in bringing the prejudices and preconceptions of the students to the surface so that the teacher can analyze them and can encourage and help the students to deal with them.

For classes in Judaism or Jewish studies, another level of discussion can be equally profitable: the expression of Jewish identity during and after the Holocaust. On the one hand, the heightening of Jewish consciousness during and after the war - as can be seen in the building of Jewish schools, synagogues and community centers - is found quite early in art, in the stress on Jewish identity through subject matter. In fact, even left-wing and/or anti-religious Jewish artists, such as Ben Shahn and William

Gropper, in the early 1940s suddenly started to depict bearded Jews wrapped in their prayer shawls, deep in prayer. The trauma of the Holocaust had a lasting effect on these artists: Gropper continued to depict Jews in prayer every year as a form of *yahrzeit* for the victims of the Holocaust, and began painting *shtetl* scenes; Shahn became involved with Jewish symbols and Hebrew texts in his works.[12]

It is possibly even more relevant to today's college students to explore the responses of younger artists to this same problem, especially as they react in an opposite manner. Instead of the Holocaust causing them to return to Judaism, several modern artists, such as Ron Kitaj, have turned to the Holocaust as part - possibly even the major part - of their rediscovery of Judaism. For such artists who lack any religious upbringing, the Holocaust experience, rather than *shtetl* life or religious observance, becomes the epitome of Judaism.[13] A discussion of this change can add a great deal to the Jewish student's understanding of his own reaction to the Holocaust and to Judaism, and of the reactions of Jewry as a whole to this trauma.

In all the above examples, care has been taken to choose artists who use a figurative mode of expression, so that their art and their messages may be more easily understood by teachers and students alike. This is especially important for students, as many of them may have a highly developed visual and esthetic sense, but neither exposure to nor understanding of the more modern modes of expression in art. The teacher needs no special art training in order to deal with the materials cited above, beyond the ability to locate the material, analyze what can be seen with the eye, and do the usual amount of background reading before introducing interdisciplinary materials into a classroom. While most of the examples have been specifically chosen for general classroom discussion, suitably trained students with an art or art history background should be encouraged to write and present papers on art-related subjects concerning the Holocaust. The students would thus apply their own strongest sense, their response to visual stimuli, to understanding the subject, and the class and the teacher would be exposed to different and perhaps new ways of looking at the material.

This analysis of the contribution that a study of visual art materials can make to courses on the Holocaust is a dual attempt - to enrich such courses with new material, and to open a dialogue between art history and other disciplines on this subject. Whereas literature has become an acceptable means of enrichment that many teachers readily use, the visual arts still remain relatively untapped, both because of the teachers' diffidence and because of the limited amount of available material - which has not, however, been adequately utilized. My own studies in the field, and those of several colleagues, are greatly enlarging the amount of useful material. It is now up to the teachers to conquer their reluctance and to find their own application for this material.

NOTES

1. For collections of drawings by camp artists, see Janet Blatter and Sybil Milton, **Art of the Holocaust** (New York: Routledge, 1981); Gerald Green, **The Artists of Terezin** (New York: Hawthorn, 1969); **Terezin** (Prague: Jewish Communities in the Czech Lands, 1965); Miriam Novitch, **Resistenza Spirituale: Spiritual Resistance 1940-1945** (Milan: Commune of Milan, 1979); Miriam Novitch, Lucy Dawidowicz & Tom L. Freudenheim, **Spiritual Resistance: Art from the Concentration Camps 1940-1945** (Philadelphia: Jewish Publication Society of America, 1981); Mary S. Costanza, **The Living Witness** (New York: Free Press, 1982); Arturo Benvenuti, **KZ** (Treviso: Trivigiana, 1983); Janina Jaworska, **"Nie wszystek umre..."** (Warsaw: Ksiazka i Wiedza, 1975); **Ueberleben und Widerstehen: Zeichnungen von Haeftlingen des Konzentrationslagers Auschwitz 1940-46** (Cologne: Pahl-Rugenstein, 1980). Many individual artists have also published books of their drawings, e.g., Avigdor Arikha, **Boyhood Drawings Made in Deportation** (Paris: Amis de l'Aliyah des Jeunes, 1971); Leon Delarbre, **Dora, Auschwitz, Buchenwald, Bergen-Belsen, Croquis Clandestins** (Paris: Michel de Romilly, 1945); Auguste Favier & Pierre Mania, **Buchenwald, Scenes pris sur le vif des horreurs Nazis** (Lyon: Imprimerie Artistique en Couleur, 1946); Alfred Kantor, **The Book of Alfred Kantor** (New York: McGraw-Hill, 1971); and Boris Taslitzky, **111 Dessins faits a Buchenwald 1944- 1945** (Paris: Bibliotheque Francaise, 1945). See also the books published by Zinovii Tolkatchev, who entered Maidanek and Auschwitz with the Russian Army.

2. For literature on artistic resistance to the Nazis, see Bologna, Museo Civico, **Arte e Resistenza in Europa,** 26 Apr. -30 May 1965; Erhard Frommhold, **Kunst im Widerstand** (Dresden; VEB, 1968); Werner Haftmann, **Banned and Persecuted** (Cologne: Dumont, 1986); Karlsruhe, Badische Kunstverein, **Widerstand statt Anpassung** (Berlin: Elefanten, 1980); Berlin, Akademie der Kuenste, **Zwischen Widerstand und Anpassung, Kunst in Deutschland 1933-1945,** 17 Sept.-29 Oct. 1978; Duesseldorf, **Bilder sind nicht verboten,** 28 Aug.-24 Oct. 1984.

3. For an analysis of the ways in which these factors work, and especially such dual responses in the work of Boris Taslitzky, see Ziva Amishai-Maisels, "The Complexities of Witnessing," **Holocaust and Genocide Studies** 2, no. 1 (1987), pp. 123-147,

and *idem*, forthcoming book on the influence of the Holocaust on the visual arts. All unfootnoted discussions in the text of this article are analyzed in detail in that book.

4. **Pablo Picasso: A Retrospective** (New York: Museum of Modern Art, 1980), p. 380.

5. For further analysis, see David G. Roskies, **Against the Apocalypse** (Cambridge, Mass.: Harvard University Press, 1984); Ziva Amishai-Maisels, "The Jewish Jesus," **Journal of Jewish Art** (1982), pp. 84-104; *idem*, "The Use of Biblical Imagery to Interpret the Holocaust," **Ninth World Congress of Jewish Studies**, 1985, Division D, vol. 2, pp. 17-24; and *idem*, "Christological Symbolism of the Holocaust," in Y. Bauer et al. (eds.), **Remembering for the Future**, Vol. 2. The Impact of the Holocaust on the Contemporary World (Oxford: Pergamon, 1989), pp. 1657-1671.

6. Paris, Galerie de France, Music: **Nous ne sommes pas les derniers**, 18 Dec. 1970-30 Jan. 1971; **Music: Opere 1946-1985** (Milan: Electa, 1985); Paris, Centre Georges Pompidou, **Music: L'Oeuvre Graphique**, 20 Jan.-20 Mar. 1988.

7. Raphael Mandelzweig (Buenos Aires: Comite de Homenage a R. Mandelzweig, 1950), pls. 40-41 and p. 51; William Gropper, **Your Brother's Blood Cries Out** (New York: New Masses, 1943), pl. 2.

8. Shalom Spiegel, **The Last Trial** (Philadelphia: Jewish Publication Society of America, 1967); *idem*, "Perur Me'Agadot Ha'Akedah," in **The Abraham Weiss Jubilee Volume** (New York: Shulsinger Brothers, 1954), pp. 653-666 (Hebrew).

9. Amishai-Maisels, "The Jewish Jesus," pp. 88-91; *idem*, "Christological Symbolism of the Holocaust" (above, n. 5); Vivian Alpert Thompson, **A Mission in Art: Recent Holocaust Works in America** (Ann Arbor: UMI, 1983), pp. 66-70; Stephen Lewis, **Art out of Agony** (Montreal: Canadian Broadcasting Company, 1984), pp. 114-115.

10. Amishai-Maisels, "The Jewish Jesus" (above, n. 9); idem, "Christological Symbolism of the Holocaust" (above, n. 5).

11. John Hayes, **The Art of Graham Sutherland** (New York: Alpine Fine Arts, 1980), pp. 24-25, 105; Ronald Alley, **Graham Sutherland** (London: Tate Gallery, 1982), pp. 34, 111.

12. Ziva Amishai-Maisels, "Ben Shahn and the Problem of Jewish Identity," **Jewish Art**, vols. 12-13 (1986-87), pp. 304-319; Louis Lozowick, **William Gropper** (Philadelphia: Art Alliance, 1983).

13. London, Marlborough Fine Art, **R.B. Kitaj**, Nov.-Dec. 1985; Marco Livingstone, **R.B. Kitaj** (New York: Rizzoli, 1985); New York, Jewish Museum, **Jewish Themes/Contemporary American Artists II**, 15 July-16 Nov. 1986.

THE HOLOCAUST AS AN APPROPRIATE TOPIC FOR INTERDISCIPLINARY STUDY

Michael Brown
Department of Humanities and Hebrew, York University, Ontario

Although interdisciplinary studies have been fashionable in certain academic quarters for some time, they are not yet universally accepted nor even altogether understood. To some of their detractors and even to some who claim to be practitioners, interdisciplinary studies are equated with the undisciplined use of methodologies with which the instructor or researcher is barely conversant, or avoidance of methodological considerations. To others, interdisciplinary studies mean the parallel presentation of different methodological approaches to an issue, without any attempt to integrate them.

Interdisciplinary studies should, of course, be none of those things. It goes without saying, that any academic course should have a conceptual framework; and that a researcher or an instructor needs to be at least literate in the language(s) he uses. In fact, one of the main impediments to interdisciplinary work is the necessity of thoroughly mastering an additional discipline or disciplines. Shallow or untenable interpretations of unfamiliar texts, works of art, behaviorisms, or other phenomena will do nothing to enlarge understanding. Rather, they will mislead the student, and perhaps even the instructor. The inability to make judgments about art and literature, or to distinguish pop from high culture, or folk religion from sophisticated theology, can lead at best to partially correct generalizations about the individuals and society reflected in such works, and at worst to complete misunderstanding. As one radical advocate of interdisciplinarity has put it,

> ... if any one of the ... disciplines is practised in ignorance of the concepts, methods, theories and problems of others, then there is a serious risk that inadequate sets of descriptive concepts will be used, problems will be poorly formulated, shallow empirical investigations will be made, woolly and obscure

metaphors and slogans will pass for explanatory theories, conceptual confusions will go undetected, and the rich store of knowledge embedded in common sense will not be properly utilised.[1]

The parallel presentation of different methodological approaches, on the other hand, has legitimacy. It should, however, be characterized as multidisciplinary rather than interdisciplinary study. Its weakness is that it tends to lead to unconnected insights, even to the fragmentation of perception.

Interdisciplinary study, ideally at least, should mean the consideration of a historical phenomenon or period (or even a natural phenomenon) through the well-fitted lenses or two or more disciplines, which together - as with eyeglasses or binoculars - help to make the object of study clearer and more comprehensible than it would be if only one lens were employed. Proponents of interdisciplinary thinking argue that compartmentalizing knowledge is an artificial approach to human experience. They believe the interdisciplinary approach to be essential for the achievement of understanding with regard to many issues, and the problems of modern societies in particular. They see those problems as so complex, that the "tunnel vision" of specialists can be dangerously misleading, if uncorrected by insights from other fields.[2] Interdisciplinarity generally involves two methodologies which do not normally intersect; psychology and history, for example. Sometimes, however, it refers to efforts to reintegrate a discipline fragmented topically - German history, Jewish history, church history, or methodologically - social, political, psychological, and the "great man theory" of history, for example.

The interdisciplinary approach is particularly useful in dealing with phenomena lacking obvious epistemological contours, such as "the Reagan era", which raises questions for historians, sociologists, economists, social psychologists, and others, or with clearly multi-faceted phenomena such as "the Great Depression", which requires the tools of historians and economists, at the least, for discussion and understanding. Interdisciplinarity is especially well suited to the examination of a culture - the study of Renaissance Italy for which historians, theologians, and art and music critics are indispensable, or of contemporary Jewry which calls for the skills of historians, sociologists, political scientists, and scholars of religion. Literature, which may offer a holistic view of a culture in operation or suggest the ambiguities inherent in it, would appear to be a natural component of almost any interdisciplinary cultural study. Although it may not provide an adequate format for the presentation of extensive, detailed, "scientific" information, literature can, under certain circumstances, be the medium for integrating the insights of several other disciplines. Interdisciplinary courses are often taught by teams, rather than by individuals. Team members are expected to work together in the various disciplines, not to "parachute in" for lectures in their own field.

Clearly, the interdisciplinary approach is appropriate for study of the Holocaust, for the complexity of that phenomenon defies one-dimensional consideration. The geographical and institutional scope of the event is too broad. And it was a historical phenomenon, perhaps even a turning point in history, that involved many aspects of the culture(s) in which it occurred. It came about when developments in philosophy and technology, in economics and military affairs, in politics and social psychology, converged and when the evil genius who could exploit those developments arose. As a result, scholars - even well-known ones - who have undertaken single-methodology studies of the Holocaust have often erred egregiously, and single-discipline courses have left students feeling that the most crucial questions have not been addressed. A few illustrations of the problems of one- dimensionality must suffice.

A historian of Germany or of the Jews, of Poland or of modern Europe, of the churches or of international relations, can offer, at best, only a partial picture of the Holocaust, an event which touched upon all of those areas. Scholars who have focused on the Jews, for example, have often claimed they were inexcusably reluctant to offer resistance to the Nazis. The accusation is found in some of the most "definitive" works on the Holocaust, such as Raul Hilberg's **The Destruction of the European Jews**). However, when the Jewish reaction to the Nazis is compared to that of other captive peoples in Europe, as Yehuda Bauer has done in his essay "Forms of Jewish Resistance During the Holocaust",[3] a proper perspective on the behavior of Jews emerges. Hilberg, whose sources were largely German documents relating to Jews, expresses the distorted view of a narrow specialist, and on that basis makes unjustified generalizations about Judaism and Jewish history. Others, such as Hannah Arendt, have followed and popularized his interpretation. Bauer, on the other hand, combines the disciplinary parameters of Jewish history and Hilberg's German sources to enlarge the picture and to add perspective.

The single-discipline approach often distorts the understanding of the role of Hitler and his relationship to the German people. Some social psychologists and historians have placed great emphasis on Hitler's charisma, on the allegedly authoritarian personality of the German people, and on the traditional German cult of the strong leader. The reader of William S. Allen's **The Nazi Seizure of Power**, which documents the ruthlessness of their political organization at the local level, comes to realize that Hitler's charisma was in part, manufactured, and that the enthusiasm of the masses was, in part, a product of manipulation and terror. Allen's work, together with that of other scholars, calls into sharp question many of the assumptions of the social psychologists.

Another example of the desirability of interdisciplinary thinking was evidenced when a prominent philosopher (Emil Fackenheim) whose works are of paramount significance to those trying to grapple with the philosophical and theological implications of the Holocaust, asked the question, "Why didn't earlier opponents of the Jews attempt their total annihilation?" His answer, cogent and convincing in its own terms, was based on an analysis of ideology. However, he did not consider the history of technology and science; for without trains, trucks, poison gas, and an impersonal bureaucracy, the final solution could not have been implemented. At the time of the Crusades the genocide of the Jewish people would have been a notion belonging to the realm of apocalyptic metaphysics. By the mid-twentieth century, however, the planning could be given over to lower-level bureaucrats and technicians. Both the technological innovations, and the relationship of people to the technology, made the situation of Jews in modern Europe more precarious than in earlier periods. It is reasonable to assume, for example, that Europeans' experience with wholesale maiming and slaughter during World War I - much of it resulting from the use of poison gas - played a role in preparing them for deliberate mass murder. Perhaps even modern medical experimentation helped lay the groundwork for murder. To be sure, the philosophical and ideological issues cannot be ignored. A study of the Holocaust which failed to deal with the theological and philosophical questions that it raised for victims and survivors, for perpetrators and bystanders, and for descendants of all of them, would be as incomplete as a study of the High Middle Ages which failed to discuss Christian thought and the role of the Church. But the philosopher or the historian of ideas, like other one-dimensional scholars, can provide only a partial view of his subject. The almost commonsense insights offered by the history of science and technology are no less necessary, if a full picture is to be obtained.

Perhaps the most disturbing example of distortion rooted in narrow specialization is the work of Bruno Bettelheim. A famed psychoanalyst, Bettelheim has been accepted by the general public and by many intellectuals as an (the?) authoritative interpreter of the behavior of Jews in the concentration camps.[4] His authority derives in part from his general reputation, in part from the fact that he spent a short period of time in an internment camp before the outbreak of war, in part from his having written about the camps before others did, and in part from other, less determinate factors. Bettelheim believes, among other things, that Jews have been conditioned to passivity by history and religion; and he argues that their behavior in the camps can best be understood as infantile regression, most obviously manifested in obsessiveness regarding food and over-eager identification with the oppressor. He generalizes from his work with autistic children and from his own brief experience in an internment camp about all camps, including those designed as machines for murder.

Despite his continuing popularity, Bettelheim has been challenged as a Holocaust scholar, and some of the most trenchant criticism has to do with his inability to transcend the parameters of his own field of specialization. Terrence Des Pres, for example, claims that no general theory can be built on the basis of Bettelheim's observations, for he draws broad conclusions from limited and even inappropriate data and, more seriously, because he was a poor observer.[5] By widening the field of vision beyond Bettelheim's recollections of what he saw and experienced, to include the memoirs of survivors and fiction dealing with death camps, internment camps, and the Russian gulags, and by subjecting the fiction and memoirs to literary and historical analysis, Des Pres argues that most of what Bettelheim observed should be classed as a misreading of idiosyncratic behavior not common to most camp inmates. Bettelheim was unfamiliar with both Jewish history and theology, and therefore unequipped to make judgments about them. His own discipline, the analysis of the behavior of individuals as it relates to their personal psycho-history, did not provide the critical tools needed to demonstrate, even to himself, that what he observed had causes other than Jewish history and thought, or an oppressive childhood. Lacking a comparative historical or sociological perspective, he could not recognize that what he observed was not typical of death camp or internment camp inmates. Furthermore, without the holistic context that the discipline of literature could have provided, he misread the meaning of isolated behavioral manifestations. Nonetheless, Bettelheim's work remains definitive for many Holocaust students, impeding understanding of the camps and, incidentally, reinforcing traditional anti-Jewish stereotypes (Jew as passive coward, Jew as ally of Satan).

Holocaust study, then, offers ready examples of the pitfalls of one-dimensionality and of the promise of interdisciplinarity. It almost seems to demand more than one methodological approach, because it was such an all-encompassing event. In the words of Jose Ortega y Gasset: "The specialist knows very well his own corner of the universe, [but] he is radically ignorant of all the rest."[6] Such narrowness and ignorance are particularly troubling in an area such as Holocaust study. Despite the difficulty of mastering two or more disciplines, even undergraduate students are likely to achieve fuller comprehension of the range and complexity of the issues raised by the Holocaust in an interdisciplinary setting. In such a framework they can develop a variety of intellectual skills and disciplinary approaches that are appropriate to complex problems posed by the Holocaust, and that can also be applied when studying other issues.

NOTES

1. A. Sloman, **Notes on the "Cognitive Studies" Programme in the School of Social Science, University of Sussex,** quoted in **Interdisciplinarity, a Report by the Group for Research and Innovation in Higher Education** (London, 1975), p. 44.

2. *Ibid*, p. 48.

3. "Forms of Jewish Resistance During the Holocaust," in Yehuda Bauer, **The Jewish Emergence from Powerlessness** (Toronto, 1979), pp. 26-40.

4. See especially, "Individual and Mass Behavior in Extreme Situations," **Journal of Abnormal and Social Psychology** (October 1943); **The Informed Heart** (Glencoe, Ill., 1960), chs. 4-7; **Surviving and Other Essays** (New York, 1979).

5. See especially, **The Survivor** (New York, 1976); "The Bettelheim Problem," **Social Research** (Winter 1979), pp. 619-647.

6. Quoted in Alvin M. White (ed.), **Interdisciplinary Teaching**, vol. 8 (San Francisco, 1981), p. 1.

THE USE OF FILM IN TEACHING ABOUT THE HOLOCAUST

Judith E. Doneson*

"I've become convinced that Lanzmann and I are fighting rear guard actions, and we have to denounce the murderous, narcissistic indifference all around us - to denounce by *showing* not by 'teaching'. The hell with 'teaching' the Holocaust! Denounce and be angry!"[1] declared Marcel Ophuls in an interview concerning his recent film **Hotel Terminus** (1988) about Nazi war criminal Klaus Barbie. Ophuls also alludes to the unbearable anguish and anger expressed in Claude Lanzmann's film **Shoah** (1985), and in Ophul's own films about the Nazi period **The Sorrow and the Pity** (1970) and **The Memory of Justice** (1976). Actually, Ophuls allowed his passion to supersede his reason, for without doubt, Claude Lanzmann and Marcel Ophuls, through their films, are teachers.

Director Erwin Leiser appreciated the power of the film maker and the film to teach when, in connection with his documentary film **Mein Kampf** (1960), he said: "A film about the past can be a film for the future. I wanted the shots and documents found for this film to speak directly to the generation for whom this bloody time had already receded into 'history'."[2] Judith Miller, correspondent for the **New York Times**, corroborated Leiser's assumption when she observed how film has been so enormously effective in kindling the interest of German students towards an attempt to comprehend the horror of the genocide against the Jews during World War II.[3]

Certainly, film offers challenging possibilities in the quest to educate students about the Holocaust. First and foremost, we are considering a filmed history of the destruction of a people for which there are no antecedents. Yet, paradoxically, in

*   Judith E. Doneson received her B.S. in Film from Boston University, and her M.A. and Ph.D. from the Institute of Contemporary Jewry of the Hebrew University of Jerusalem, where she specialised in Holocaust history. She is the author of **The Holocaust in American Film** (Philadelphia: The Jewish Publication Society of America, 1987).

contrast to the vast amount of material filmed prior to and during World War II, there is little footage of the actual process of destruction, and none of the death camps - a revealing fact emanating from a regime in which film was accorded a primary role. We have, therefore, to examine Nazi footage, liberation footage, newsreels, post-Holocaust fictional and non-fictional movies and television as we investigate this filmed history.

The analysis of all this material must consider both content and context. It must utilize the tools of the visual media, and refer to historical knowledge of the Holocaust as well. One might suggest that esthetic criteria also play a role in our discussion, but perhaps it is more relevant for our purpose to focus on the function of film in the society that produced it. (What esthetic value, one may ask, can there be in the footage shot by SS camera crews in the Warsaw Ghetto, focusing on starving diseased Jews?) Our concern must be dual: the role of the film as it confronts history, and the moral issues involved in any depiction of the Final Solution.

We view the camera as a documenter through whose eye we examine history. Indeed, every film is a source of knowledge and evidence, as well as a symbol of its culture. Yet each film is only a fragment of history. The British BBC TV film **Warsaw Ghetto** (1968), frequently screened in the classroom as *the* history of the Jewish ghetto in Warsaw, is merely one reflection of existence within its walls. But what a story its images tell: nothing of the organized life in the ghetto, the food kitchens, the self-help groups, the clandestine meetings, the inexhaustible strategies for survival; only what the Nazis wished to export as antisemitic propaganda. The instructor must be cognizant of the source of the filmed images along with what the camera does not show.

In other words, when we use film in the teaching of the Holocaust, we begin with a cardinal principle: film must be treated seriously. Just as a historian, for example, would balk at an untrained mind teaching his subject, so he must respect the discipline of film. Film in the classroom is neither a diversion or entertainment, nor a mere illustration. Under optimal conditions the teacher who uses film has some knowledge of film techniques such as camera angles and editing; of film theories, among them structuralism and semiotics; of the function of film as evidence; of the society and culture in which the particular film was made. In short, he is film-literate and has a broad comprehension of the film in question. He is aware that just as documentary film can distort the truth, fictional film may reveal hidden realities. The instructor should not screen a film unless he is prepared to provide an analysis of the raison d'etre for his choice.

Along with his command of film, the informed instructor has a goal in mind. He is the guide leading the students through a maze of possibilities. His objectives must be clear. Is he using newsreels to show how the war was portrayed to Americans? Does he screen German newsreels for the purpose of examining Nazi propaganda? Might he wish to explain Hollywood's treatment of the Nazi persecution of the Jews in the late 1930s and 1940s? Perhaps he is screening Nazi antisemitic films in order to explain how the release of these films in 1940 was coordinated with plans for the "Final Solution" of the Jewish problem. Is he interested in postwar interpretations of the Holocaust in fiction film? Each of the preceding motivations is valid, for the educational potentialities of film - in the right environment - are endless. We must, however, learn to identify modes of film analysis which can minimize subjective viewing.[4] We must fight the misuse of film in education. As British historian Paul Smith concludes: "There is much ignorance about what sort of material is available, what it can provide, and how it can be employed both in research and in teaching."[5]

Historical Films

Historical films are not simply a matter of recreating the past, as is so often assumed, but rather, as French historian Pierre Sorlin has indicated, a reorganizing of the present. Paul Smith informs us that "to a large extent attention is concentrated upon what [historian] Arthur Marwick has described as its [film's] 'unwitting testimony' upon the information that can be derived from it about the mental and social world of its makers and audiences. All categories of film can be examined from this point of view, from the 'factual' to the 'fantastic'."[6] In other words, in the dual analysis of content and context, there is the salient level of the film that deals with content or subject, and there is the latent level that explains the context, the popular attitudes at the time of the film's appearance. As an illustration, we might briefly examine the Nazi antisemitic film **Jud Suess** (1940).

Jud Suess is a historical recreation of the life of Suess Oppenheimer, who in the eighteenth century was a court Jew to Duke Karl Alexander of Wuerttemberg. The depiction of the film's characters, in particular the image of the conniving, dark Jew in juxtaposition to the pure, blonde German, offers a lesson to the German viewer in 1940: the film ends as the Jews are deported from Wuerttemberg. The ideology and function of this film in Nazi Germany were so blatant that its director, Veit Harlan, was tried for war crimes. Harlan claimed that he was not an antisemite and that he was forced by Propaganda Minister Joseph Goebbels to make the film. However, historian Marc Ferro commented that the astute observer would have noticed that the positioning of images in specific transition shots affirms the true, if sometimes cryptic, antisemitic voice of the director.[7]

The ability to "read" film is imperative if it is to be used in the classroom. Let us consider, for instance, three films, each decidedly different yet nonetheless sharing some of the same visual content. **The House of Rothschild** (1934), produced in the United States, is a historical recounting of the rise of the Rothschild dynasty. The objective of the film was to fight contemporary antisemitism by showing the Rothschilds as a metaphor for the American dream: they worked hard for their fortune, gave charity, and contributed gratefully to the society that permitted them to advance. Still, the film's image of the Jew is ambivalent, a reflection of American attitudes towards the Jew in the 1930s. This ambivalence allowed Dr. Franz Hippler to incorporate segments of **The House of Rothschild** into his Julius Streicher- style, antisemitic film **The Eternal Jew** (1940). This pseudo- scientific "documentary" was intended to convince the German people of the urgency of solving the Jewish problem once and for all. Its most obscene footage was filmed by Nazi cameramen in Warsaw and other Nazi-created Jewish ghettos, to be used as antisemitic propaganda vindicating German anti-Jewish policies. Twenty-eight years later, the BBC in Britain utilized this same antisemitic propaganda footage in its film **Warsaw Ghetto** (1968) for the purpose of arousing sympathy for Jews persecuted during the war.

No doubt, this interchangeability of images in films with distinctly contradictory goals poses a serious problem requiring careful analysis. Holocaust historian Lucy Dawidowicz concludes that regardless of the BBC's attempts to change the point of view of these images by adding sympathetic music and narration, "the photographic images [of the Jews] remain what they were intended to be - pictures that elicit disgust and revulsion". Film writer Jay Leyda would concur: "I have never seen this strong Nazi material used for equally strong anti-Nazi purposes".[8] Films like **Warsaw Ghetto** are frequently used in teaching about the Holocaust, and unless there is proper analysis, the danger exists of the viewer receiving the wrong message, that is, the one the Nazis intended. To reiterate: in analyzing film, content should not be divorced from context. Charlie Chaplin's **The Great Dictator** (1940) serves as a fine illustration of the function of both content and context in the analysis of a film.

The Great Dicatator had its premier in October of 1940, only one short month after **Jud Suess**. While **Jud Suess** was filmed in order to convince the German population of the urgency of the "Final Solution" against the Jews, Chaplin wrote, produced and directed the lone Hollywood film during the war years openly to confront and focus on the Nazi persecution of the Jews. In his film he beseeched the public to demand a sane world, a world of peace and freedom, while it was still possible. He saw in the German victimization of the Jew a symbol of man's inhumanity to man.

As Chaplin prepared to battle the Nazi threat through **The Great Dictator**, he received warnings not to mock Hitler or defend the Jews. The film came under attack during the 1941 congressional hearings that accused Hollywood of putting pro-war propaganda in its films. Senator Gerald P. Nye of North Dakota, the sponsor of the bill calling for the hearings, admitted under examination that the only film he had seen was **The Great Dictator**.[9] This brief account demonstrates how the study of Chaplin's film can offer an illuminating insight into American society before and during the war.

Newsreels

The newsreel offers a fascinating illustration of the manner in which the Holocaust was presented to the American public. During the late 1930s and 1940s, movie attendance reached a peak in the United States. (Television had not yet become a factor in the American home.) Several major film studios produced newsreels that were shown prior to the main feature in most movie houses throughout the country. For many Americans, images of the war were shaped by these newsreels.[10]

It is through newsreels filmed by cameramen who accompanied the Allied armies liberating the concentration camps that the first images of the Holocaust entered the public consciousness. When the Universal Studios newsreel called *Nazi Atrocities* was issued in April 1945, managers were warned that the film contained "real-life horror pictures revealing the unbelievable atrocities committed by the Nazis in the murder camps".[11] Interestingly, as the first visual icons of the Holocaust - the skeletal survivors, the plows heaving bodies into open pits, the stacks of personal belongings - began to shape public memory, a phenomenon was occurring that would, in the early postwar era, impede historical memory and universalize the Holocaust.

Liane Richter, a Library of Congress researcher, wrote in her "notes on newsreels" of 25 April 1945:

> Like the majority of fictitious films, newsreels are made for showing to audiences of all ages, many varied political, ideological and religious denominations, every conceivable national and occupational group... The result is the same in fiction and actuality films: In order to serve such a large and heterogeneous public and in their anxiety to offend nobody, the film makers reduce their standards to the lowest common denominator intellectually and avoid making any controversial statement.[12]

This translates into a continuation in postwar newsreels of the unwritten wartime guidelines "enforced" in Hollywood films, namely, not to focus on the Jews as specific targets of Nazi persecution. (This approach was also expressed in such political applications as America's policy at the 1938 Evian Conference on refugees and the quota system applied to refugees entering the United States.) The narration in the newreels makes only casual, if any, reference to the Jews being the specific prey of the Nazis, thus abetting postwar universalization of the Holocaust. In any case, because of their horrifying images, and the American public's desire to forget the war, these atrocity newsreels were packed away into film vaults, not to surface again for some ten years.[13]

Fictional Films

Considering how little actual footage exists of the Final Solution, fictional films can be an important source for studying the post-Holocaust discourse. **The Wannsee Conference** (1984), produced in Germany, offers an interpretation of an event which the camera had not recorded, namely, the meeting at Wannsee on 20 January 1942, which formalized the "Final Solution". The film is structured to match the length of the original meeting - eighty-five minutes. Since no official minutes exist, the film makers could only guess at what was discussed. Historian Raul Hilberg has pointed out many flaws in this film. Nonetheless, we conjecture that this film will be screened in the classroom as an authentic representation of that fateful meeting at Wannsee. In reality, it should be used to understand the process and function of recreating history though film. Hilberg himself said: "The makers of 'The Wannsee Conference' did not cling to the structure and chronology of the historical record. They made a hybrid film. Yet they approached the subject seriously and left us a fascinating experiment."[14]

A large number of fictional films provide an enticing source for investigation into cinematic interpretations of the Holocaust. East European film makers, particularly those from Poland and Czechoslovakia, frequently turn to World War II themes depicting the severe suffering under Nazi occupation. The motif of the shared experience of war is more readily accepted by the strict censors. The Holocaust, therefore, becomes a metaphor for contemporary problems, a means of disguising a modern message. Following the release of Marcel Ophuls' documentary **The Sorrow and the Pity** (1970), which challenged the myth of the French as a nation of resisters, a series of French fictional films pursued the polemic raised by Ophuls' film. A thoughtful study of **Lacombe, Lucien** (1974), **Black Thursday** (1974), and **Mr. Klein** (1976) informs us of the French view of the Holocaust, and also provides insights into French society in the 1970s.

Television, too, offers a reflection of the culture from which it emanates, and is a marvelous tool for classroom instruction. Television has transformed postwar America as well as much of the Western world.[15] "Because of the pervasiveness of television in American life," observed journalist Lance Morrow, "the entire nation is now getting its history, therefore its collective memory, sifted and packaged by technicians in Burbank and Century City."[16] With regard to the proliferation of "simulated" and "real" legal cases on television, Harvard Law Professor Alan Dershowitz has wisely remarked: "This phenomenon may help explain why I - and some other law professors... try to catch as many episodes of these legal soaps as we can. After all, professors should always stay at least one step ahead of their students."[17] Dershowitz's rule would apply to teachers of the Holocaust as well. With the availability of video, it is relatively simple to rent the numerous dramas and television talk shows that address the Holocaust and screen them in the classroom. In this way, we can attempt to measure the impact of the Holocaust as it is reflected through the popular medium of television.

The original format of a film is an added element to be taken into consideration in the use of film for teaching. It is essential to project Leni Riefenstahl's masterpiece of Nazi propaganda **Triumph of the Will** (1936) on a large screen, to view it as nearly as possible as an audience in Nazi Germany would have seen it. The power of Riefenstahl's images is lost on a small screen. In contrast, the American-produced NBC TV production of **Holocaust** (1978) can be watched on a television-size screen, just as it was seen throughout America and Western Europe. In other words, it is important to approximate, as much as one can, the original format of a film.

A somewhat more complex approach to the use of film in teaching about the Holocaust, is that of the history professor who makes his own historically accurate films for students. This has been done in Britain through the Inter-University History Film Consortium and by academics from Britain's Open University.[18] Such films are used by their producers for instruction in their own classes, and can also be transmitted to other educational institutions.

Finally, at its simplest, history can speak for itself through film. We can watch Neville Chamberlain's nervous smile after Munich, or the flaming inferno of Warsaw, or the testimonies from the Holocaust Survivors Video Project at Yale University. As Jay Leyda has noted, the spectator becomes an active participant in history.[19]

The possibilities for using film to teach about the Holocaust are infinite. The overriding requirement is that the instructor speak the language of film. At a time when the media dominate our lives, we might hope for increased visual skills to sift through and evaluate the limitless material available. Following historian Carl Becker, who maintains that "the proper function of the historian is not to repeat the past but to make use of it,"[20] we may add that the purpose of studying films on the Holocaust is to provide an invaluable source for analyzing a traumatic era in history in order to give meaning to the present.

NOTES

1. Michael Ciment, "Joy to the World! An Interview with Marcel Ophuls," **American Film** (September 1988), p. 42.

2. Quoted in Jay Leyda, **Films Beget Film** (1964) (Reprint: New York: Hill and Wang, 1971), p. 92-93.

3. Judith Miller, "Erasing the Past: Europe's Amnesia About the Holocaust," **New York Times Magazine** (16 November 1986), p. 110.

4. William Hughes, "The Evaluation of Film as Evidence," in Paul Smith (ed.), **The Historian and Film** (Cambridge: Cambridge University Press, 1976), p. 74.

5. Paul Smith, "Introduction," in **The Historian and Film**, *ibid.*, p. 3.

6. Smith, pp. 7-8.

7. Marc Ferro, **Cinema et histoire** (Paris: Denoel/Gontier, 1977), p. 51. There is a growing bibliography dealing with Nazi film propaganda, including Nazi antisemitic films. These include: David Stewart Hull, **Film in the Third Reich: A Study of the German Cinema 1933-1945** (Berkeley: University of California Press, 1969); Erwin Leiser, **Nazi Cinema** (New York: Collier Books, 1975); Richard Taylor, **Film Propaganda: Soviet Russia and Nazi Germany** (London: Croom Helm, 1979); and David Welch, **Propaganda and the German Cinema 1933-1945** (London: Oxford University Press, 1983).

8. Lucy Dawidowicz, "Visualizing the Warsaw Ghetto: Nazi Images of the Jews Refiltered by the BBC," **Shoah: A Review of Holocaust Studies and Commemorations**, vol. 1, no. 1, p. 6; Leyda (above, n. 2), pp. 50-51.

9. For further discussion on Hollywood's view of World War II and of the Holocaust, see Judith E. Doneson, **The Holocaust in American Film** (Philadelphia: The Jewish Publication Society of America, 1987); and the works edited by K.R.M. Short: **Film and Radio Propaganda in World War II** and **Feature Films as History** (Knoxville: University of Tennessee Press, 1981).

10. K.R.M. Short, "American Newsreels and the Collapse of Nazi Germany," in K.R.M. Short & Stephan Dolezel (eds.), **Hitler's Fall: The Newsreel Witness**, (London: Croom Helm, 1988).

11. Short (above, n. 10), pp. 11-12.
12. Short (above, n. 10); Liane Richter, Appendix 2, "Notes on Newsreels," (25 April 1945), p. 23.
13. Leyda (above, n. 2), p. 73.
14. Raul Hilberg, "Is it History, or is it Drama?" **New York Times** (13 December 1987).
15. Judith Murphey & Ronald Gross, **Learning by Television** (New York: The Fund for the Advancement of Education, 1966), pp. 10-11.
16. Lance Morrow, "The History-Devouring Machine," **Horizon** (July 1978), p. 20.
17. Alan Dershowitz, "The Verdict," **American Film** (December 1987), pp. 15-18.
18. Anthony Aldgate, **Cinema and History: British Newsreels and the Spanish Civil War** (London: Scholar Press, 1979), p. 13.
19. Leyda (above, n. 2), p. 92.
20. Carl L. Becker, "What Is Evidence?" in Robin Winter (ed.), **The Historian as Detective: Essays on Evidence** (New York: Harper & Row, 1970), p. 21.

INTEGRATING THEOLOGICAL ANALYSIS INTO A COURSE ON THE HOLOCAUST

James F. Moore
Department of Theology, Valparaiso University, Indiana

Yehuda Bauer has said on more than one occasion that the Nazi war against the Jews was an ideological war, meaning that it was sustained by a system of ideas as its sole justification.[1] The plans devised to forward that ideology were not subject to rational argument or empirical evidence. The central Nazi ideology became the sole arbiter of truth, immune from any other claim or counter-argument. This does not mean that the Nazis were unaware of the real world in which they strove to put their plan into effect (far from it), but that ideology held a primary place in every critical interpretation and important decision.

If Bauer is correct, and I think he is, then any analysis of the Holocaust, any course on the Holocaust, must include as a primary component an analysis of this ideology - its roots, its implementation, and its effects. Such an analysis is necessarily complex, requiring a variety of different approaches to the material. One approach that is essential to an understanding of the roots of Nazi ideology and its peculiar nature is theological analysis.

What is Theological Analysis?

The discipline of theology is a complex of sub-disciplines that are practiced by a variety of theologians.[2] One of those sub-disciplines is the analysis of the historical development of theological ideas from their traditional religious roots, through various hermeneutical processes and theological inquiry. This inquiry follows a pattern similar to the analysis of the general history of ideas (cultural history), with specific attention paid to the way religious ideas arise and are disseminated.

Beyond such simple historical description, theological analysis also aims to judge whether those ideas are consistent with the basic principles of the religious tradition, and what influence those ideas have on the shaping or changing of religious traditions and the broader culture. Such judgments can aid the investigation of any cultural, historical event in that they help evaluate what is held to be true in any culture and show how religious ideas and institutions influence the course of events.

One major claim can stand as an example: the idea that there is a Judeo-Christian tradition. It is claimed that this tradition has shaped the values and judgments of much of the Western world since the fourth century C.E. Theological analysis can dispel the notion that there is a single, unified, Judeo-Christian tradition, and recognize a plurality of religious views.[3] On the other hand, certain values imbedded in many national traditions in the Western world can be attributed to religious sources - common perspectives that help people in our cultures make decisions and value judgments. Understanding the source and strength of those values contributes to the analysis of socio-historical events such as the Holocaust.

Religious Ideas and the Holocaust

There can be little doubt that there is a relationship between religious ideas and the events of the Holocaust. The Nazis used both religious ideas and religious thinkers as a rationale for their ideology. In turn, religious organizations used religious ideas as justification for either action or inaction, complicity or non-complicity. Victims of the onslaught used traditional religious ideas, or explicitly rejected them, as a means for coping. Each of these three uses of religious ideas is a significant component of the events we call the Holocaust; each is distinct and requires separate treatment although there is overlap.

This overlap appears in our investigations as a series of questions. How were the Nazis able to use religious tradition as a justification for genocide? How could the great majority of Christians and Christian leaders either lend support to the Nazi effort or simply choose to do and say nothing? How was it possible for some to use religious convictions as a justification for resistance to Nazism and aid to the Jewish victims, while so many others did not? Was the religious tradition of the victims a source of strength or a road to disaster? None of these questions can be given a simple answer even though theological analysis of the events can provide some patterns of consistency and some startling conclusions.

The answers to these questions can also become a springboard for examining the impact of the Holocaust on religious traditions and traditional religious ideas. The old philosophical rule that there is no necessary relationship between the "is" and the "ought" holds here; the effect of religious ideas during the Holocaust does not necessarily mean that those ideas will later be altered. Nevertheless, the knowledge that religious ideas produced the justification for atrocity and complicity could lead post-Holocaust thinkers to ponder changes in theological thinking. This must also be considered when studying the full meaning of the Holocaust.

This comment leads to a final relationship between religious ideas and the Holocaust, namely, the religious ideas of the traditions are used to give meaning to the events that occurred. Certain ways of construing the meaning of the Holocaust can be called specifically religious and as such can be analyzed theologically and judged on the basis of fact. Even more, this analysis can produce further judgments about the meaning of the Holocaust complementing the results of historical, sociological, and psychological analyses.

The integration of theological analysis into a course on the Holocaust would require an exploration in depth of each of these three areas of investigation - the use of religious ideas in either justifying or coping, the impact of the Holocaust upon religious ideas and traditions, and the use of religious ideas to explain and therefore give meaning to the events of the Holocaust. The following sections will provide an example of each, and will show some of the ways in which theological analysis can be used.

The Use of Religious Ideas for Justifying Action

Shortly after the end of World War II the French historian, Jules Isaac, began a study of the reasons for the massive silence of Christians and the organized Christian Church regarding the Holocaust. The results of that study are now well known to any student of the Holocaust.[4] Isaac uncovered the long history of a systematic teaching of anti-Jewish ideas in every level of Christian instruction. In fact, he concluded that the general nature of Christian instruction had been so thoroughly anti-Jewish that the silence of the war years was simply an extension of centuries of Church teaching and practice. Isaac called this the "teaching of contempt". In a systematic study written some time later, Rosemary Radford Ruether, a Christian theologian, showed that Christian scripture was the foundation of this teaching of contempt.[5] In a startling conclusion she claimed that "anti-Judaism is the left hand of Christology" - of Christian teaching about Jesus.[6] Charlotte Klein's study of German theology and Church teaching is only one of many studies showing the blatant anti-Judaism in the thinking of the leading theologians of this century.[7]

The presence of anti-Judaism in Christian theology does not mean that Christianity produced the Holocaust. Indeed, many other factors contributed to change radically the intent of Christian teaching for the purpose of Nazi genocide. However, the fact that throughout the centuries Christians had taught and learned that Jews were and are responsible for the death of Jesus certainly made it possible to conclude that Jews deserved whatever punishment they received. This teaching made countless social, moral, political, and economic solutions to the "Jewish problem" acceptable to Christians, and divorced from what they might consider appropriate moral behavior in general. As much as any other single factor in Western history, the idea that Jews were a special case, scapegoats for society, and particularly despicable, was fostered by Christian teaching.

How were religious ideas used as a justification for action? The relationship between the centuries-long implantation of religious hatred of the Jews by the Church, and the ideology of Jew-hatred formulated by the Nazis is difficult to define. There can be little doubt, however, that various Nazi leaders used the thinking of Christian theologians to promote and justify their ideology.[8] The question remains whether such arguments could realistically have convinced an entire nation. The problem lies in determining how many were directly involved in implementing the plan and how many others knew of the full extent of the genocide - questions which are subjects for historical study.

Much more significant for our purposes is the connection between the "teaching of contempt" and Christian indifference. Is the history of Christian anti-Judaism sufficient to explain the tacit assent of masses of Christians to the Nazi program against the Jews? The more basic question is how vital the teaching of contempt is to Christian theology and religious life. Ruether's claim is significant in reaching a judgment. If Christian anti-Judaism has been developed theologically as "the left hand of Christology," as Ruether argues, the conclusion must be that the teaching of contempt is a vital component of Christian thinking. (Whether or not it ought to be is another question.) Christians of various levels of theological sophistication would view, for various reasons, the affirmation of Jesus as the Christ, and the denunciation of the Jews as inextricably intertwined. Given this perception, there would be little reason for Christians to aid Jews in trouble, even if such action were secondarily seen as an important feature of Christian morality.

The deadening of Christian moral sensitivity was compounded by centuries of social and political/legal practice that made the actions of the Nazis seem little more than an extension of the normal state of affairs.[9] Still, the connection between the consistent linking of contempt for Jews and of devotion to Jesus must be seen as a major force contributing to the context in which the Holocaust occurred. Few would deny this claim, but a full appreciation of the relative ease with which Nazis were able to enforce their policies is difficult without the theological analysis provided by Ruether or other historians of religious ideas, such as Franklin Littell.[10]

Still other important theological resources are useful additions to any course. The study of Jewish reaction to the Holocaust during the war, especially the response of the victims of Nazi atrocity, requires an analysis of the ideas of the religious life prevalent within Jewry, especially in Eastern Europe during the first half of the century, and the requirement to maintain strict rules of Jewish religious observance, even in the harshest of circumstances. Similarly, an analysis of the action of the rescuers, especially Christians, requires some understanding of the religious background of these people and how they were able to establish moral priorities contrary to those common within the majority population. The case can be made with some force that theological analysis of at least the most rudimentary form is necessary to understand how religious ideas were used to justify the differing actions of religious people.

The Impact of the Holocaust on Religious Ideas and Traditions
It is clear from even a cursory analysis that the Holocaust not only emerged from religious and/or quasi-religious ideas, but has also shaped and modified religious ideas and traditions. Surely, the Christian image of the Jew is forever altered as a result of becoming aware of the events of the Holocaust and the background of Christian anti-Judaism. Just as surely, the composition and character of Judaism have been radically altered by the Holocaust. These important features of any study of the reaction to the Holocaust by Jews and Christians can be understood fully only through analysis of the religious ideas of both groups, and how they have been challenged by the Holocaust.

Perhaps even more significant for teaching a general course on the Holocaust is the question of how Jews, and also Christians, interpreted the genocide while it was in progress. In some cases, theological analysis can be valuable for understanding the importance of religious ideas as reflected by writers of diaries, such as Etty Hillesum.[11] Theological analysis is also a significant critical tool for understanding a memoir such as Elie Wiesel's **Night**.[12] A brief account of such an analysis may illustrate what I mean.[13]

Wiesel's book is clearly more than just a personal memoir; it is also a theological comment on the impact of the Holocaust on the religious convictions of the victim and the survivor (surviving community). The literary structure of the book is fascinating, but the theological structure is far more profound. Its key elements are the image of night, the notion of obedience (observance), the father-son relationship, and the basic foundation of covenant-revelation.

Wiesel's use of the image of night is both a literary device and a theological comment. "Never will I forget the night, the first night in camp."[14] The image works like a refrain throughout the book, appearing at every significant turn except one - the death of the father. The literary device bears theological import since night is linked dramatically in the book to two stories of Jewish tradition - the *Seder*, and the *Akeda*, (the sacrifice of Isaac). It is not by coincidence that the first real turning point of the book occurs at night, the night of the Saturday before Pentecost just after the Passover. (Indeed, the Passover occurred at night.) It is no coincidence that in the relationship of father and son, a central motif of the book, critical challenges occur at night. (Abraham left before dawn from Mount Moriah.) The image of night is fused with the biblical story of redemption. **Night** is a memoir of the fate of those imprisoned in the "Kingdom of the Night".

Wiesel connects that symbol to a running commentary on obedience. The radical change in Moshe the Beadle's notion of observance is a foretaste of what is to come.[15] The issue of choice is only barely evident at the beginning of the story. Both observance and obedience require choice; but the central feature of the Holocaust, for the Jews, is their lack of choice. The victim is labelled by the Nazis as a Jew regardless of his or her choice. The fate of the Jew is sealed not by the choice of the individual but by the choice made two generations earlier. Thus, the obedience of the Jew is merely a charade within the larger charade. This realization is at the heart of the growing religious consciousness of the victim, as recalled by Wiesel. What happens to the notion of Jewish uniqueness when choice is taken away and uniqueness means only a sentence of death? Surely obedience means something different, and that is Wiesel's point.

The relation of father and son is a context for observing the transformation of the religious view brought on by the Holocaust. The significance of obedience is called into question through the painstaking unravelling of this central relationship. The father is initially the son's hope for survival, yet later he becomes the cause of the son's demise. Redemption comes only with the death of the father. This is the only place in the text in which there is no night; instead night is replaced by the dawn of the only day marked with a date in the book.

The image of father-son is used by Wiesel in the context of the familiar *Akeda* story. Three factors make this imagery a startling theological commentary. First, the ultimate challenge in Wiesel's story is not whether the father will offer up the son, but whether the son will be forced to sacrifice the father. Second, the challenge comes not because of a command from God, but only because the choice to be an observant Jew has been twisted into a non-choice, a liability. The connection with God becomes the liability - a key issue for post-Holocaust Judaism. Third, in Wiesel's story there is no redemption, but only death or survival by cunning, stealth, or accident. An incredible amount of material for theological analysis resides in this treatment of the Holocaust experience. The point, in simplest terms, is that the normal, traditional Jewish view of history is turned upside down.

Thus, the final image, that of covenant, presents the final challenge - the relation of God to His people. Wiesel's work does not resolve that question. He makes the point that the Holocaust challenges every traditional image of that relationship. No simple use of traditional language is possible since all previous religious solutions and theodicies fail in part when viewed from within the Kingdom of the Night.

The theological commentary offered by Wiesel is initially a negative one. He questions the various resources of the tradition and leaves the people to their own resources in combatting the forces of evil in the Holocaust. Subsequent writings by Wiesel provide evidence that he has not ceased reflecting about these issues.[16] Wiesel is not alone in the attempt to interpret the events of the Holocaust and to analyze the shifting view of the victims when confronted by unbounded evil. Both Eliezer Berkovits and Richard Rubenstein have offered views of a different sort.[17] A theology course will certainly take these efforts to understand the dynamics of faith in the camps with utmost seriousness. In addition, many other courses on the Holocaust can legitimately use these theological analyses as a way of explaining an important dimension of the Holocaust.

The Use of Religious Ideas to Give Meaning to the Holocaust

There are those who argue that the Holocaust cannot be adequately understood. The events are so unique that no analogies can help us give it meaning. Others argue that the Holocaust is merely another of many tragic events of Western history, especially Jewish history, and can be understood just like all other such events. Depending on which discipline one follows for understanding the Holocaust, one might fall nearer one extreme than the other; theologians can be found at any point of the spectrum between the extremes, and theological views are among many options offered for understanding the events of the Holocaust.

One prominent contention regarding the meaning of the Holocaust is that the event represents the moral failure of the Western world, particularly Christianity. Rosemary Ruether's argument falls within this position. Judgments about this theory must, however, first be grounded in historical analysis. How much of the blame for Nazi success can be placed on Christian anti-Judaism? How significant was the moral/political influence of Christianity on the masses in the early to mid-twentieth century?[18] These questions and others can provide important factual bases for making judgments about the moral failure of Christianity.

Even so, ultimately such a judgment must be made in part on the basis of a theological analysis of Christian principles, their social and political implications, and their importance in the shaping of theological views during and immediately after the Holocaust. Irving Greenberg claims that the Holocaust is an indictment of the Christian principle of love. Determining whether Greenberg is correct requires some understanding of the meaning of the Christian love commandment, and how significantly that perspective shaped the views of both passive bystanders and active rescuers.[19] Indeed, the Protestant theological tradition was radically divided regarding the centrality of the love command, if one is to judge by the leading Christian thinkers of this century. Uncertainty about what was required of Christians under normal circumstances might easily create confusion in times of extraordinary moral challenge. Thus, the moral failure of Christianity, if there was one, might be seen as much more of a crisis in leadership than widespread moral erosion.

However, the judgment may be more than historical. If it is also a theological judgment, the issue is not simply whether a moral failure was evident, but what such a failure means for subsequent generations of Christians. The extreme position would be a thoroughgoing indictment of Christianity in particular and of religions in general. A less harsh stance might be a call for a re-examination of those teachings that created the rationale for anti-Judaism and led to moral ambivalence. Given this view, the meaning of the Holocaust is not so much contained within the event but rather a matter of the consequences of that event. Recent work has focused on Christology and Christian moral philosophy as avenues for re-examination.[20]

*   *   *

Do these reflections warrant inclusion in a general course on the Holocaust? Naturally, each instructor will make an individual judgment. It is my belief that as much as a discussion of the establishment of the State of Israel is a legitimate extension of a course on the Holocaust, so too is a discussion of the present state of Jewish-Christian dialogue, together with new reflections on both Jewish and Christian thought.

Theological analysis, employed with varying degrees of sophistication and attention, introduces another dimension to the teaching of the Holocaust, and can lend valuable assistance to anyone in making critical judgments about those events. Such analysis is not solely the prerogative of the theologian, nor is it to be relegated to courses on religion or to theological schools. Theological analysis, as described in this article, has a legitimate place and value within the context of courses in history departments and departments of Jewish and literary studies. A serious study of the Holocaust approached from the vantage of any of these disciplines can be enriched by considering the Holocaust from the different perspective and analysis of the theologian.

NOTES

1. See, e.g., Yehuda Bauer, **The Holocaust in Historical Perspective** (Seattle: The University of Washington Press, 1978).
2. For a discussion of the nature of theology, see David Tracy, **The Analogical Imagination** (New York: Crossroad Press, 1981), Part I.
3. The classic text may be Arthur A. Cohen, **The Myth of the Judeo-Christian Tradition** (New York: Schocken, 1969).
4. Jules Isaac, **The Teaching of Contempt: Christian Roots of Anti-Semitism** (New York: Holt, Rinehart and Winston, 1964).
5. See especially, Rosemary Radford Ruether, **Faith and Fratricide** (New York: Seabury, 1974).
6. Rosemary Radford Ruether, **To Change the World** (New York: Crossroad, 1983), p. 31.
7. Charlotte Klein, **Anti-Judaism in Christian Theology** (Philadelphia: Fortress Press, 1978).
8. Raul Hilberg, **The Destruction of the European Jews** (New York: Harper & Row, 1961), Part 1.
9. This argument was made forcefully by Harry James Cargas, **A Christian Response to the Holocaust** (Denver: Stonehenge Books, 1981).
10. Franklin Littell, **The Crucifixion of the Jews** (New York: Harper & Row, 1975).
11. Etty Hillesum, **An Interrupted Life** (New York: Washington Square Press, 1984).
12. Elie Wiesel, **Night** (New York: Bantam Books, 1960).
13. Much of the basic analysis suggested here came from conversations with Rabbi Joseph Edelheit of Chicago.
14. Wiesel, p. 32.
15. Wiesel, pp. 4-5.
16. Elie Wiesel, **Messengers of God** (New York: Summit Books, 1976).
17. Eliezer Berkovits, **With God in Hell** (New York: Sanhedrin Press, 1979; Richard Rubenstein, **After Auschwitz** (Indianapolis: Bobbs-Merrill, 1966); Richard Rubenstein & John Roth, **Approaches to Auschwitz** (Atlanta: John Knox Press, 1987).

18. See Littell, **The Crucifixion of the Jews** (above, no. 10).

19. Irving Greenberg, "Cloud of Smoke, Pillar of Fire: Judaism, Christianity and Modernity After the Holocaust," in Eva Fleischner (ed.), **Auschwitz: Beginning of a New Era?** (New York: Ktav, 1974).

20. Johann Metz, **The Emergent Church** (New York: Crossroad, 1980), pp. 17ff; John Pawlikowski, **Christ in the Light of the Christian-Jewish Dialogue** (New York: Paulist Press, 1982), pp. 136ff.; Roy Eckardt & Alice Eckardt, **Long Night's Journey into Day** (Detroit: Wayne State University Press, 1982).

II.   SELECTED SYLLABI

I. THE COURSE

THE HOLOCAUST: ORIGINS, HISTORY AND REACTIONS

David Bankier
Department of Contemporary Jewry, The Hebrew University of Jerusalem

II. ACADEMIC CONTEXT OF THE COURSE
This course is offered at the School for Overseas Students of the Hebrew University, for English-speaking students who take summer courses at the university. Most of the students are from the United States and Canada; some are from European countries. The majority complete their studies in their respective universities and get credit for the courses they take in Jerusalem. The course is intended for undergraduates, but, sometimes, graduate students also enroll. Some basic previous knowledge in modern Jewish history is required. The number of students ranges from 15 to 25.

III. OUTLINE OF THE COURSE
1. Introduction: Europe - the seedbed of the Holocaust

Required reading
Jacob Talmon, "European History as the Seedbed of the Holocaust," **Holocaust and Rebirth** (Jerusalem, 1974), pp. 11-76.

2. Political and racial antisemitism

Required reading
Paul Massing, **Rehearsal for Destruction** (New York, 1949), pp. 227-310.

3. The Jews in Nazi ideology and policy

Required reading
Eberhard Jaeckel, **Hitler's Weltanschauung, A Blueprint for Power** (Middletown, Conn., 1972), Ch. 1-3.

4. Nazi antisemitic policy

Required reading
Helmut Krausnick, "The Persecution of the Jews," in Helmut Krausnick et al. (eds.), **Anatomy of the SS State** (London, 1978), pp. 1-124.

5. Jewish life in Nazi Germany

Required reading
Jacob Boas, "Germany or Diaspora? German Jewry's Shifting Perceptions in the Nazi Era 1933-1938," **Leo Baeck Institute Yearbook** XXVII (1982), pp. 109-126.

6. German public reactions to the persecution of the Jews

Required reading
Ian Kershaw, "The Persecution of the Jews and German Popular Opinion in the Third Reich," *ibid.* XXVI (1981), pp. 261-289.

7. The reaction of the churches

Required reading
Guenter Lewy, **The Catholic Church and Nazi Germany** (New York, 1964), Ch. 10.

8. The process of destruction

Required reading
Karl Schleunes, **The Twisted Road to Auschwitz** (Urbana, 1970).

Hans Mommsen, "The Realization of the Unthinkable," in Gerhard Hirschfeld (ed.), **The Policies of Genocide** (London, 1986), pp. 97-144.

Eberhard Jaeckel, **Hitler in History** (Hanover and London, 1984), pp. 44-65.

9. Life in the ghettos

Required reading
Yisrael Gutman, **The Jews of Warsaw 1939-1943: Ghetto, Underground, Revolt**
(Indiana, 1984), Ch. 3.

10. The problem of the Jewish Councils

Required reading
Isaiah Trunk, "The Typology of the Judenraete in Nazi Europe," in Y. Gutman &
C.J. Haft (eds.), **Patterns of Jewish Leadership in Nazi Europe 1933-1945**
(Jerusalem, 1979), pp. 17-30; 43-60.

Raul Hilberg, "The Ghetto as a Form of Government," in Yehuda Bauer & Nathan
Rotenstreich (eds.), **The Holocaust as Historical Experience** (New York, 1981),
pp. 155-172.

11. The death camps

Required reading
Aharon Weiss, "Categories of Camps - Their Character and Role in the Execution
of the 'Final Solution of the Jewish Question'," in Y. Gutman & A. Saf (eds.),
The Nazi Concentration Camps (Jerusalem, 1984), pp. 115-132.

12. The bystanders

Required reading
Yisrael Gutman, "The Attitude of the Poles to the Mass Deportation of Jews from
the Warsaw Ghetto in the Summer of 1942," in Y. Gutman & E. Zuroff (eds.),
Rescue Attempts During the Holocaust (Jerusalem, 1977), pp. 399-422.

13. Jewish resistance

Required reading
Yitzhak Arad, "Jewish Armed Resistance in Eastern Europe - Its Character-
istics and Problems," in Y. Gutman & L. Rothkirchen (eds.), **The Catastrophe of
European Jewry** (Jerusalem, 1976), pp. 490-517.

Yehuda Bauer, **The Jewish Emergence from Powerlessness** (Toronto, 1979), pp. 26-40.

14. Responses to the Holocaust

Required reading
Walter Laqueur, "Hitler's Holocaust, Who Knew What, When and How," **Encounter** 55 (1980), pp. 6-25.

Henry Feingold, **The Politics of Rescue** (New Brunswick, NJ, 1970), pp. 3-69.

David Wyman, **The Abandonment of the Jews: America & the Holocaust 1941-1945** (New York, 1986), Ch. 15.

15. Rescue attempts

Required reading
David Wyman, "The American Jewish Leadership and the Holocaust," in Randolph Braham (ed.), **Jewish Leadership During the Nazi Era** (New York, 1985), pp. 1-28.

Bela Vago, "Some Aspects of the Yishuv Leadership Activities During the Holocaust," *ibid.*, pp. 45-66.

IV. REQUIREMENTS OF THE COURSE
Students are expected to take a final examination. Those who need graduate credit are also expected to write a paper.

V. CONCEPTUAL FRAMEWORK OF THE COURSE
The course analyzes the fate of the Jews in the modern era from a historical perspective, focusing mainly on the antagonism between the Jews and the surrounding society in the period between the granting of emancipation and the Holocaust.

The major issues discussed are: The reasons for the persistence of anti-Jewish feelings after the eighteenth century. The secularization of religious anti-Judaism and its transformation into modern racial and political antisemitism. The uniqueness of Nazi antisemitism; the place of Judaism in Nazi ideology and policy, showing its centrality for Hitler's worldview. How the solution of the Jewish Question (the Jews perceived by the Nazis as the source of antinatural universalistic ideologies) became the focus of Hitler's expansionist policy. The reactions of the Germans, the European nations under occupation, the Allies, and the Yishuv in Palestine to the persecution of the Jews and their extermination. In this context the responses of the Churches are analyzed in particular. Another main issue discussed in class (with the aid of video material) is Jewish behavior in response to Nazi policy; from the responses of German Jewish leaders to those of the Judenraete in the ghettos. Alternative responses, such as resistance, are also examined.

The process of persecution and destruction from the discriminatory legislation to the death camps, is examined in the light of the contesting interpretations of intentionalist and functionalist historians. (I wish to note that I intentionally do not incorporate other aspects related to the Holocaust such as theology, art and literature, since I consider them to be beyond the scope of the course.)

I. THE COURSE

SEMIOLOGY OF NAZISM: DACHAU CONCENTRATION CAMP

Izidoro Blikstein
Faculty of Philosophy, Literature and Humanities, University of São Paulo, Brazil

II. ACADEMIC CONTEXT OF THE COURSE

The course is given in Portuguese. It is offered at a graduate level in the Faculdade de Filosofia, Letras e Ciencias Humanas for students who have majored in several areas of the Humanities. The faculty's postgraduate system requires the students to take a certain number of courses and to choose a research theme upon which they must present a Master's dissertation or a Ph.D. thesis. The faculty offers graduate courses in approximately 20 disciplines, including languages, literature, linguistics, history, geography, philosophy, and anthropology. The department of Hebrew Language, Jewish Culture and Literature has been recently created and comprises courses in Hebrew Language, Hebrew Literature, Jewish History, and Jewish Culture. These incorporate the Holocaust as a major theme.

It is within the context of the Holocaust that the course "Semiology of Nazism: Dachau Concentration Camp" is placed. The fundamental goal is to guide the students applying the theoretical and methodological apparatus of semiology to the interpretation of the administrative system of Dachau concentration camp, against the background of Nazism's macro-system.

This is a one-semester course, comprising 60 hours. The prerequisites are a general background in Modern European History, in Jewish History and in Linguistics and Semiology.

III. OUTLINE OF THE COURSE

1. Praxis, ideology, stereotypes, perception and language

Reading
R. Arnheim, **Visual Thinking** (Berkeley: University of California Press, 1969).

R. Barthes, **Aula** (São Paulo: Cultrix, 1971).

I. Blikstein, **Kaspar Hauser ou A Fabricação da Realidade** (São Paulo: Cultrix, 1985).

E. Buyssens, **Semiologia e Comunicação Linguistica** (São Paulo: Cultrix, 1982).

E. Conseriu, **El hombre y su lenguaje** (Madrid: Gredos, 1977).

U. Eco, **Tratado de semiótica general** (Barcelona: Lumen, 1977).

M. Foucault, **Surveiller et Punir** (Paris: Gallimard, 1975).

A.J. Greimas, **Sémantique structurale** (Paris: Larousse, 1977).

E. Hall, **The Silent Language** (New York: Anchor Books, 1973).

A. Schaff, **Language et connaissance** (Paris: Anthropos, 1974).

2. The Nazi discourse in the ideological molds of Aryanism, of "verticality," of "purity," of "rectitude" and of "alignment": the semantic "corridor" of anti-semitism

Reading

H. Arendt, **The Origins of Totalitarianism** (New York: Meridian Books, 1969).

S. Berstein, **Le nazisme** (Paris: MA Ed., 1985).

C. David, **Hitler et le nazisme** (Paris: PUF, 1979).

L. Flem, **Le racisme** (Paris: MA Ed., 1985).

S. Freud, **Group Psychology and the Analysis of the Ego** (New York & London: W.W. Norton & Company, 1959).

A. Guyot & P. Restellini, **L'art nazi** (Bruxelles: Ed. Complexe, 1988).

A. Hitler, **Minha Luta** (São Paulo: Moraes, 1977).

F. Jordão, **Dossiê Herzog** (São Paulo: Global Ed., 1979).

M. Jahoda & N.W. Ackerman, **Distúrbios Emocionais e Anti-semitismo** (São Paulo: Perspectiva, 1969).

S. Kracauer, **De Caligari a Hitler** (Barcelona: Paidos, 1985).

H. Michel, **Les fascismes** (Paris: PUF, 1977).

P. Milza, **Le fascisme** (Paris: MA Ed., 1986).

P. Milza & S. Berstein, **Le fascisme italien (1919-1945)** (Paris: Seuil, 1980).

B. Phillips, **Swastika, Cinema of Oppression** (New York: Warner Books, 1976).

J. Ch. Petitfils, **L'extrême droite en France** (Paris: PUF, 1983).

—————, **La droite en France (de 1789 à nos jours)** (Paris: PUF, 1973).

L. Poliakov, **O Mito Ariano** (São Paulo: Perspectiva, Edusp, 1974).

—————, **De Voltaire a Wagner** (São Paulo: Perspectiva, 1985).

A. Portela, **Salazarismo e Artes Plásticas em Portugal** (Lisboa: Instituto de Cultura Portuguesa, 1982).

R. Lionel, **Le nazisme et la culture** (Bruxelles, Ed. Complexe, 1988).

P. Sorlin, **L'antisemitisme allemand** (Paris: Flammarion, 1969).

M.L. Tucci Carneiro, **O Anti-Semitismo na Era de Vargas 1930-1945** (São Paulo: Ed. Brasiliense, 1988).

L. Winckler, **A Função Social da Linguagem Fascista** (Lisboa: Estampa, 1969).

3. Praxis and ideological molds of European Jewry

<u>Reading</u>
A Biblia de Jerusalem (São Paulo: Ed. Paulinas, 1985).

A Lei de Moisés (tradução, explicações e comentarios pelo Rabino Meir Masliah Melamed) (Rio de Janeiro: Gráfica Americana, S.A., 1962).

I. Bashevis Singer, **A Crown of Feathers and Other Stories** (New York: Penguin Books, 1980).

——————, **Um Amigo de Kafka** (A Friend of Kafka and Other Stories) (Porto Alegre: L & PM Ed., 1987).

J. Pinsky, **Origens do Nacionalismo Judaico** (São Paulo: Hucitec, 1978).

C. Roth, **Histoire du Peuple Juif** (Paris: Stock, 1980).

UNESCO (1969), **Vida e Valores do Povo Judeu** (Social Life and Social Values of the Jewish People) (São Paulo: Perspectiva, 1972).

4. Dachau concentration camp within Nazism's ideological macro-system. Semiological obsession: the classification of prisoners through a code of symbols

<u>Reading</u>
P. Berben, **Histoire du camp de concentration de Dachau 1933-1945** (Bruxelles: Comité Internationale de Dachau, 1976).

B. Distel, **Le camp de concentration de Dachau** (Bruxelles: Comité Internationale de Dachau, 1972).

B. Distel & R. Jakusch (eds.), **Concentration Camp Dachau 1933-1945** (Bruxelles: Comité Internationale de Dachau, 1978).

Z. Garber, A.L. Berger & R. Libowitz (eds.), **Methodology in the Academic Teaching of the Holocaust** (Lanham, New York & London: University Press of America, 1988).

M. Gilbert, **Atlas of the Holocaust** (Jerusalem, Tel-Aviv & Haifa: Steimatzky's Agency Ltd., 1982).

I. Gutman & A. Saf (eds.), **The Nazi Concentration Camps** (Jerusalem: Yad Vashem, 1984).

I. Gutman & L. Rothkirchen (eds.), **The Catastrophe of European Jewry** (Jerusalem: Yad Vashem, 1976).

IV. REQUIREMENTS OF THE COURSE FOR GRADING
Participation in a seminar on one of the major themes of the course; a paper (8-10 pages), usually an analysis of one bibliographical source; a final examination.

V.   CONCEPTUAL FRAMEWORK OF THE COURSE
This course offers a very particular perspective in research and teaching of the Holocaust, namely the semiological point of view in the interpretation of the deeper meaning which underlies the signs and the symbols of Nazi discourse.

The starting point of the course is the interpretation of the deeper meaning of Dachau prisoners' classification chart. Controlled by a code of diagrams (▽ ⊙) and color (red, brown, pink, black) combination, this chart is an authentic semiological system the signs of which indicate, in a clear and precise way, the prisoners' sociocultural and psychological characteristics, such as ethnic origin, ideology, religion, behavior and personality. In searching for a semiological explanation for the prisoners' signs or marks, it becomes evident how this system of classification contributed to the larger context of the Dachau concentration camp's administrative structure. This structure, in turn was part of a macro-system: Nazism's administrative organization. The relationship among these systems justifies semiological investigation, since a micro-system of signs and symbols can only be understood and interpreted within the sociocultural and ideological dimensions of the macro-system in which it is situated.

The course falls into four parts (coinciding with the four months of study), each informed by a conceptual framework as follows:

Part one: The course aims at demonstrating how our perceptions and our minds are conditioned and controlled by language and symbolic systems, which are in themselves tied up with a network of stereotypes, semantic "corridors" and ideological molds. Thus, the human mind perceives and captures a symbolic "reality" which has been *fabricated* by the network of stereotypes and semantic "corridors." To arrive, therefore, at the deeper meaning of symbolic systems, it is necessary to detect the whole network of stereotypes, semantic "corridors" and ideological molds which underlies them.

Part two: The students are guided through an analysis of the ideological molds and semantic "corridors" which trigger off the discourse and the symbolic systems of Nazism: Aryanism, purity, verticality, alignment, etc. This analysis enables us to understand how the semantic "corridor" of antisemitism is in the very center of the network of stereotypes and semantic "corridors" of Nazism: in fact, anti-semitism was a necessity for the Nazi ideology.

Part three: The course analyzes the cultural universe of European Jewry and the ideological molds which governed its *Weltanschauung*. In this way the course draws out the implications of the conflict between two great semantic "corridors": *aryanism* and *semitism*, a conflict "solved" in the system of the concentration camps and in the Holocaust.

Part four: The course tries to demonstrate the coherence of the relationship between the three systems: the macro-system of Nazism, the system of the Dachau concentration camp, and the Dachau prisoners' classification chart. This chart is a microcosm of the ideological postulates of Nazism. To analyze the chart of Dachau is to unveil the way in which a totalitarian system controls the mind and behavior of humans and legitimates any and every kind of violence.

I. THE COURSE

THE HOLOCAUST AND CANADIAN JEWISH LITERATURE

Rachel Feldhay Brenner
Stong College, York University, Toronto

II. ACADEMIC CONTEXT OF THE COURSE

This is an undergraduate course and no previous knowledge of the subject is assumed. It is geared to the considerable Jewish student body at York University. Stong College focuses on cultural studies in a multi-cultural context. The College encourages studies of various ethnic groups, and as such is receptive to exploring issues pertaining to the Jewish experience in Canada.

The course focuses on the impact of the Holocaust on Canadian Jewish postwar writing. Emphasis is also placed on the Canadian response to the European tragedy in the context of Jewish experience in Canada in the 1930s and the 1940s.

III. OUTLINE OF THE COURSE

1. Canadian response to the rise of Nazism

Required reading
Lita-Rose Betcherman, **The Swastika and the Maple Leaf: Fascist Movements in**

Canada in the Thirties (Toronto, 1978).

Stanley R. Barrett, **Is God a Racist? The Right Wing in Canada** (Toronto, 1987), Part I.

Recommended reading
Merrily Weisbord, **The Strangest Dream: Canadian Communists, the Spy Trials, and the Cold War** (Toronto, 1983).

2. Canadian response to the Jewish plight in Europe

Required reading
Irving Abella and Harold Troper, **None Is Too Many: Canada and the Jews of Europe 1933-1948** (Toronto, 1982).

M. Weinfeld, W. Shaffir & I. Cottler (eds.), **The Canadian Jewish Mosaic**, Part I: "Early Encounters" (Toronto, 1981).

3. Literary representations of Jewish immigrant experience in Canada

Required reading
Adele Weisman, **The Sacrifice** (Toronto, 1972).

——————, **Crackpot** (Toronto, 1982).

Irving Layton, "Waiting for the Messiah," **Canadian Literature** 101 (1984) pp. 7-14.

Mordecai Richler, **The Street** (Harmondsworth, 1977).

Edna Paris, **Jews: An Account of Their Experience in Canada** (Toronto, 1980).

4. The Holocaust: survivors' literary responses

Required reading
Elie Wiesel, "Why I Write," in Alvin H. Rosenfeld & Irving Greenberg (eds.), **Confronting the Holocaust: The Impact of Elie Wiesel** (Bloomington, 1978).

——————, **Night** (New York, 1970).

Shirley Neuman (ed.), **Henry Kreisel: Another Country** (Edmonton, 1985).

Henry Kreisel, **The Rich Man** (Toronto, 1961).

——————, **The Betrayal** (Toronto, 1982).

Recommended reading
Sidra Ezrahi, **By Words Alone: The Holocaust in Literature** (Chicago, 1978).

5. A.M. Klein: Canadian response to the European tragedy

Required reading
M.W. Steinberg & Usher Caplan (eds.), **A.M. Klein: Beyond the Sambation: Selected Essays and Editorials 1928 - 1955** (Toronto, 1982).

A.M. Klein, "Hath Not a Jew," "Poems," "The Hitleriad," in Miriam Waddington (ed.), **The Collected Poems of A.M. Klein** (Toronto, 1974).

Recommended reading
Usher Caplan, **Like One That Dreamed: A Portrait of A.M. Klein** (Toronto, 1982).

6. Holocaust consciousness in postwar Canadian Jewish writing

Required reading
Irving Layton, **Fortunate Exiles** (Toronto, 1987).

Mordecai Richler, **St. Urbain's Horseman** (Toronto, 1972).

———————, **Joshua Then and Now** (New York, 1981).

———————, **Shovelling Trouble** (London, 1973).

Leonard Cohen, **Let Us Compare Mythologies** (Toronto, 1956).

———————, **Flowers for Hitler** (Toronto, 1964).

Sheldon Oberman & Elaine Newton (eds.), **Mirror of the People: Canadian Jewish Experience in Poetry and Prose** (Winnipeg, 1985), Parts IV and V.

Recommended reading
Alan Berger, **Crisis and Covenant: The Holocaust in American Jewish Fiction** (Albany, 1985).

7. Canadian Jewish response to the State of Israel

Required reading
A.M. Klein, **The Second Scroll** (Toronto, 1969).

—————, **Beyond the Sambation** (Toronto, 1982).

Irving Layton, **Taking Sides** (Oakville, 1977).

Mordecai Richler, "This Year in Jerusalem: An Israeli Journal, March 31, 1962," **Hunting Tigers Under Glass** (Toronto, 1968).

Recommended reading
Emil L. Fackenheim, **God's Presence in History: Jewish Affirmations and Philosophical Reflexions** (New York, 1970).

IV. REQUIREMENTS OF THE COURSE FOR GRADING
Students are expected to write two short essays during the first term, one long essay in the second term, and also to present two oral reports.

V. CONCEPTUAL FRAMEWORK OF THE COURSE
The rationale for this course stems from the view that the study of Holocaust representations in literature can counteract the evolving process of reductive abstraction of that mammoth tragedy. As the distance from the event increases, systematic study of creative response to it underscores the emotional impact of the tragic loss on the postwar world. Exploration of literary responses to the Holocaust not only keeps the memory alive, but also helps us to understand the extent to which historical consciousness determines our social relationships today.

The course focuses on the impact of the Holocaust on Jews who witnessed the destruction of European Jewry from the safe distance of the North American continent. In that respect, Canadian Jewish literature offers an interesting case study. Canadian writers-outsiders, unlike writers-survivors who often display reluctance to deal with their experience, demonstrate a tendency to explore the implications of the tragedy on the Jewish psyche in the postwar world.

For the most part, Canadian writers are sons and daughters of an immigrant generation. The consciousness of the pogroms in Eastern Europe, transmitted through the collective experience of the parental generation, compounded the sense of fear and anxiety provoked by the awareness of rekindled Jewish suffering in Europe. The sense of insecurity was further deepened by the direct experience of surging anti-semitism in Canada itself. The emergence of the fascist movement in Quebec in the 1930s augmented the sense of rejection and alienation of the Jewish minority vis-a-vis general society.

The convergence of disturbing local antisemitic phenomena and the consciousness of Jewish victimization in Europe has generated an increasingly problematic issue of self-identity for the Canadian Jew. The problem manifests itself, perhaps most clearly, in the conflict-ridden response to the State of Israel. The desire to escape the fate of the Jewish victim, symbolized by the Holocaust, is demonstrated in literary representations of constant vacillation between the pole of nationalism, as represented by the Jewish State, and the pole of liberal universal humanism.

The study of literary responses to the recent tragic history of the Jewish people aims at clarification and exploration of issues which engage the Jewish individual at present. While drawing on past experience, the course invariably directs the student to analytical examination and comprehension of the historical, sociological, and emotional components of his/her interaction with all mankind.

I. THE COURSE

HOLOCAUST PERSPECTIVES

Michael Brown
Division of Humanities, York University, Canada; Department of History and Judaic Studies Program (visiting), University of California at San Diego.

II. ACADEMIC CONTEXT OF THE COURSE

Two 80-minute meetings a week for one 10-week quarter, including occasional lectures, but mostly in the form of seminar-discussions.

UCSD is a medium-sized (c. 15,000 students) state university, considered one of the best in the University of California system. An upper-division course, "Holocaust Perspectives" was designed for third-year and fourth-year students, 25 of whom enrolled.

Students included a number taking the course as an elective and others who were History or Judaic Studies majors. Several had some familiarity with the subject matter. Since Judaic Studies majors at UCSD concentrate in Bible, even they did not necessarily know much about modern Jewish history. About half the students were Jewish.

III. OUTLINE OF THE COURSE

<u>Books Required for Purchase</u>
William S. Allen, **The Nazi Seizure of Power.**
Hannah Arendt, **Eichmann in Jerusalem.**
Lucy Dawidowicz, **The War Against the Jews.**
Primo Levi, **Survival in Auschwitz.**
Emanuel Ringelblum, **Notes from the Warsaw Ghetto.**
Andre Schwarz-Bart, **The Last of the Just.**

A. The Setting
   1. Introduction: Europe, the seedbed of the Holocaust

   Required reading
   "Emancipation" and "Europe", in **Encyclopedia Judaica**.

   Michael Marrus, "The Theory and Practice of Anti-Semitism," **Commentary** (August 1982), pp. 38-42.

   Suggested reading
   Shmuel Ettinger, "Jew-Hatred in Its Historical Context," **Immanuel** (Fall 1980), pp. 81-94.

   Jacob Katz, **From Prejudice to Destruction: Anti-Semitism, 1700-1933**.

   James Parkes, **Antisemitism**.

   Leon Poliakov, **The History of Antisemitism**.

   Jacob Talmon, "European History as the Seedbed of the Holocaust," in **Holocaust and Rebirth, A Symposium**, pp. 11-76.

   2. Jews in Germany

   Required reading
   Peter Gay, "German Jews in Wilhelmian Culture," in **Freud, Jews and Other Germans**, pp. 93-168, or in **Midstream** (February 1975), pp. 23-65.

   Gershom Scholem, "Jews and Germans" in W.J. Dannhauser (ed.), **On Jews and Judaism in Crisis**, pp. 71-92.

   Dawidowicz, pp. 29-62.

   Suggested reading
   George Mosse, **The Crisis of German Ideology**.

   Sanford Ragins, **Jewish Responses to German Anti-Semitism 1870-1914**.

Jehuda Reinharz, **Fatherland or Promised Land?**

Fritz Stern, **Dreams and Delusions: The Drama of German History.**

3. Jews in Germany

Required reading
Andre Schwarz-Bart, **The Last of the Just.**

Suggested reading
Seymour Cain, "The Holocaust and Christian Responsibility," **Midstream** (April 1982), pp. 20-27.

Rosemary Radford Ruether, "Anti-Semitism and Christian Theology," in Eva

Fleischner (ed.), **Auschwitz: Beginning of a New Era?** (New York: Ktav, 1974), pp. 79-92.

Uriel Tal, **Christians and Jews in Germany.**

B. The Event
    4. Hitler, the man and leader

Required reading
Dawidowicz, pp. 3-28.

Film: *The Triumph of the Will.*

Suggested reading
Alan Bullock, **Hitler.**

John Toland, **Adolf Hitler.**

5. The Nazi seizure of power

Required reading
William S. Allen, **The Nazi Seizure of Power.**

Dawidowicz, pp. 63-92.

Suggested reading
Karl A. Schleunes, **The Twisted Road to Auschwitz.**

Wendelgard van Staden, **Darkness Over the Valley,** pp. 1-50.

Bernt Englemann, **In Hitler's Germany,** pp. 3-165.

6. The banality of evil

Required reading
Hannah Arendt, **Eichmann in Jerusalem,** pp. 1-134.

Dawidowicz, pp. 93-116.

Kazimierz Moczanski, "Conversations with a Hangman," **Midstream** (November 1980), pp. 31-41.

Suggested reading
Michael Kater, **The Nazi Party.**

Albert Speer, **Inside the Third Reich: Memoirs.**

7. Responses of the outside world

Required reading
Irving Abella & Harold Troper, "'The Line Must Be Drawn Somewhere', Canada and the Jewish Refugees 1933-39," **Canadian Historical Review** (June 1979), or in M. Weinfeld, W. Shaffir, & I. Cottler (eds.), **The Canadian Jewish Mosaic,** pp. 49-78.

Dawidowicz, pp. 117-171, 201-223.

Suggested reading
Irving Abella and Harold Troper, **None Is Too Many.**

Henry L. Feingold, **The Politics of Rescue.**

Bernard Wasserstein, **Britain and the Jews of Europe 1939-1945.**

David Wyman, **Paper Walls,** and **The Abandonment of the Jews: America & the Holocaust 1941-1945.**

8. Under fire

   Required reading
   Robert Weltsch, "The Yellow Badge, Wear It With Pride" (tr. from **Juedische Rundschau,** 4 April 1933).

   Yehuda Bauer, "Jewish Resistance During the Holocaust," **The Jewish Emergence from Powerlessness.**

   Emanuel Ringelblum, **Notes from the Warsaw Ghetto.**

   Dawidowicz, pp. 227-461.

   Suggested reading
   Moshe Flinker, **Young Moshe's Diary.**

   Anne Frank, **The Diary of a Young Girl.**

   Yisrael Gutman, **The Jews of Warsaw 1939-1943. Ghetto, Underground, Revolt.**

   Phillip P. Hallie, **Lest Innocent Blood Be Shed.**

   John Hersey, **The Wall.**

   Janusz Korczak, **Ghetto Diary.**

   Michael Marrus & Robert O. Paxton, **Vichy France and the Jews.**

   Nehama Tec, **Dry Tears.**

Isaiah Trunk, **Judenrat: The Jewish Councils in Eastern Europe under Nazi Occupation.**

9. The camps

<u>Required reading</u>
Bruno Bettelheim, **The Informed Heart**, Chs. 4-7.

Primo Levi, **Survival in Auschwitz: The Nazi Assault on Humanity.**

Dawidowicz, pp. 173-200, 463-479.

<u>Suggested reading</u>
Terrence Des Pres, **The Survivor.**

Viktor Frankl, **Man's Search for Meaning.**

C. The Aftermath
   10. Distortions and appropriations of the Holocaust

<u>Required reading</u>
Edward Alexander, "Stealing the Holocaust," **Midstream** (November 1980), pp. 46-51.

Robert Alter, "Deformations of the Holocaust," **Commentary** (February 1981), pp. 48-54.

Hannah Arendt, **Eichmann in Jerusalem**, pp. 135-256.

<u>Suggested reading</u>
William Styron, **Sophie's Choice.**

Jacob Neusner, "Wanted: a New Myth," **Moment Magazine** (March 1980), pp. 34-35, 61, or his **Stranger at Home**, pp. 82-91.

IV. REQUIREMENTS OF THE COURSE FOR GRADING

Mid-term examination (25%); research paper (topic open, subject to the approval of the instructor) 10-12 pp. (30%); final examination (30%); the remainder of the grade (15%) based on class presentations and participation.

Example of examination questions:

1. In the context of this course, identify as fully as you can in the time allotted, *five* of the following   (45 minutes, 25 marks).

Alberto	Denmark
Anne Frank's family	Rudolf Kastner
Butz, Faurisson & Roeder	Georg Simmel
the thirteen	Robert Weltsch
Miss Blumenthal	Adam Czerniakow
Moslem	Kosow, Galicia
Szmuel Zygelboim	Home Army (Armija Krajowa)

2. Answer *one* of the following (45 minutes, 25 marks).
   A. Compare the views of Hannah Arendt and Primo Levi regarding the psychology of Europe's Jews during and prior to the Holocaust.
   B. Compare the views of Bruno Bettelheim and Yehuda Bauer with regard to Jews' willingness to revolt against the Nazi oppression.

3. Answer *one* of the following (45 minutes, 25 marks).
   C. What do revisionist approaches have to contribute to the understanding of the Holocaust?
   D. In what ways, if at all, did the responses of the "free world" affect Nazi policy between 1933 and 1942?

4. Answer *one* of the following (45 minutes, 25 marks).
   E. "The Holocaust was a German - and not a Jewish - event." Discuss with appropriate and extensive references to readings and class discussions.
   F. "The Holocaust was a Christian - and not a Jewish - event." Discuss with appropriate and extensive references to readings and class discussions.

V.   CONCEPTUAL FRAMEWORK OF THE COURSE

This is a course in the history of the Holocaust and in the dimensions of history. It is designed to encourage students to view the Holocaust in a number of contexts (Jewish history, German history, Christian-Jewish relations, and international relations) through a variety of methodological approaches (political, social and psycho-history; the "great man" theory, and the history of ideas) and types of material (historical texts, memoirs, documents of the period, and the historical novel). These different perspectives make evident the complexity of the Holocaust as an event which had many different "causes," and which altered human life in many different ways. The Holocaust is seen as a new departure in history, the kind of turning point that occurs only when the way has been prepared through philosophical, political, social, and technological developments. As a result, it can be comprehended only by considering several aspects of human life.

The final week of the course is devoted to a discussion of the aftermath of the Holocaust, to the ways in which the Holocaust is "used" in contemporary culture and ideologies as an illustration of "the uses and abuses of history".

I. THE COURSE

MODERN ANTISEMITISM AND THE HOLOCAUST

Richard I. Cohen
Department of Jewish History, The Hebrew University of Jerusalem
Jewish Theological Seminary, New York (visiting)

II. ACADEMIC CONTENT OF THE COURSE

This course was prepared for a summer session at the Jewish Theological Seminary, New York. Classes were held three times a week, on consecutive days, limiting the possibility of extensive reading. Emphasis was thus placed on the sources examined at each session. Students were not required to have a background in modern Jewish history or European history. Documentary sources marked with an asterisk were to be photocopied and brought to class in the relevant session.

III. OUTLINE OF THE COURSE

1. Introduction

    Can the Holocaust be studied? Are memory and scholarship reconcilable? Interrelationship between the history of antisemitism and the Holocaust; theories of antisemitism. Inevitability of the Holocaust; could it have been prevented? The place of the Jews in the study of the Holocaust - not only what was done to the Jews, but their response to the persecution in various countries. Some theoretical hypotheses on the causes of the Holocaust from psychological and sociological perspectives.

2. The historical background

    The integration of the Jews in Europe from the eighteenth century until the outbreak of modern antisemitism in the second half of the nineteenth century. Sources of confrontation - social and ideological. Achievement of political emancipation in western and central Europe. Expectations of Jews by theorists of Jewish emancipation.

<u>Required reading</u>
Jacob Katz, **From Prejudice to Destruction: Anti-Semitism 1700-1933** (Cambridge, Mass., 1983), pp. 51-63; 74-92. Optional: *Ibid.*, pp. 63-73; 92-104.

*P. Mendes-Flohr & J. Reinharz (eds.), **The Jew in the Modern World** (New York, Oxford, 1980), pp. 27-36; 44-46.

3. The rise of political antisemitism in Western and Central Europe
Revolutions of 1848 and their impact on modern antisemitism. Beginnings of a political antisemitic movement in Germany, Austria, Hungary and France. Major ideological and social tendencies; central figures and positions. Inter-relationships between the movements and their ideologies. Peak of political success at the end of the century. Reasons for decline. Comparative analysis of the movement in Germany and France.

<u>Required reading</u>
Peter Pulzer, **The Rise of Political Antisemitism in Germany and Austria, 1870-1914** (New York, 1964), pp. 37-59.

*Mendes-Flohr & Reinharz, pp. 268-273; 276-278; 280-284.

4. Patterns of Jewish response to modern antisemitism (1870-1914)
Comparative inquiry into the ways Jews responded to antagonistic expressions on the part of European society. The meaning of Jewish "passive" behavior, "assimilatory" and political responses; the nationalist response. What can be defined as a "response" to antisemitism? What can be seen as an outgrowth of the process of political integration in the host society?

<u>Required reading</u>
Ben Halpern, "Reactions to Antisemitism in Modern Jewish History," J. Reinharz (ed.), **Living with Antisemitism** (Hanover, London, 1987), pp. 3-15.

Choose one of the following:
<u>France</u>: Michael Marrus, **The Politics of Assimilation** (Oxford, 1971), ch. 8.
<u>Germany</u>: Ismar Schorsch, **Jewish Reactions to German Anti-Semitism, 1870-1914** (New York, Philadelphia, 1972), pp. 53-79.

Austria: J. Toury, "Defence Activities of the Osterreichisch-Israelitische Union before 1914," in Reinharz (ed.), pp. 167-192.

5. Hitler and the "Final Solution" - the problem and its interpretations
The role of Hitler in the evolution of National Socialism and its Jewish policy. The sources and the historical debate. Was ideology a central force in the success of the National Socialists? Discussion will focus on Hitler's writings and on their interpretation by various schools of thought.

Required reading
Eberhard Jaeckel, **Hitler's Weltanschauung, A Blueprint for Power** (Middletown, 1972), pp. 47-66, or **Hitler in History** (Hanover, London, 1984), pp. 44-65.

Michael Marrus, **The Holocaust in History** (Hanover, London, 1987), pp. 9-18.

Optional: Martin Broszat, "Hitler and the Genesis of the 'Final Solution': An Assessment of David Irving's Theses," **Yad Vashem Studies** XIII, 1979, pp. 73-125.

6. The road to destruction: twisted or straight?
Related to the previous discussion is the nature of the National Socialist drive to exterminate the Jews. Was it built into the structure of the movement, or did it evolve after all other possibilities of "removing the Jews from German society" had been exhausted? Was it ideologically enunciated, or a product of practical developments? Basic Nazi legislation. The historical debate on this question has assumed serious proportions, and it too will be analyzed.

Required reading
Raul Hilberg, **The Destruction of the European Jews** (New York, 1985), pp. 27-38.

Karl Schleunes, **The Twisted Road to Auschwitz** (Urbana, 1970), pp. 92-132. (Skim details if too much reading.)

*Y. Arad, Y. Gutman & A. Margaliot (eds.), **Documents on the Holocaust: Selected Sources on the Destruction of the Jews of Germany and Austria, Poland and the Soviet Union** (Jerusalem, 1981), Nos. 8-10; 30-34; 53.

7. From theory to practice: towards the "Final Sólution"
   War was a central weapon used by the Nazis to achieve their political and social goals. How did this influence the decision to bring about the "Final Solution"? Who were the figures involved in this decision, and when was it actually taken? The connection between the war in the Soviet Union and the "Final Solution."

   Required reading
   Christopher R. Browning, **Fateful Months: Essays on the Emergence of the Final Solution** (New York and London), 1985, pp. 8-38.

8. Conquering Europe - the fall of Poland
   The consequences of German occupation in Eastern Europe, as seen in the densely populated Jewish community of Poland. Establishment of ghettos. Internal Jewish structure.

   Required reading
   Lucy Dawidowicz, **The War Against the Jews, 1933-1945** (New York, 1975), pp. 197-222.

   *Arad, Gutman, Margaliot (eds.), Nos. 65-68.

   Optional: Yisrael Gutman, **The Jews of Warsaw, 1939-1943. Ghetto, Underground, Revolt** (Bloomington, 1982), pp. 3-48.

9. Conquering Western Europe - the fate of France
   Germany's military victories wrought havoc no less in Western Europe. Test-case for study: France underwent an internal revolution of its own, occasioned by the defeat and by internal social and political problems. Comparative look at different countries in an analogous situation.

Required reading
M.R. Marrus and R.O. Paxton, **Vichy France and the Jews** (New York, 1981), pp. 3-21.

10. Public opinion and the "Final Solution"
Recent historical research has focused on the nature of societies under National Socialism and shied away from the traditional concept of "totalitarian societies". What is "public opinion" in a society where freedom of speech is severely curtailed? How does one gauge its impact? What did people in Germany and elsewhere know about the "Final Solution"?

Required reading
Ian Kershaw, "The Persecution of the Jews and German Popular Opinion in the Third Reich," **Leo Baeck Institute Yearbook** XXVI (1981), pp. 261-289.

Optional: M.R. Marrus, **The Holocaust in History**, pp. 84-107.

11. The Allies and the Holocaust
The role of the bystanders in the Holocaust, the position of the American government in particular, has been seriously questioned in recent years. This relates both to the prewar period, when immigration possibilities were greater, and to the war period when unorthodox types of assistance were required. Evian, Bermuda, and the War Refugee Board are discussed. Could Auschwitz have been bombed?

Required reading
David Wyman, **The Abandonment of the Jews: America & the Holocaust, 1941-1945** (New York, 1984), pp. 124-156; 288-307. Optional: 104-123.

Bernard Wasserstein, **Britain and the Jews of Europe, 1939-1945** (Oxford, 1979), pp. 197-222.

12. Jewish responses to the Holocaust
How did the Jewish communities across Europe face the advent of Nazism, and how did they function? Excessive debate has accompanied the attempt to arrive at an understanding of the internal dilemmas of the Jewish community.

Required reading
Hilberg, op. cit., pp. 295-305.

I. Trunk, **Judenrat** (New York, 1972, 1982), pp. 14-35. Optional: pp. 115-185.

*Arad, Gutman, Margaliot (eds.), Nos. 109; 119-121; 127-130.

13. Jewish resistance to Nazism
    How to define resistance? Under what circumstances was physical resistance
    utilized by Jewish groups against the Nazis? Moral and social considerations
    involved in deciding to opt for resistance. Attitude of Judenraete to resis-
    tance.

    Required reading
    Y. Gutman, **The Jews of Warsaw, 1939-1945. Ghetto, Underground, Revolt**
    (Bloomington, 1982), pp. 283-307; 336-363.

    *Arad, Gutman, Margaliot, Nos. 134-152 (Selected).

14. Halakhic and cultural issues during the Holocaust

    Required reading
    I.J. Rosenbaum, **The Holocaust and the Halakhah** (New York, 1976), pp. 17-46.

IV. REQUIREMENTS OF THE COURSE FOR GRADING
    Class participation and a final examination paper.

V. CONCEPTUAL FRAMEWORK OF THE COURSE
    This course explores major problems in the history of the Holocaust, and their
    antecedents in modern antisemitism of the late nineteenth century. Each segment
    focuses on a major theme in the history of antisemitism and the Holocaust, and
    draws on a variety of primary and secondary sources.
        The major questions posed and the unfolding themes are incorporated in section
    III, Outline of the Course.

I. THE COURSE

PROBLEMS IN THE STUDY OF THE HOLOCAUST

David Engel
Department of History, Tel Aviv University
University of Pennsylvania (visiting)

II. ACADEMIC CONTEXT OF THE COURSE
This course was presented under the auspices of the Joseph Meyerhoff Visiting Professorship in Modern Jewish History at the University of Pennsylvania. The University of Pennsylvania is a private institution of some 16,000 students; its admissions policy is highly selective, and it is generally regarded as an elite institution. The Meyerhoff Visiting Professorship was established in 1987 in order to enable the History Department, which is noted for strengths in, inter alia, modern European, German, and Russian-Soviet history, to offer courses in the history of the Jews in modern Europe.

The course was offered as a weekly three-hour seminar for senior majors in history and was limited in advance to fifteen students. It was assumed that all of the students would have taken courses in the history of Europe in the twentieth century (although not in the history of European Jewry) and would have been exposed to the rudiments of historical method. It was further assumed that at least some of the students would later pursue advanced degrees in history. In the event, over half of the students had previously taken a course on the history of the Third Reich; none had studied any Jewish history; and three applied to graduate school (two in history, one in German literature). The class consisted of eleven Jews and four non-Jews.

III. OUTLINE OF THE COURSE
1. The ideological roots of total murder

Required reading
Y. Arad, Y. Gutman & A. Margaliot (eds.), **Documents on the Holocaust**

67

(Jerusalem. 1978), nos. 1-5.

Lucy S. Dawidowicz, **The War Against the Jews** (New York, 1975), ch. 1.

Eberhard Jaeckel, **Hitler's World View** (Cambridge, 1981), chs. 2-6.

2. The Holocaust and antisemitism - continuity and difference

    Required reading
    Dawidowicz, ch. 2.

    Karl A. Schleunes, **The Twisted Road to Auschwitz** (Urbana, 1970), ch. 1.

    Ismar Schorsch, "German Antisemitism in the Light of Post-War Historiography," **Leo Baeck Institute Yearbook** XIX (1974).

    Shulamit Volkov, "Antisemitism as a Cultural Code," **Leo Baeck Institute Yearbook** XXIII (1978).

3. Why Germany?

    Required reading
    Karl Dietrich Bracher, **The German Dictatorship** (New York, 1970), pp. 3-49, 67-79.

    Ian Kershaw, "The Persecution of the Jews and German Popular Opinion in the Third Reich," **Leo Baeck Institute Yearbook** XXVI (1981).

    Otto Dov Kulka, "Public Opinion in Nazi Germany and the Final Solution," **Jerusalem Quarterly** 26 (1983).

    Schleunes, ch. 2

4. German Jewish policy, 1933-1944 - preset or improvised?

    Required reading
    Arad et al., nos. 6-12, 30-36, 43, 45-48, 52-53.

Dawidowicz, chs. 3-5.

Gerhard Hirschfeld (ed.), **The Policies of Genocide** (London, 1986), pp. 77-129.

Schleunes, chs. 3-7.

5. The proximate origins of the Final Solution

Required reading
Arad et al., nos. 65-70, 75-77, 87-92, 97, 105-108, 160-163, 169.

Martin Broszat, "Hitler and the Genesis of the Final Solution," **Yad Vashem Studies** XIII (1979).

Dawidowicz, chs. 6, 8.

Gerald Fleming, **Hitler and the Final Solution** (Berkeley, 1984), pp. vii-xxxiii, 66-106.

Hirschfeld, pp. 1-29.

6. The Judenraete

Required reading
Arad et al., nos. 72, 74, 81, 94, 100-101, 109-112, 118, 120-21, 165, 187-190, 192, 194-95.

Dawidowicz, chs. 11, 14.

Helen Fein, **Accounting for Genocide** (New York, 1979), ch. 5.

Isaiah Trunk, **Judenrat** (New York, 1972), Introduction, chs. 16, 19, 21.

7. **Resistance - Armed and Other**

Required reading
Arad et al., nos. 78-80, 82-86, 93-96, 98-99, 102-104, 116-18, 125-29, 131, 135, 157, 172-73, 185-86, 191, 198-200.

Dawidowicz, chs. 12, 13, 15.

Fein, chs. 8, 9.

Shmuel Krakowski, **The War of the Doomed** (New York, 1984), chs. 1, 12.

8. Information and knowledge

Required reading
Yehuda Bauer, **The Holocaust in Historical Perspective** (Seattle, 1979), ch. 1.

Walter Laqueur, **The Terrible Secret** (Boston, 1980), chs. 1, 2, 4, 5, Conclusion.

9. The response of World Jewry

Required reading
Henry L. Feingold, **Did American Jewry Do Enough During the Holocaust?** (pamphlet).

Laqueur, ch. 6.

David Wyman, **The Abandonment of the Jews: America & the Holocaust 1941-1945** (New York, 1984), pp. 61-103, 143-77, 345-47.

10. The response of the Western Allies

Required reading
David Engel, "The Western Allies and the Holocaust," **Polin** I (1986).

Fein, ch. 7.

Laqueur, ch. 3.

Bernard Wasserstein, **Britain and the Jews of Europe 1939-1945** (Oxford, 1979), pp. 134-221.

Wyman, pp. 104-42, 178-206.

11. The response of the immediate bystanders

Required reading
Chimen Abramsky, Maciej Jachimczyk & Antony Polonsky (eds.), **The Jews in Poland** (Oxford, 1986), chs. 13-15.

Bauer, ch. 3.

Fein, chs. 2-4, 6.

12. The uniqueness and universality of the Holocaust

Required reading
Bauer, ch. 2.

Fein, ch. 1.

Uriel Tal, "On the Study of the Holocaust and Genocide," **Yad Vashem Studies** XIII (1982).

IV. REQUIREMENTS OF THE COURSE FOR GRADING
Each student is required to prepare a written bibliography of secondary literature on his assigned topic, to make an oral presentation on his topic at a class session, and to submit a written paper (20-30 typwritten pages) on a specific aspect of his topic.

V. CONCEPTUAL FRAMEWORK OF THE COURSE
In accordance with the anticipated profile of the students, the course is designed primarily to identify some of the central questions concerning the Holocaust that have occupied the attention of professional historians in recent years and to

convey a sense of the debates that these questions have aroused. Attention is paid to the types of available evidence that might throw light on the problems under discussion and to the way in which various historians employed such evidence in formulating their positions on these issues.

Each of the topics listed above is assigned to one or two students, who are responsible for initiating discussion during the week in which the topic is treated. The vehicle for accomplishing this task is a bibliography of relevant secondary literature (books and journal articles) that each student prepares on the topic that he has been assigned, and distributes to the entire class. Each student opens the discussion for which he is responsible by commenting upon the most significant works listed in his bibliography. All students are expected to have read the listed core readings in preparation for each session, so that they have the necessary background to participate intelligently in the discussions.

On the level of content, the course begins from the premise that the Holocaust is, in the first instance, a case of murder and that therefore the initial tasks of the investigator are to establish the murderer's motive and opportunity. From this exordium the course examines various explanations that have been advanced by professional historians. Whereas investigation of motive involves, primarily, consideration of the murderer, investigation of opportunity also involves consideration of the victim and the bystanders.

Beyond the content level, the course also operates on the level of method. It is designed to demonstrate how the tools of the academic historian can be put to use in understanding a phenomenon as formidable as the Holocaust and to give students practice in using those tools on a rudimentary level in a structured, supervised setting. In the process of pursuing this goal, students will also, it is hoped, become aware that the historical discipline has limits as a tool for understanding the Holocaust, and an effort is made to bring them up against those limits. This situation is encountered especially in the discussions under rubrics 1, 3, 7 and 8, although it is evident in other discussions as well.

I. THE COURSE

LITERATURE AND HISTORICAL MEMORY: HOLOCAUST LITERATURE AND THE LANGUAGE OF CATASTROPHE

Sidra Ezrahi
Institute of Contemporary Jewry, The Hebrew University of Jerusalem

II. ACADEMIC CONTEXT OF THE COURSE

Versions of this course have been taught in different academic contexts at the Hebrew University and at Duke University. In the graduate program of the Institute of Contemporary Jewry, courses on Holocaust literature are taught in Hebrew to students who are presumed to have a rich background in Jewish texts. A general survey course in "Literature and Historical Memory" has alternated with a more specific course in "The Lamentation Tradition and the Holocaust in Hebrew Literature". These courses are generally offered as two semester courses that meet once a week for an hour and a half (or sometimes as a semester course that meets twice weekly). They are organized as seminars with an emphasis on discussion and student presentations on texts related to the material under consideration.

The other context in which versions of the course on "Literature and Historical Memory" have been offered is the one-year program of the Rothberg School for Overseas Students. The students here represent a cross-section of the American (Jewish) student body - coming from many universities and diverse backgrounds. Although most of the students are Jewish, one cannot presume any specific level of competence regarding Jewish culture and texts, and the levels of sophistication vary tremendously in such a heterogeneous student population. The course is limited to 25-30 students in order to protect the opportunity for discussion of what is both emotionally and intellectually challenging material.

The reading for all these courses comprises imaginative and critical texts written in several languages. Depending on the linguistic competence of the individual students, the material is read in the original or in Hebrew or English translation.

One characteristic common to the courses offered both in the regular University program and in the Overseas program is the diversity of disciplines represented by the students. Although prerequisites for the Overseas course include some familiarity with the historical material and some competence in literature, many of the students who take these courses are not literature majors, and terms of reference must be established as we proceed.

III. OUTLINE OF THE COURSE
1. Introduction: violence, persecution and destruction as themes in contemporary literature
    Critical discussions of the impact of   World War I on Western literature and selected readings from the literature of that war.

2. The language of catastrophe
    Kafka and/or inter bellum texts such as Werfel's **Forty Days of Musa Dagh.**

3. Holocaust literature: documentary literature
    Peter Weiss, **The Investigation** or Rolf Hochhuth, **The Deputy.**

4. "Concentrationary realism"
    Tadeusz Borowski, **This Way to the Gas, Ladies and Gentlemen.**

5. Literature of survival
    Ilona Karmel, **An Estate of Memory**
                    or
    Jurek Becker, **Jacob the Liar.**

6. Myth
    Pierre Gascar, **The Season of the Dead**
                    or
    Jorge Semprun, **The Long Voyage.**

7. "Lamentation literature"
    Readings from:
        The Book of Lamentations
        Bialik's poem on Kishinev
        Elie Wiesel, **Night**

S.Y. Agnon, "The Sign"
Paul Celan, selected poems
Abraham Sutzkever, selected poems
Dan Pagis, selected poems
Aharon Appelfeld, **The Age of Wonders**

The course on Lamentation Literature includes a wide range of Israeli writers from Bialik through to Grossman as well as background reading in the biblical, midrashic and medieval Hebrew literary responses to catastrophe.

IV. REQUIREMENTS OF THE COURSE FOR GRADING

In the graduate course taught at the Institute, the students are expected to deliver presentations on texts related to topics under discussion. Final papers are either short (10-15 pp., referred to at the Hebrew University as a "referat"), or long seminar papers (ranging in length from 30 to 80 pp., depending on the subject and the student, and requiring a fair amount of research and interpretive depth).

In the undergraduate course in the Overseas Program, students are expected to write a mid-term essay, a long (15-20 pp.) research paper on a topic of their choosing, and a final take-home examination.

V. CONCEPTUAL FRAMEWORK OF THE COURSE

These courses are founded on two conceptual premises. The first is that this literature cannot be studied outside of the larger cultural contexts in which it evolves. The attempt is to challenge the critical isolation in which this material is often considered, and to view it as part of the modernist and postmodernist project which began with World War I, if not earlier. Kafka is read not as "prophetic" of future events, but as one of those who, early in the century, helped to establish the literary and philosophical vocabulary that was to inform the literature of the latter part of the twentieth century.

The second conceptual premise derives from the typology I developed in my book on Holocaust literature, **By Words Alone**, which places the literature along a mimetic spectrum stretching from "documentary" to "myth"; this presupposes a "displaced literature" of (survivor) writers writing, for the most part, in adopted languages. A second, parallel structure is the "lamentations" tradition which draws on literary responses to catastrophe that are grounded in the biblical Book of Lamentations and punctuate 2000 years of Jewish creative responses to persecution.

Much of the reading and discussion in class considers the polarized articulation of the challenge of "Holocaust" literature as "history versus the imagination" or "testimony versus aesthetics" or "memory versus metaphor".

I. THE COURSE

NAZI WAR CRIMES: LAWS AND TRIALS

Henry Friedlander
Department of Judaic Studies, Brooklyn College, City University of New York

II. ACADEMIC CONTEXT OF THE COURSE
CUNY is a public university whose senior colleges, including Brooklyn College, are financed by the State of New York and the City of New York.

   The students are usually upper-level juniors or seniors taking the course as an elective. They come from all arts and sciences departments, but always include majors in history, political science, and pre-law. General background in modern history and in government is required. About half have taken a previous course on the Holocaust.

   At the time of its introduction at Brooklyn College in the early 1980s, "Nazi War Crimes" appeared to have been the first course on this topic to be taught at an American university. The available literature in English is limited, and thus there are not many options for reading assignments. The object of the course is to make students think about Nazi crimes in legal terms.

III. OUTLINE OF THE COURSE
Reference
John R. Lewis, comp., **Uncertain Judgment: A Bibliography of War Crimes Trials** (Santa Barbara & Oxford, 1979).

Norman E. Tutorow, comp., **War Crimes, War Criminals and War Crimes Trials: An Annotated Bibliography and Source Book** (New York, Westport & London, 1986).

General Reading
Henry Friedlander, "The Trials of the Nazi Criminals: Law, Justice and History," **Dimensions: A Journal of Holocaust Studies**, vol. 2, no. 1 (1986), pp. 4-10

1. The Allied war crimes trials

Documents
The Moscow Declaration (1943).
The London Agreement (1945).
Control Council Law No. 10 (1945).

Proceedings and Evidence
Nazi Conspiracy and Aggression [Red Series], 8 vols. & 2 suppl., Washington, 1946-48.

Trial of the Major War Criminals before the International Military Tribunal [Blue Series], 42 vols., Nuremberg, 1947.

Trials of War Criminals before the Nuremberg Military Tribunals under Control Council Law No. 10 [Green Series], 14 vols., Washington, 1949-50.

Earl W. Kintner (ed.), **The Hadamar Trial** (London, 1949).

Raymond Phillips (ed.), **The Belsen Trial** (London, 1949).

Readings
Bradley Smith, **Judgment at Nuremberg** (New York, 1979).

Telford Taylor, **Final Report to the Secretary of the Army on the Nuremberg War Crimes Trials under Control Council Law No. 10** (Washington, 1949).

2. Postwar trials in West Germany

Documents
The Statutory Criminal Law of Germany with Comments (Washington: Library of Congress, 1947).

Proceedings and Evidence

(Selected cases are summarized in class.)

Proceedings are not kept in German trials; there are only short summaries. Indictments are long and detailed. Indictments and summaries of proceedings are not published and are available only in manuscript form, as are decisions, which are not routinely published. Similarly, the evidentiary documentation is only available in Germany. However, selected appeals decisions are published in **Bundesgerichtshof in Strafsachen (BGHSt)** (annual editions), and selected decisions in cases involving Nazi crimes of homicide are available in: Adelheid L. Rueter-Ehlermann & C.F. Rueter (eds.), **Justiz und NS-Verbrechen; Sammlung deutscher Strafurteile wegen nationalsozialistischer Toetungsverbrechen** 22 vols. (Amsterdam: University Press, 1968-81).

Readings

Adalbert Rueckerl, **The Investigation of Nazi Crimes** (Heidelberg & Karlsruhe, 1979).

Henry Friedlander, "The Judiciary and Nazi Crimes in Postwar Germany," **Simon Wiesenthal Center Annual** 1 (1984), pp. 27-44.

Henry Friedlander, "The Deportation of the German Jews: Postwar Trials of Nazi Criminals," **Leo Baeck Institute Yearbook** XXIX (1984), pp. 201-26

3.   US denaturalization, deportation and extradition

Court Decisions

United States v. Feodor Fedorenko, 455 F. Supp. 893 (1978).

United States v. Feodor Fedorenko, 597 F. 2nd, 946 (5th Cir. 1979).

Feodor Fedorenko v. United States, 449 U.S. 490 (1981).

United States v. John Demjanjuk, 518 F. Supp, 1362 (N.D. Ohio 1981), aff'd, 680 F.2nd 32 (6th Cir. 1982), cert. denied, 459 U.S. 1036 (1982).

In re Demjanjuk, No. A8-237-417 (Immigration Court, Cleveland, Ohio, 23 May 1984).

In re Demjanjuk, No. A8-237-417 (BIA, 14 February 1985).

In re Demjanjuk, Brief of Amicus Curiae, The International Human Rights Law Group (Washington, 9 April 1984), filed 10 April 1984, 603 F. Supp. 544 (N.D. Ohio 1985), 612 F. Supp. 544 (N.D. Ohio 1985).

In re Demjanjuk, 603 F. Supp. 1463 (N.D. Ohio, 6 December 1984); Supplemental Order, 11 December 1984; and 603 F. Supp. 1468 (N.D. Ohio 21 February 1985).

In re Demjanjuk, 612 F. Supp. 544 (N.D. Ohio 15 April 1985, as amended 30 April 1985).

Demjanjuk v. Petrovsky, 612 F. Supp. 571 (N.D. Ohio 17 May 1985), 612 F. Supp. 571 (N.D. Ohio 17 May 1985), 106 S. Ct. 1198 (24 Feb. 1986), cert. denied.

Demjanjuk v. Meese, 784 F.2nd 1114 (D.C. Cir. 27 February 1986, as amended 7 March 1986).

Readings
Henry Friedlander & Earlean McCarrick, "Nazi Criminals in the United States: The Fedorenko Case," **Simon Wiesenthal Center Annual** 2 (1985), pp. 63-93

Henry Friedlander and Earlean McCarrick, "Nazi Criminals in the United States: Denaturalization after Fedorenko," **Simon Wiesenthal Center Annual** 3 (1986), pp. 47-85

Henry Friedlander and Earlean McCarrick, "The Extradition of Nazi Criminals: Ryan, Artukovic, Demjanjuk," **Simon Wiesenthal Center Annual** 4 (1987), pp. 65-98.

IV. REQUIREMENTS OF THE COURSE FOR GRADING
Students are required to submit one essay on a topic chosen in consultation with the lecturer, and to take a final examination.

V. CONCEPTUAL FRAMEWORK OF THE COURSE

The object of the course is to make students think about Nazi crimes in legal terms. First, students are presented with a topology of Nazi crimes and a history of how these crimes have been judged under international and under national law. For this purpose the course is divided into three chronological topics. The first treats the Allied postwar trials, and thus looks at how the international community has dealt with these crimes under international law. The second treats the way national law has dealt with these crimes. For this topic the postwar trials in German courts have been chosen as an example, both because no special (retroactive) legislation was applied, and because more trials took place there than anywhere else. The third treats the current American proceedings. These illustrate both the application of national civil proceedings (denaturalization and deportation), and the application of treaty law (extradition).

In each topic students study three kinds of sources. First, they analyze the laws that serve as the basis for legal proceedings against Nazi criminals. Second, they study portions of proceedings that present information on laws, procedures, crimes, perpetrators, and legal interpretations. Third, they read the secondary literature.

Discussion and analysis focuses on three central themes. First, the nature of the crimes: individual criminal acts, crimes committed under orders, crimes involving physical violence (murder, manslaughter, assault, etc.), crimes that do no not involve attack on persons (arson, theft, illegal detention, etc.). This also involves a discussion of how "genocide" or "crimes against humanity" can be defined and judged. Second, the motives of the perpetrators (both perpetrators on the scene and bureaucratic perpetrators): following orders, ideological commitment, peer pressure, etc. This also involves an analysis of defense arguments advanced by perpetrators (duress under orders, error of law). Third, the legal basis for the proceedings. This involves a discussion of international law (Nuremberg, extradition, etc.), and the penal code as applied under national law.

I.   THE COURSE

RESPONSES TO THE HOLOCAUST

Zev Garber
Program in Jewish Studies, Los Angeles Valley College

II.   ACADEMIC CONTEXT OF THE COURSE
This course is one of the 20 Jewish Studies classes offered in a two-year span by the Program in Jewish Studies at Los Angeles Valley College. This was the first program in the United States to offer an A.A. degree in Jewish Studies at a public institution. The college was established in June 1949, and is one of nine public colleges of the Los Angeles Community College District. Currently, there are more than 20,000 students enrolled at LAVC.

The course is conducted over one semester (20 weeks), in five 60-minute sessions per week. Some knowledge is assumed in the outlook and philosophy, values and ideals of European Jews - as taught in other Jewish Studies classes; however, there is no prerequisite for enrollment. The student composition is about 75 per cent Jewish; 25 per cent non-Jewish.

III.   OUTLINE OF THE COURSE
1.   Defining the subject
    Is the *Shoah* different only in degree, not in kind, from previous and contemporary acts of man's inhumanity to man?

Readings
Zev Garber, "Teaching the Holocaust: The Introductory Course," in Z. Garber, A. Berger & R. Libowitz (eds.), **Methodology in the Academic Teaching of the Holocaust** (Lanham: University Press of America, 1988), pp. 25-55.

Zev Garber & Bruce Zuckerman, "Why Do We Call the Holocaust 'the Holocaust'? An Inquiry into the Psychology of Labels," in Y. Bauer et al., **Remembering for the Future**. Theme II: **The Impact of the Holocaust on the Contemporary World** (Oxford: Pergamon, 1988), pp. 1879-1892.

John Fox, "The Holocaust, A Non-Unique Event for All Humanity," in Y. Bauer et al. **Remembering for the Future. Theme II: The Impact of the Holocaust on the Contemporary World** (Oxford: Pergamon, 1988), pp. 1863-1878.

Irwin L. Horowitz, "Many Genocides, One Holocaust?" **Modern Judaism**, vol. 1, no. 1 (1981), pp. 74-89.

Steven Katz, "The Unique Intentionality of the Holocaust," **Modern Judaism**, vol. 1 no. 2 (1981), pp. 161-183.

Yehuda Bauer, "Whose Holocaust?" **Midstream** (November 1980), pp. 42-46.

Emil Fackenheim, Foreword to Yehuda Bauer, **The Jewish Emergence from Powerlessness** (Toronto, 1979).

Yehuda Bauer, **The Holocaust in Historical Perspective** (Seattle, 1978), pp. 30-49.

2. Understanding antisemitism and the nature of prejudice
    The unifying link of antisemitism, yesterday, today, and forever, is the "dislike of the unlike".

Readings
Saul Friedlander, "From Antisemitism to Extermination," **Yad Vashem Studies XVI** (1984), pp. 1-50.

Jacob Katz, **From Prejudice to Destruction: Anti-Semitism 1700-1933** (Cambridge, Mass., 1983), pp. 1-10, 74-91, 303-327.

Michael R. Marrus, "The Theory and Practice of Antisemitism," **Commentary**, vol. 74, no. 2 (August 1982), pp. 38-42.

Ben Halpern, "What Is Anti-Semitism?" **Modern Judaism**, vol. 1 no. 3 (1981), pp. 251-262.

Shmuel Ettinger, "The Origins of Modern Anti-Semitism," in Y. Gutman & L. Rothkirchen (eds.), **The Catastrophe of European Jewry** (Jerusalem, Yad Vashem, 1976), pp. 3-39.

Jacob L. Talmon, "European History as the Seedbed of the Holocaust," **Midstream** (May 1973), pp. 3-25.

3. Nihilism of murder
How to explain the role of the Jews in Nazi ideology and policy?

Readings
Emil Fackenheim, "Holocaust and Weltanschauung: Philosophical Reflections on Why They Did It," **Holocaust and Genocide Studies**, vol. 3 no. 2 (1988), pp. 191-208.

Raul Hilberg, **The Destruction of the European Jews** (student edition) (New York, 1985), selections.

Gerhard Fleming, **Hitler and the Final Solution** (Berkeley, 1984).

Randolph L. Braham, "What Did They Know and When?" Y. Bauer and N. Rotenstreich (eds.), **The Holocaust as Historical Experience** (New York, 1981), pp. 109-132.

Jacob Katz, "Was the Holocaust Predictable?" Y. Bauer & N. Rotenstreich (eds.), **The Holocaust as Historical Experience**, pp. 23-41.

Lucy Dawidowicz, **The War Against the Jews, 1933-1945** (New York, 1975), selections.

Eberhard Jaeckel, **Hitler's Weltanschauung, Blueprint for Power** (Wesleyan, Conn., 1972), chs. 1-3.

4. The biblical response
The structure and dimensions of the Bible have much to say about human suffering. What can Creation, *Akedah* ("Binding of Isaac"), "the Hidden Face," Test of Job, Valley of the Bones, Sinai, and other biblical selections tell us about the silence of Auschwitz?

Readings
Selections from the *TaNaK* (Bible)

5. The rabbinic response
   The Rabbis endured the destruction of the Temple and Jerusalem in the year 70
   C.E. and the tragedy of the abortive revolt of Bar-Kochba in 135 C.E. How does
   the classical rabbinic mind respond to the Holocaust?

   Readings
   Selections from Mishnah, Gemara, and Midrash.

6. The mystical response
   In every generation there have been those who contemplated the problem of evil
   in a context which, while not obliterating its reality, diminished its power by
   virtue of a cosmic or mythic perspective. What is a Kabbalistic response to the
   Shoah?

   Readings
   David R. Blumenthal, **Understanding Jewish Mysticism: The Merkabah Tradition and the Zoharic Tradition** (New York, 1978), pp. 141-180.

   Maimonides, **Guide of the Perplexed**, Part III, Chapter 51 (S. Pines, trans.),
   (Chicago, 1963).

7. The hasidic response
   Hutzpah and *Ahavat Yisrael* - courage bordering on the reckless and love of the
   Jewish people - are characteristics of the tales about R. Levi Yitzhak of
   Berditchev. How does Hasidic optimism prevail against impossible odds?

   eadings
   Yaffa Eliach, **Hasidic Tales of the Holocaust** (New York, 1982).

   Anonymous, "The Last Song of the Jewish Community of Lublin".

8. The literary response
   The literary imagination does not merely deal with the Holocaust as *Historie*:
   controlled, objective facts of historiography. Rather, it sees the Holocaust as

Geschichte: a paradigm, above the historical; attached to history but by no means limited by it. What are some of the responses of the creative artist "to show what cannot be shown, to explain what is not to be explained, to recapture an experience that cannot be relived" (Elie Wiesel).

Readings
Alan L. Berger, **Crisis and Covenant: The Holocaust in American Jewish Fiction** (New York, 1985).

Sidra Ezrahi, **By Words Alone: The Holocaust in Literature** (Chicago, 1980).

Elie Wiesel, **Night** (New York, 1982).

Jerzy Kosinski, **The Painted Bird** (New York, 1981).

Andre Schwarz-Bart, **The Last of the Just** (New York, 1973).

9. Film response
    In recent years, significant films on the destruction of European Jewry have been produced for television and theatre release, including *Sophie's Choice, Genocide, Night and Fog, Who Shall Live and Who Shall Die? The Wall, Inside the Third Reich, Skokie, The Wannsee Conference, Shoah, Weapons of the Spirit*, etc. How does filmography contribute to our understanding of the Holocaust?

    Readings
    Judith E. Doneson, **The Holocaust in American Film** (Philadelphia, 1987).

    Annette Insdiorf, **Indelible Shadows; Film and the Holocaust** (New York, 1983).

10. The traditionalist response
    Many notable rabbis endured the Nazi era and later wrote about it. Leo Baeck commenced his study of **This People Israel** in Theresienstadt. Ignaz Maybaum contemplated the **Face of God After Auschwitz**. Ephraim Oshry wrote voluminous responsa in the ghetto of Kovno, in the midst of Lithuanian fascistic cruelty. Emil Fackenheim reaffirmed **God's Presence in History**. Eliezer Berkovits responded with **Faith After the Holocaust**. What is the quality of faith and Halachah in response to the Holocaust?

Readings

Eliezer Berkovits, **With God in Hell** (New York, 1979).

Irving Greenberg, "Cloud of Smoke, Pillar of Fire: Judaism, Christianity and Modernity After the Holocaust," in E. Fleischner (ed.), **Auschwitz: Beginning of a New Era? Reflections on the Holocaust** (New York, 1977), pp. 7-55.

Irving J. Rosenbaum, **The Holocaust and Halachah** (New York, 1976), pp. 17-46.

Eliezer Berkovits, **Faith After the Holocaust** (New York, 1973), pp. 37-85.

Emil Fackenheim, **God's Presence in History: Jewish Affirmations and Philosophical Reflections** (New York, 1970), pp. 67-104.

11. The humanist response

For the religious theist, responding to the Holocaust is intolerable. How could the Guardian of Israel have failed to intervene? For the religious humanist, responding is no less agonizing. How could Man have done it? What are the responses of Jewish humanists, e.g., Martin Buber, Mordecai Kaplan, Richard Rubenstein, and others, to the Holocaust?

Readings

Richard Rubenstein, **After Auschwitz** (Indianapolis, 1966).

12. The Christian response

Whether or not we take the extreme view that there is a direct causal link between two thousand years of the "teaching of contempt" and the *Shoah*, Christian culpability for the Holocaust cannot be denied. What is the Christian response to the *Shoah*?

Readings

Paul M. van Buren, "Ecclesia Semper Reformanda: The Challenge of Israel," in R. Libowitz (ed.), **Faith and Freedom: A Tribute to Franklin H. Littell** (Oxford, 1987), pp. 119-125.

Eugene Fisher, "Theological Education and Christian- Jewish Relations," in Z. Garber (ed.), **Methodology in the Academic Teaching of Judaism** (Lanham, MD, 1986/87), pp. 189-200.

Alice Eckardt, "Post-Holocaust Theology: A Journey Out of the Kingdom of Night," **Holocaust and Genocide Studies**, vol. 1, no. 2 (1986), pp. 229-240.

Norman Ravitch, "The Problem of Christian Anti-Semitism," **Commentary**, vol. 73 no. 4 (1982), pp. 41-52.

Rosemary Radford Ruether, "Anti-Semitism and Christian Theology," in E. Fleischner (ed.), **Auschwitz: Beginning of a New Era? Reflections on the Holocaust** (New York, 1977), pp. 79-92.

Franklin H. Littell, **The Crucifixion of the Jews: The Failure of the Christians to Understand the Jewish Experience** (New York, 1975), pp. 24-99.

13. The American Jewish response
How effective was the American Jewish response to the Holocaust? Why did a prestigious Holocaust fact-finding group, made up of prominent Jews and headed by former Supreme Justice Arthur J. Goldberg "split up in anger and dissension" (New York Times, week of 2 January, 1983) while investigating the American Jewish community's response to the Nazi extermination program?

Readings
Henry L. Feingold, "Did American Jewry Do Enough During the Holocaust?" **B.G. Randolph Lecture in Judaic Studies**, Syracuse University, April 1985, 33 pp.

David Wyman, **The Abandonment of the Jews: America & the Holocaust 1941-1945** (New York, 1984), selections.

Yehuda Bauer, **American Jewry and the Holocaust** (Detroit, 1981).

Walter Laqueur, **The Terrible Secret** (Boston, 1980).

14. A dialogue response

For centuries the Jewish community in Poland prospered, but memories of the Holocaust have tainted the relationship. Can looking honestly at the past begin the healing? Or must one conclude that anti-Jewish prejudice is very strong among Poles in and outside Poland, the land of Auschwitz?

Readings

Claude Lanzmann, **Shoah**, New Yorker Films; Pantheon Books, 1985.

Ronald Modras, "Jews and Poles: A Relationship Reconsidered," **America** (January 1982).

J. Kermisz and S. Krakowski, **Polish-Jewish Relations During the Second World War** (Jerusalem, 1974), selections.

15. An Israeli response

Never since 1948 has one campaign and one massacre - the summer of 1982 Peace for Galilee Operation and the Phalangist murder of Palestinian refugees at Sabra and Shatila - caused so many in and outside Israel to raise questions concerning Israeliness and Jewishness, Israeli state and Jewish state, and to suggest that "Judaism does *not* need a political entity in the Land of Israel to survive worldwide. A State of Israel that can conspire with Phalangist thugs is *not* a proper response to the Holocaust. And we are *not* one people if that means condoning blatantly immoral Israeli acts" (Eugene B. Borowitz writing in **Sh'ma**, 5 November, 1982). Similarly, the *Intifada* ("Uprising") of 1987-88 tests Jewish morality. Can Jewish morality and Jewish power coexist in the land of Zion, in the second generation after Auschwitz?

Readings

Zev Garber, "Triumph on the Gallows," **Israel Today** (Perspective column) (August 1987); "Blood and Thunder: Israel Under Siege," (March 1988).

Kahan Commission Report, **Jerusalem Post** (9 November, 1983).

Jacobo Timerman, **The Longest War: Israel in Lebanon** (New York, 1982).

Elie Wiesel, **Dawn** (New York, 1982).

Yehuda Bauer, **The Jewish Emergence from Powerlessness** (Toronto, 1979), pp. 41-78.

Emil Fackenheim, **The Jewish Return into History** (New York, 1978), pp. 129-286.

16. Can it happen again?
    The question of whether or not the *Shoah* could happen again depends for an answer upon our model of an "I and Thou" society. The major traits of Hitlerism - isolation, vilification, expulsion, slavery, and extermination - are not the will of heaven but the act of Everyman, the bitter fruits of the freedom he has abused. Consequently, man can stamp out these evils if he so chooses by demonstrating intelligence, wisdom, and moral will. This then, is the command-ment after the Great Tragedy: All are made in the image of God, and the inter-dependence of humankind is the only rational road to survival.

Readings
Zev Garber, "Auschwitz: The Real Problem," **Israel Today** (15 April, 1988).

Zev Garber, "Sinai and not Cyanide: Witness and not Survivor," remarks given at the Utah State Capitol Rotunda on 19 April, 1985, in conjunction with the Governor's proclamation of Holocaust Memorial Week 1985 (5745).

"Teshuvah," a Hasidic sermon by Yehuda Leib Alter (1847-1905), in Barry W. Holtz (ed.), **Back to the Sources, Reading the Classic Jewish Texts** (New York, 1984), pp. 393-399.

Irving Greenberg, "Religious Values After the Holocaust," in A.J. Peck (ed.), **Jews and Christians After the Holocaust** (Philadelphia, 1982), pp. 63-86.

Simon Wiesenthal, **The Sunflower** (New York, 1977).

"The Indestructible Dignity of Man," (The Last Musar Lecture in Slabodka), **Judaism**, vol. 19 no. 3 (1970), pp. 262-263.

IV. REQUIREMENTS OF THE COURSE FOR GRADING
    Students are expected to do a take-home final examination (10 pages). In addition, a synthesizing project is required. (A synthesizing project permits a direct

encounter of student with material, and can serve as an option or alternative to a writing-only presentation - as found in most Holocaust course offerings. It permits the student to pursue his/her own special academic preference - art, music, religion, psychology, literature, sociology, etc. - in whatever medium he/she deems most productive - short story, collage, audio-visual, etc. - for showing the relationship between these disciplines and some aspect of Holocaust studies. If done properly, a synthesizing project can weave a thread of continuity into complex and diversified material, and make the course content more particular and personal.)

V. CONCEPTUAL FRAMEWORK OF THE COURSE

The subject of the Holocaust, the destruction of the Jews of Europe, and others, at the hands of the Nazis and their collaborators, is one of great moral significance in the history of human civilization. Genocide, the obliteration of all members of a national group, is the most horrible of crimes and one of the most difficult to deal with in the field of social studies, revealing the human race in its worst perspective.

Some say that all speaking about the Holocaust and its consequences is thoroughly inadequate and sacrilegious to the memory of the millions murdered, maimed, and orphaned. Others say that silence is ultimately a posthumous victory for Hitlerism. However, all agree that education is the key to understanding the *Shoah*. But how is one to teach a subject that most educators believe is like no other course taught in the basic college curriculum of today?

"Responses to the Holocaust" seeks to address the issues of human life and meaning in the post-Holocaust world. Through a variety of approaches and disciplines, the units are united by a fundamental recognition that after the *Shoah*, the entire enterprise of being human has been called into serious question.

Conceived as an introductory (i.e., lower division) course within a program in Jewish Studies (also Religious Studies), it is an attempt to tackle the questions of "What can we learn?" and "How do we teach about the *Shoah* and its lessons?"

The conceptual framework of the course is divided into three sections. The first (topics 1, 2, 3) raises questions of meaning, terminology, and methodology. The second section (topics 4, 5, 6, 7, 10, 11, 12) speaks about theological and religious responses to the *Shoah* from a variety of approaches, including Jewish, Christian and humanist. The final part (topics 8, 9, 13, 14, 15) is designed to be an "open-end" section which probes a number of responses to Judaism's perpetual dilemma and tragedy. It concludes (topic 16) with a personal ideology suggesting a post-Auschwitz second generation committed to life, hope, and action.

The subject of the Holocaust is universally broad and cannot be encompassed within any one course. This course does not attempt to cover all of the relevant history, sociology, psychology, philosophy and theology. Rather, it offers a context for asking questions, and provides a frame of reference for insights on the background, meaning, and practice of antisemitism. The unique nature of the *Shoah* and its significance for Jews and non-Jews are developed; the complicated religious and theological problems of *contra-Judaeos*, and the search for a better understanding of Jewish-Christian relations are highlighted; the changes and development of Jewish self-definition, including religious experiences and theology, are illuminated; and, using the materials presented and discussed in this course, the question whether a holocaust can happen again is considered.

The emphasis is on tolerance, diversity, and understanding. The course focuses on the student, and endeavors to heighten his/her awareness of ethical themes and of human tendencies toward racial and religious prejudices.

The method employed includes analysis of historical data and literature; newspapers, TV programs, movies, plays (where and when applicable); linguistic and rhetorical evidence; reports from local survivors and liberators of the camps, group discussions and written evaluations.

The following observations will serve to further explain the approach which informs this course:

The essence of Holocaust thinking is "dislike of the unlike". It is the recognition of this force in our lives that is at the core of this course's alternative approach to presenting the Holocaust.

The message of the Holocaust for the generation after and for future generations, is not survival alone. There is something more important than survival, and that is preventing moral bankruptcy. When Auschwitz (survival at any price) contends with Sinai (a moral standard), Sinai must prevail. Nazi Germany is an example of what can happen when Auschwitz prevails.

Rigorous academic standards are followed. Students are made aware of the laborious work involved in a critical, disciplined study of origins, sources and materials, and encouraged to obtain skills in oral and written presentations on a given problem in Holocaust studies. Yet the readings selected are not difficult ones, so that the students' feelings, and thus, interest, may be engaged. Consequently, the class hour takes seriously the four sequential steps of learning: confrontation, analysis, interaction and internalization. The belief is that students will learn better and gain more understanding of the subject matter if they are actively involved in learning rather than if they are passive auditors of lectures. It is my view that an overly elitist, academic approach tends to turn the lecturer into an accountant of facts, rather than a teller of history. I hold that it can, and has, led to depersonalization in the classroom. I prefer passionate objectivity. It is especially needed now that academic life has become so technological and bureaucratic.

I. THE COURSE

THEOLOGICAL ISSUES ARISING OUT OF THE HOLOCAUST

Jocelyn Hellig
Department of Religious Studies, University of the Witwatersrand (South Africa)

II. ACADEMIC CONTENT OF THE COURSE

The University of the Witwatersrand is a liberal institution which has always protested against racial inequality in South Africa and against segregated universities. In recent years it has been given permission to admit black students, and while they are still far from forming the majority, there are increasing numbers of black students in all faculties each year.

This course is proposed as an undergraduate course within the Faculty of Arts, to be given to third-year students in the Department of Religious Studies or to undergraduate students in the Department of Jewish Studies. In the first case, it would presuppose a knowledge of the major world religions and the conflicting ideas of Judaism, Christianity and Islam. The students would be of diverse religious, racial and cultural backgrounds. In the second case, most of the students would be Jewish. They would have a knowledge of Jewish history, but would not necessarily have a thorough grasp of the conflicting truth-claims of world religions.

The main focus of the course is on the theological issues associated with the Holocaust, both in terms of the religious roots of antisemitism and the theological responses to the question of God and the Holocaust. Since the mid-1980s have witnessed an upsurge of antisemitism in South Africa, in both left- and right-wing circles, accompanied by denials of the Holocaust, it will be of value to examine this phenomenon in the light of the religious roots of antisemitism.

III. OUTLINE OF THE COURSE

1. Why the Jews? The theological roots of antisemitism
   a. What is "antisemitism"?
   b. Pre-Christian anti-Judaism
   c. The role of the New Testament in the demonization of the Jew

d. Subsequent development of the anti-Jewish stereotype in the Church:
The Patristic *Adversos Judaeos* tradition
Martin Luther
e. Nazi antisemitism

Required reading
Rosemary Ruether, "Anti-Semitism and Christian theology," in Eva Fleischner (ed.), **Auschwitz: Beginning of a New Era?** (New York, 1977), pp. 79-92.

Raul Hilberg, "Introduction," **The Destruction of the European Jews** (New York, 1961), pp. 1-31.

Cuthbert Carson Mann, "Hitler: A Clue to History," **Judaism** (Winter 1988), pp. 9-21.

Norman Ravitch, "The Problem of Christian Anti-Semitism," **Commentary** (April 1982), pp. 41-52.

Michael Marrus, "The Theory and Practice of Antisemitism," **Commentary** (August 1982), pp. 38-42.

2. Some methodological problems associated with study and recording of the Holocaust
a. The word "Holocaust"
b. The incomprehensibility of the Holocaust
c. Recording of the Holocaust - literature and films
d. Trivialization of the Holocaust
e. Artists and writers as "profiteers of torment"
f. Those who were there and those who were not

Required reading
Alice Eckardt & Roy Eckardt, "Studying the Holocaust's Impact Today: Some Dilemmas of Language and Method," **Judaism** (Spring 1978), pp. 502-505.

Dan Magurshak, "The 'Incomprehensibility' of the Holocaust: Tightening Up Some Loose Usage," **Judaism** (Spring 1980), pp. 233-242.

Eliezer Berkovits, "Approaching the Holocaust," **Judaism**, Winter 1973, pp. 18-20

In discussing the problem of trivialization it would be valuable, for comparative purposes, to view the following films:
The television series *Holocaust*
Claude Lanzmann's *Shoah*
Alain Resnais' *Night and Fog*

3. The problem of theodicy with special reference to the Holocaust
   Areas of theodicy
   > God's omnipotence
   > God's omnibenevolence
   > The existence of evil
   Covenant
   Chosenness
   Reward and punishment

   Required reading
   Zwi Werblowsky, "Judaism," in C. Bleeker & G. Widengren (eds.), **Historia Religionum**, vol II (Leiden, 1971).

   Maurice Samuel, "Prejudice and the Chosen People," **The Reconstructionist** (6 April, 1962), pp. 9-14.

4. A survey of some of the more important theological responses to the Holocaust, with specific relation to theodicy
   These will range from the fideistic to the radical and will include such thinkers as: Ignaz Maybaum, the Lubavitcher Rebbe, Eliezer Berkovits, Emil Fackenheim, Martin Buber, Elie Wiesel, and Richard Rubenstein.
   Some Christian responses to theodicy generally, and the Holocaust in particular: John Hick, John K. Roth, and Jurgen Moltmann.

   Required reading
   Michael Berenbaum, "Elie Wiesel and Contemporary Jewish Theology," **Conservative Judaism** (Spring 1976), pp. 19-39.

Israel Ben Yosef, "Jewish Religious Responses to the Holocaust," **The Journal of Religion, Southern Africa** (January 1987).

Benny Kraut, "Faith and the Holocaust," **Judaism** (Spring 1982), pp. 185-201.

Emil Fackenheim, "Jewish Faith and the Holocaust," **Commentary** (August 1968), pp. 30-36.

Jocelyn Hellig, "Richard L. Rubenstein: Theologian of the Holocaust," Proceedings of the Seventh Judaica Conference, University of the Witwatersrand, 1984.

5. Resurgence of antisemitism and neo-Nazism
Discussion of the emergence of right-wing antisemitism and neo-Nazism in South Africa; left-wing anti-Zionisim.

Required reading
Robert Wistrich, "The Anti-Zionist Masquerade," **Midstream** (Aug./Sept. 1983).

——————, **Hitler's Apocalypse** (London, 1985).

Ragnar Kvam, "Among Two Hundred Survivors from Auschwitz," (Otto Reinert, trans.), **Judaism** (Summer 1979), pp. 283-292.

Selected Bibliography

Theological Responses to the Holocaust
Ignaz Maybaum, **The Face of God After Auschwitz** (Amsterdam, 1965).

Emil Fackenheim, **God's Presence in History: Jewish Affirmations and Philosophical Reflexions** (New York, 1970).

——————, **The Jewish Return into History** (New York, 1978).

Eliezer Berkovits, **Faith After the Holocaust** (New York, 1973).

Michael Berenbaum, **The Vision of the Void: Theological Reflections on the Works of Elie Wiesel** (Middletown Conn., 1979).

Richard Rubenstein, **After Auschwitz** (Indianapolis, 1966).

Martin Buber, **I and Thou** (R.G. Smith, trans.) (Edinburgh, 1958).

------------, **Eclipse of God** (New York, 1957).

Elie Wiesel, **Night** (London, 1960).

John Roth, **A Consuming Fire: Encounters with Elie Wiesel and the Holocaust** (Atlanta, 1979).

Juergen Moltmann, **The Crucified God** (London, 1974).

Robert McAfee Brown, **Elie Wiesel: Messenger to all Humanity** (Notre Dame, 1983).

Steven Katz, **Post-Holocaust Dialogues** (New York, 1983).

Antisemitism
Rosemary Radford Ruether, **Faith and Fratricide** (New York, 1974).

Franklin Littell, **The Crucifixion of the Jews** (New York, 1975).

Jules Isaac, **The Teaching of Contempt: Christian Roots of Anti-Semitism** (New York, 1962).

History
Martin Gilbert, **The Holocaust** (London, 1986).

Raul Hilberg, **The Destruction of the European Jews** (New York, 1961).

Lucy Dawidowicz, **The War Against the Jews 1933-1945** (New York, 1975).

Post-Holocaust Implications
Eva Fleischner (ed.), **Auschwitz: Beginning of a New Era?** (New York, 1977), pp. 79-92.

Paul van Buren, **Discerning the Way: A Theology of the Jewish-Christian Reality** (New York, 1980).

Robert Wistrich, **Hitler's Apocalypse** (London, 1985).

Richard Rubenstein and John Roth, **Approaches to Auschwitz** (London, 1987).

IV. REQUIREMENTS OF THE COURSE FOR GRADING
The students will be expected to write one essay of 8-10 pages and take a final examination based on lectures, readings and tutorials.

V. CONCEPTUAL FRAMEWORK OF THE COURSE
The primary focus of this course is on the theological implications of the Holocaust, both in terms of the religious causes of antisemitism and the question of God and the Holocaust. It does not deal with the history of the Holocaust *per se*, although such readings have been included.

This approach is regarded as important, since the depth, persistence and irrationality of antisemitism cannot be understood in isolation from its religious roots. An occurrence of the magnitude of the Holocaust would be inexplicable without reference to Christendom's role in the promulgation of the negative stereotype of the Jews, and the demonization of the Jews which derives from the New Testament and was elaborated by the Church Fathers and later Christian tradition. Hitler's antisemitism must be seen as an extension of Christendom's negative evaluation of the Jews. Even though Hitler was anti-Christian, or rather *because* he was anti-Christian, he could appropriate Christendom's anti-Jewish stereotype unhindered by Christian moral restraints.

As a corollary, emphasis will be placed on the particularly Jewish aspects of the tragedy. While one realizes that other people did die, failure to see the Holocaust as a particularly Jewish tragedy minimizes its impact and relevance. Attempts to appropriate the Holocaust as a general category of human evil and, broadly speaking, as a "crime against humanity," universalize it into vague categories. This results in failure to appreciate its particularity and minimizes the fact that real violence was done to real people. The particularity of the

Holocaust has universal implications in that failure to recognize that there was a specific target-group may blind us to the specificity of another target-group, should one arise in other circumstances.

Since the Jewish aspect of the Holocaust is to be emphasized, one must consider whether there is anything in the dynamics of Judaism itself which predisposes to Jew-hatred. Hence, pre-Christian anti-Judaism must be examined with a view to isolating it from the more virulent form of antisemitism developed by Christendom.

Having examined the question of the centrality of the Jews, problems with regard to study of the Holocaust must be raised. To what extent does the word "Holocaust" falsify the events in terms of its having reference to a "burnt offering"? Equally seriously, how adequate is *any* term in any language to describe the real Nazi intention so well encapsulated in the single German word "*Judenvernichtung*"? Trivialization becomes a major issue in the problem of recording the Holocaust. Should trivialization be accepted as part of a wider program to make people aware of the Holocaust, or does it serve to minimize the reality of the Holocaust and desensitize people to the enormity of Jewish suffering? Bearing in mind that the Holocaust must be written about, recorded on film, and examined in order to perpetuate awareness of it, it must be questioned to what extent writers on the Holocaust and film makers using it as a central or peripheral theme are "profiteers of torment". With regard to the "incomprehensibility" of the Holocaust, must it be regarded as an event which defies human understanding, or can it be comprehended in ways that will help us to avoid its repetition?

Finally, with regard to the question of God and the Holocaust, to what extent are the statements of those who were *not* there admissible as part of the theological discourse? If, to use Eliezer Berkovits' words, loss of faith by those who were not there mocks the faith of millions who went to their deaths believing, and the retention of faith by those who were not there desecrates "the holy disbelief of those whose faith was murdered," of what validity are the statements of theologians who have grappled with the question of God and the Holocaust? While recognizing this dialectical tension, the conviction which underlies this course is that *some* theological statement is essential if we are to understand the realities of twentieth-century Jewish existence. Hence, a survey of the major theological responses to the question of God and the Holocaust will be undertaken. This will be preceded by consideration of theodicy and whether the Holocaust fits into normative Jewish responses to evil and suffering. The responses dealt with will serve to underscore the enormity of the problem by revealing that, ultimately, one response is less inadequate than the others. Despite the limitations of the discipline, it is not one that can and should be avoided. It will be found that the views of individuals, both survivors and others, correspond to the conclusion of the major theologians who have grappled with the problem, thereby indicating the significance of theological discourse in relation to ongoing Jewish existence.

As Jewish existence can never reside in a vacuum, Christian responses to the question of God and the Holocaust will be examined. Consideration of Christian responses will aid students to moderate their views on the negative relationships between Judaism and Christianity which arise in Section One of the course. This type of study also aids interreligious dialogue.

Since there has been a worldwide trend of renewed antisemitism and denial of the Holocaust, and since these aspects have taken on tangible forms on both sides of the political spectrum in the struggle for a nonracist, post-apartheid South Africa, the phenomenon must be examined not only in terms of Christian antisemitism but in terms of Arab antisemitism and the consequent demonization of the Jew in Islam which has received wide currency since the Six Day War. Anti-Zionism as a barely disguised form of antisemitism is a significant feature of anti-Jewish feeling in South Africa. Likewise, conspiracy theories have become commonplace. This leads full-circle back to the problem of the religious roots of antisemitism and makes clear the relevance of the theological approach of this syllabus to the problem of antisemitism and to studying the implications of the Holocaust.

I. THE COURSE

HOLOCAUST SURVIVOR COMMUNITIES IN THE UNITED STATES

William B. Helmreich
Sociology Department, The City University of New York,
City College Graduate Center

II. ACADEMIC CONTEXT OF THE COURSE

This course is offered in the Sociology Department at the City University of New York Graduate Center. The students taking it are pursuing either an M.A. or Ph.D. degree, usually the latter. Some of the students are Jewish and some are not. A few may be Black, Hispanic, or Asian. While most are likely to be enrolled in the Sociology Department, others can come from anthropology, history, political science, or various ethnic studies graduate programs. Almost all are residents of New York City or its suburbs. Most will have read something, but not a great deal, on the Holocaust.

In designing the course, the following factors or realities are considered: The students come from a wide variety of backgrounds. Therefore, readings must address both the beginner and those who know more. Both types of readings appear in the Suggested Reading. Since almost all of the students' prior knowledge relates to the Holocaust itself, it is certain that none of the readings will be repetitious in terms of their theme.

Because this course is a graduate seminar with small classes, there are no examinations, simply a paper and class presentations of assigned readings.

III. OUTLINE OF THE COURSE

1. From the DP camps to the United States

   Required reading
   Leonard Dinnerstein, **America and the Survivors of the Holocaust** (New York: Columbia University Press, 1982), chs. 1 and 2.

Simon Schochet, **Feldafing** (Vancouver: November House, 1983).

Suggested reading
Paul Friedman, "The Road Back for the DPs: Healing the Psychological Scars of Nazism," **Commentary** (December 1948), pp. 502-510.

Maurice R. Davie, "Immigration and Refugee Aid," **American Jewish Yearbook 1948-49**, Vol. 50 (Philadelphia: Jewish Publication Society, 1949), pp. 223-236

2. Adaptation and adjustment in the United States

Required reading
Mary Russak, "Helping the New Immigrant Achieve His Own Beginning in the U.S.," **Journal of Jewish Communal Service** (December 1949), pp. 239-254.

Herman J. Levine and Benjamin Miller, **The American Farmer in Changing Times** (New York: Jewish Agricultural Society, 1966), Chs. 1, 2 and 3.

David Crystal, **The Displaced Person and the Social Agency** (New York: United HIAS Service, 1958), Chs. 1 & 2.

Suggested reading
Myron Fenster, "The Nitra Rav," **Present Tense** (Summer 1985), pp. 26-29.

Doris Kirschmann & Sylvia Savin, "Refugee Adjustment - Five Years Later," **Jewish Social Service Quarterly** (Winter 1953), pp. 197-201.

3. Occupational patterns

Required reading
Allan J. Cowett, "Casework Elements in Dealing with Job Refusals by New-comers," **Jewish Social Service Quarterly** (June 1952), pp. 428-433.

Arthur Goldhaft, **The Golden Egg** (New York: Horizon Press, 1957), pp. 251-272.

Suggested reading

Isaac Trainin, **In My People's Service, Vol. 3, Communal Diary** (New York: Commission on Synagogue Relations, 1981), Part One.

4. Family life of Holocaust survivors

Required reading

Helene Frankle, "The Survivor as a Parent," **Journal of Jewish Communal Service** (Spring 1978), pp. 241-246.

Ira O. Glick, Robert S. Weiss and C. Murray Parkes, **The First Year of Bereavement** (New York: Wiley, 1974), chs. 3 and 4.

J.R. Leon et al., "Survivors of the Holocaust and their Children: Current Status and Adjustment," **Journal of Personality and Social Psychology**, vol. 41 (1981), pp. 468-478.

Suggested reading

Helen Epstein, **Children of the Holocaust** (New York: Putnam, 1979).

Judith Kestenberg, "Psychoanalytic Contributions to the Problem of Children of Survivors from Nazi Persecution," **Israel Annals of Psychiatry and Related Disciplines** vol. 10 no. 4 (1972), pp. 311-325.

5. Education

Required reading

Helen Epstein, **A Study in American Pluralism Through Oral Histories of Holocaust Survivors,** Report of Wiener Oral History Collection (American Jewish Committee), selected readings.

Deborah S. Portnoy, "The Adolescent Immigrant," **Jewish Social Service Quarterly** (December 1948), pp. 268-273.

Suggested reading

Alfred Werner, "The New Refugees," **Jewish Frontier** (July 1946), pp. 21-23.

6. Communal life of survivors

Required reading
Eugene Kaufman, "A Social, Educational, and Recreational Program in the Adjustment of Adult Newcomers," **Jewish Social Service Quarterly** (March 1950), pp. 404-409.

Hannah Kliger, "Traditions of Grass-Roots Organization and Leadership: The Continuity of Landsmanshaften in New York, **American Jewish History** vol. 76, No. 1, pp. 25-39.

Suggested reading
Selected issues of **The Jewish Farmer**, published between 1945-1947.

7. Survivors' contributions to American Jewish life

Required reading
William B. Helmreich, "Postwar Adaptation of Holocaust Survivors in the United States," **Holocaust and Genocide Studies** vol. 2, no. 2 (1987), pp. 307-315.

----------, "The Impact of Holocaust Survivors on American Society: A Socio-Cultural Portrait," in Y. Bauer et al. **Remembering for the Future: Jews and Christians During and After the Holocaust** (Oxford/New York: Pergamon, 1988), pp. 363-384.

Suggested reading
I. Harry Levin, "Vineland - A Haven for Refugees," **The Jewish Poultry Farmers Association of South Jersey, Tenth Anniversary Journal** (n.d.).

8. Social, religious and political attitudes of survivors

Required reading
Robert Reeve Brenner, **The Faith and Doubt of Holocaust Survivors** (New York: The Free Press, 1980), chs. 1, 2, 3, and 4.

William B. Helmreich, "Postwar Adaptation..." (loc. cit.).

Selections from Wiener and Yad Vashem oral history collections.

Suggested reading
Dorothy Rabinowitz, **New Lives: Survivors of the Holocaust Living in America**
(New York: Avon, 1976).

9. Long-range implications

   Required reading
   Aaron Antonovsky et al., "Twenty Five Years Later: A Limited Study of Sequelae of the Concentration Camp Experience," **Social Psychiatry** vol. 6, no.
   4 (1971), pp. 186-193.

   Elmer G. Luchterhand, "Early and Late Effects of Imprisonment in Nazi Concentration Camps," **Social Psychology** 5 (1970), pp. 102-109.

   Yael Danieli, "On the Achievement of Integration in Aging Survivors of the
   Holocaust," **Journal of Geriatric Psychiatry** vol. 14, no. 2 (1982), pp.
   191-210.

   Suggested reading
   Gail Sheehy, **Spirit of Survival** (New York: Morrow and Co., 1986).

   Sarah Moskovitz, **Love Despite Hate** (New York: Schocken Books, 1983).

IV. REQUIREMENTS OF THE COURSE FOR GRADING
In addition to the presentation of several oral reports during the course of the
semester, students are expected to write a 25-50 page paper based on in-depth
interviews as well as readings.

V. CONCEPTUAL FRAMEWORK OF THE COURSE
Our primary goal is to understand the Holocaust survivors as a community, in the
sociological and historical sense. Between 1945-52 about 137,000 Holocaust survivors came to the United States. Although they are an important and numerically
significant group, very little is known about them as a group. Our course proceeds
with the following organizing themes:

Immigration to the US and Adaptation: We begin by trying to understand the reasons that went into the DPs' decision to come to the United States, why others opted for Palestine/Israel, and why still others stayed in Europe or went elsewhere. We look at structural factors as well as the personal reasons of the immigrants. Through interviews already done we examine the journey to America and its implications for adaptation. We also consider the many places in which the immigrants settled and ask what were the factors that went into these decisions. We ask how the immigrants lived in these places. There were, for example, immigrants who studied in universities, and there were others who became farmers. Some lived in cities with large Jewish populations, others did not.

Community, Family, Education: We examine various socializing institutions in America, the impact they had on the immigrants, and how the immigrants influenced them. We seek to understand how the immigrants adapted to life in the new land while at the same time trying to create a certain degree of social living space. One way was reviving the sometimes dormant *landsmanshaften*; another was starting their own organizations made up entirely of new immigrants. We observe how synagogues, Jewish community centers, and other organizations enabled the immigrants to make the transition from the old to the new. Schools, too, were socializing agents, particularly for those who attended part-time at night classes, and were avenues of upward mobility for those who saw them as springboards for careers. Finally, our examination of family explores both the pathology in survivor families and the strengths of these families. We look for principles that explain certain types of interaction, while at the same time being careful not to generalize.

Religious, Social, and Political Attitudes: Sociologists measure a community by the views and opinions of its members. In this way it becomes possible to gauge how it is likely to act, and to comprehend how the community has been influenced by the experiences of its members. It is of particular interest to know how the Holocaust has affected the survivors' view of religion and their religious behavior. It is also of importance to know how their religious beliefs have affected their ability to adapt to life in the post-Holocaust era. We study the attitudes of survivors on many other issues, including antisemitism, Israel, tolerance for others, politics, and materialism.

Long-Range Adaptation: Finally, we want to know how successful the survivors were in their efforts to rebuild their shattered lives. Their modes and patterns, plus the strategies they selected, will, hopefully, tell us much about how human beings can cope with tragedy in general.

I. THE COURSE

THE HOLOCAUST: HISTORICAL PERSPECTIVES

Paula E. Hyman
The Undergraduate Program in Judaic Studies, Yale University

II. ACADEMIC CONTEXT OF THE COURSE

This course has been offered in two different academic contexts - in a large American university and in a Jewish institution of higher learning. In both cases the course was offered as a seminar to advanced undergraduates. No previous knowledge was assumed, but preference was given to students who had taken courses in either European or Jewish history. In the university setting this course attracted a heterogeneous student body, of Jews and Gentiles, children of Holocaust survivors, and the merely curious. I offer this course as a seminar because I believe that students must confront this subject actively rather than simply acquire information passively; the seminar format encourages discussion and provides me with immediate feedback as to students' perceptions and concerns. The course does not aspire to comprehensiveness. Instead, it focuses on central issues in the historiography of the Holocaust.

III. OUTLINE OF THE COURSE

1. The rise of Nazism
   Week 1 The legacy of German antisemitism

   Paul Massing, **Rehearsal for Destruction**, pp. 1-109, 277-310.

   Week 2 Hitler and Nazi ideology

   *Adolf Hitler, **Mein Kampf**, pp. 284-329.

   *George Mosse, **Nazi Culture**, pp. 1-40, 57-91, 263-316.

*Yehuda Bauer & N. Keren, **A History of the Holocaust**, pp. 73-92.

Film: *Triumph of the Will.*

Week 3 Prelude to the Final Solution

Karl Schleunes, **The Twisted Road to Auschwitz.**

*Lucy Dawidowicz, **A Holocaust Reader**, pp. 35-53.

2. The Holocaust
Week 4 The bureaucratization of death

*Raul Hilberg, **The Destruction of the European Jews**, pp. 43-308.

*Dawidowicz, **The War Against the Jews**, pp. 117-171.

*————, **Reader**, pp. 55-103.

Week 5 Life in the ghettos

*Emanuel Ringelblum, **Notes from the Warsaw Ghetto.**

*Chaim Kaplan, **The Scroll of Agony**, pp. 207-250, 255-269, 273-284, 290-314, 347-350, 383-385.

*Dawidowicz, **War**, pp. 327-252.

Week 6 **Role of the Jewish Councils**

*Isaiah Trunk, **Judenrat**, pp. 14-35, 43-60, 388-450, 475-527.

*Dawidowicz, **Reader**, pp. 235-287.

Week 7 The death camps

*Hilberg, pp. 555-669.

*Primo Levi, **Survival in Auschwitz,**

or

*Elie Wiesel, **Night.**

Rudolf Hoess, Commandant of Auschwitz.

Film: *Night and Fog.*

3. Responses to the Holocaust
    Week 8   Witnesses and bystanders

    *Bauer, pp. 279-302, 309-325.

    Guenter Lewy, **The Roman Catholic Church and Nazi Germany,** selections.

    Richard Gutteridge, **The German Evangelist Church and the Jews,** selections.

    David Wyman, **The Abandonment of the Jews,** pp. 311-340.

    *Phillip Hallie, **Lest Innocent Blood Be Shed,** selections.

    Week 9   Jewish responses: individual and communal

    *Dawidowicz, **Reader,** pp. 143-170.

    Isaiah Trunk, **Jewish Responses to Nazi Persecution,** pp. 3-74, 122-134, 221-228.

    *Irving Rosenbaum, **The Holocaust and Halakhah,** pp. 1-59, 77-119.

    Week10   Resistance

    *Dawidowicz, **Reader,** pp. 329-380.

    *Bauer, pp. 245-277

Israel Gutman, **The Jews of Warsaw, 1939-1943**, pp. 283-430.

*Terrence Des Pres, **The Survivor**, pp. 111-174.

4. Confronting the Holocaust
   Week11   A sociological approach

   *Helen Fein, **Accounting for Genocide**.

   Week12   Literary responses

   *Sidra Ezrahi, **By Words Alone: The Holocaust in Literature**.
   or
   Alvin Rosenfeld, **A Double Dying**.

   Week13   Theological responses

   *Irving Greenberg, "Cloud of Smoke, Pillar of Fire: Judaism, Christianity, and Modernity after the Holocaust," in Eva Fleischner (ed.), **Auschwitz: Beginning of a New Era?** pp. 7-55.

   *Richard Rubenstein, **After Auschwitz**, pp. 47-58.

   *Eliezer Berkovits, **Faith after the Holocaust**, pp. 67-85.

   Jacob Neusner, **Stranger at Home**, pp. 85-98.

NOTE: Readings preceded by asterisks are available in paperback.

IV. REQUIREMENTS OF THE COURSE FOR GRADING

Students are expected to complete each reading assignment before the class and to participate in class discussion. They are required to write two short (3 page) papers on the films, and a 15 page research paper on a topic to be chosen in consultation with the instructor.

V. CONCEPTUAL FRAMEWORK OF THE COURSE

The course is designed to examine major issues in the history of the Holocaust through an analysis of both primary documents and secondary sources. It begins with a consideration of the development of modern political antisemitism and its role in German politics at the end of the nineteenth century. After exploring the themes of various types of antisemitism and the way in which antisemites constructed reality, the course investigates the role of antisemitism in Hitler's ideology and in Nazi culture. It raises the questions of the connection between stereotype and social reality as well as between nineteenth-century antisemitism and the rise of Nazism. The film *Triumph of the Will* serves as a text to discuss the impact of Nazism upon the German public. Turning to early years of Nazi rule, the course discusses the intentionalist and functionalist approaches to the development of the Final Solution.

The course then focuses on the destruction of European Jewry, with special emphasis on the Polish experience. The central issue of the Holocaust - how it was possible, from both an institutional and a human point of view, to commit genocide - is discussed with reference to the Nazi perpetrators and their Jewish victims. Critiques of Jewish perceptions and behavior during the Holocaust (Arendt, Bettelheim, and Hilberg) are evaluated within the specific historical context. Special attention is also paid to diaries and memoirs as historical testimony, and to the potential conflict of interpretation between the contemporary observer and the historian.

The rubric "Responses to the Holocaust" permits discussion of the role of such witnesses and bystanders as the Allies, the churches, world Jewry, and individual Europeans. Here the course explores the issue of contemporary knowledge of the Holocaust and the factors constraining activity on behalf of the victims. This section of the course also deals with the range of responses of the Jewish victims and pays particular attention to definitions of resistance as well as to study of particular instances of resistance.

The course concludes with consideration of the ways in which different disciplines have attempted to define the meaning of the Holocaust. Although the juxtaposition of primary and secondary sources throughout the syllabus encourages discussion of methodological issues, this concluding section, whose readings have varied widely, enables students to recognize the multiplicity of approaches to historic reality and to consider how discipline affects the framing of questions and the interpretation of human experience. It also permits some discussion of the impact of the Holocaust on contemporary Jewish thought.

I. THE COURSE

THE DESTRUCTION OF EUROPEAN JEWRY

Leon A. Jick
Department of Near-Eastern and Judaic Studies, Brandeis University

II. ACADEMIC CONTEXT OF THE COURSE

The course is offered in the Department of Near Eastern and Judaic Studies of Brandeis University. Brandeis University is a non-sectarian Jewish-sponsored university with approximately 2800 undergraduates and 750 graduate students in the arts and sciences.

For the past ten years the course has attracted between 150 and 200 students, which is an unusually large number for a small university and for a course which is an elective. The students come from all departments and possess a wide range of backgrounds in general and Jewish history. In order to compensate for the diversity in backgrounds, weekly discussion sections are divided according to prior knowledge.

III. OUTLINE OF THE COURSE

1. Observations on the study of the Holocaust, uniqueness and universalism in the historic Jewish experience

Required reading

Yehuda Bauer, "Against Mystification," **The Holocaust in Historical Perspective**, pp. 30-49.

Shmuel Ettinger, "The Origins of Modern Anti-Semitism," in I. Gutman & L. Rothkirchen (eds.), **The Catastrophe of European Jewry**, pp. 3-39.

Shaul Esh, "The Dignity of the Destroyed: Towards a Definition of the Period of the Holocaust," *ibid.*, pp. 346-361.

Saul Friedlander, "Some Aspects of the Historical Significance of the Holocaust," **The Jerusalem Quarterly** (Fall 1976), pp. 36-59.

Recommended reading
Jacob Katz, "Was the Holocaust Predictable?" **Commentary** (May 1975).

——————————, **Exclusiveness and Tolerance**, pp. 3-48, 169-182.

2. The impact of modernization on European Jewry

Required reading
Jacob Talmon, "Mission and Testimony: The Universal Significance of Modern Anti-Semitism," in I. Gutman & L. Rothkirchen, *loc. cit.*, pp. 127-174.

Lucy Dawidowicz, **The War Against the Jews 1933-1945**, Part I, 1 & 2, pp. 3-47 (pages refer to hard cover edition).

Yehuda Bauer & N. Keren, **A History of the Holocaust**, pp. 3-73.

Recommended reading
Hannah Arendt, **The Origins of Totalitarianism**, pp. 3-122.

3. Between the wars: Germany and Europe 1918-1933

Required reading
Bauer & Keren, *loc. cit.*, pp. 73-93.

A.J. Nicholls, **Weimar and the Rise of Hitler**, especially pp. 144-171.

Recommended reading
George Mosse, **The Crisis of German Ideology**, pp. 237-317, or **Germans and Jews**, pp. 34-60, 77-115.

Leon A. Jick, **A Study of Betrayal**, pp. 10-46.

4. The Third Reich 1933-1939

Required reading
Dawidowicz, pp. 48-106, 169-196.
  and/or
Bauer & Keren, pp. 93-139.

"Chronological Table of Events 1933-1945," in I. Gutman & L. Rothkirchen, loc. cit., pp. 705-738.

Abraham Margaliot, "The Struggle for Survival of the Jewish Community in Germany in the Face of Oppression," in H. Druks (ed.), **Jewish Resistance During the Holocaust**, pp. 100-122.

Nathan Feinberg, "Jewish Political Activities Against the Nazi Regime in the Years 1933-1939," *ibid.*, pp. 74-99.

Recommended reading
Raul Hilberg, **Documents of Destruction**, pp. 8-36.

John L. Snell (ed.), **The Nazi Revolution**, pp. 117-154, 173-185.

5. The coming of war 1939-1941

Required reading
Dawidowicz, pp. 107-128, 197-278.
  and/or
Bauer & Keren, pp. 139-193.

Jacob Robinson, "The Holocaust," in I. Gutman & L. Rothkirchen, *loc. cit.*, pp. 243-282.

Jick, pp. 47-80.

Recommended reading
Gerald Reitlinger, **The Final Solution**, pp. 3-52.

6. From horror to Holocaust: 1941-1945

Required reading
Dawidowicz, pp. 129-166, 279-353.
 and/or
Bauer & Keren, pp. 193-245.

Helen Fein, **Accounting for Genocide**, pp. 3-31.

Jick, pp. 81-116.

Recommended reading
Raul Hilberg, **The Destruction of European Jewry**, 1st ed., pp. 31-39.

Reitlinger, pp. 123-155, 183-272.

7. Reactions and resistance

Required reading
Leni Yahil, "Jewish Resistance - An Examination of Active and Passive Forms of Jewish Survival in the Holocaust Period," **Jewish Resistance During the Holocaust**, pp. 35-45.

Yitzhak Arad, "Jewish Armed Resistance in Eastern Europe - Its Characteristics and Problems," in I. Gutman & L. Rothkirchen, *loc. cit.*, pp. 490-517.

Marc Dworzecki, "The Day to Day Stand of the Jews," **Jewish Resistance During the Holocaust**, pp. 152-190.

Bauer & Keren, **History**, pp. 245-279.

Isaiah Trunk, "The Attitude of the Judenrats to the Problem of Armed Resistance Against the Nazis," in I. Gutman & L. Rothkirchen, *loc. cit.*, pp. 422-450.

Recommended reading
Terrence Des Pres, **The Survivor**.

8. The bystanders: reactions and failures to react

Required reading
Helen Fein, "Socio-Political Responses During the Holocaust," in **Encountering the Holocaust**, Byron Sherwin & Susan Ament (eds.), pp. 84-140.

Bauer & Keren, **History**, pp. 279-303.

Yehuda Bauer, "The Holocaust and American Jewry," in **The Holocaust in Historical Perspective**, pp. 7-29.

David Wyman, **The Abandonment of the Jews**, pp. 178-206.

Recommended reading
(choose one of the following)
Henry Feingold, **The Politics of Rescue**.

Yehuda Bauer, **American Jewry and the Holocaust**.

David Wyman, **The Abandonment of the Jews**.

Arthur Morse, **While Six Million Died**.

9. The final chapter (1944-1945)

Required reading
Livia Rothkirchen, "The Final Solution in Its Last Stages," in I. Gutman & L. Rothkirchen, *loc. cit.*, pp. 319-345.

Bauer & Keren, **History**, pp. 303-337.

——————, "The Mission of Joel Brand," in **The Holocaust in Historical Perspective**, pp. 94-155.

Wyman, pp. 235-254. 288-307.

Recommended reading
Raul Hilberg, **Documents of Destruction**, pp. 187-202.

Ira Hirschmann, **Lifeline to a Promised Land**, pp. 3-172.

10. The war ends - the struggle for redemption (1945-1948)

Required reading
Bauer & Keren, **History**, pp. 337-351.

Marie Syrkin, **Blessed is the Match**, pp. 309-360.

"Journal of Kibbutz Buchenwald," Leo Schwartz, ed., **The Root and the Bough**, pp. 309-345.

Recommended reading
Leo Schwartz, **The Redeemers**.

I.W. Stone, **Underground to Palestine**.

Ira Hirschmann, **Lifeline to a Promised Land**, pp. 173-208.

Hannah Arendt, **Eichmann in Jerusalem**, pp. 232-256.

11. The ongoing scourge

Required reading
Ben Halpern, "Anti-Semitism in the Perspective of Jewish History," in Charles Stember (ed.), **Jews in the Mind of America**, pp. 273-299.

Yehoshua Gilboa, **The Black Years of Soviet Jewry**.

12. "Watchman - What of the Night?"

Required reading
Jacob Katz, "Was the Holocaust Predictable?" **Commentary**, May 1975.

Leni Yahil, "The Holocaust in Jewish Historiography," in I. Gutman & L. Rothkirchen, *loc. cit.*, pp. 651-667.

Emil Fackenheim, "Jewish Faith and the Holocaust," **Commentary**, August 1968,
pp. 30-36.

Abba Kovner, "The Mission of the Survivors," in I. Gutman & L. Rothkirchen,
loc. cit., pp. 671-683.

Alfred Kazin, "The Heart of the World," in E. Fleischner (ed.), **Auschwitz:
Beginning of a New Era?**

IV. REQUIREMENTS OF THE COURSE FOR GRADING

Students are expected to attend lectures each week, to participate in a weekly
discussion section, and to attend film showings.

Two examinations are given, and lists of study questions are distributed prior
to each examination. (See examples of study questions, below.) Students are expected to deal with issues rather than to repeat factual information. In addition, a
paper of 10-15 pages is required, reviewing one of the many personal accounts by
Holocaust survivors and relating the individual experience to the larger context of
the period. The following are examples of memoir literature from which students may
choose. They may also select from a more complete list of memoir literature to be
found in **The Holocaust, an Annotated Bibliography**, by David M. Szonyi, held on
reserve in the library.

Suggested list of Survivors' Memoirs and Accounts of the Holocaust

A. Memoirs, diaries, photographs, and drawings

Berg, Mary. **The Warsaw Ghetto**, S.L. Schneiderman (ed.) (New York: L.B. Fisher,
1945).

Brand, Sandra. **Between Two Worlds** (New York: Shengold, 1983).

Czerniakow, Adam. **The Warsaw Diary of Adam Czerniakow: Prelude to Doom.** R. Hilberg, S. Staron & J. Kermisz (eds.) (New York: Stein & Day, 1979; Scarborough pb., 1982).

David, Janina. **A Square of Sky and A Touch of Earth** (New York: Penguin Books, 1981).

Kaplan, Chaim A. **The Scroll of Agony** (reprinted in paperback as **The Warsaw Diary of Chaim Kaplan**) A. Katsh & C. Kaplan (eds.), (New York: Macmillan, 1965; Collier pb., 1981).

Korczak, Janusz. **Ghetto Diary** (New York: Holocaust Library, 1978: pb. 1981).

Ringelblum, Emanuel. **Notes from the Warsaw Ghetto** (New York: McGraw-Hill, 1958; Schocken pb., 1974).

B. Death camps and death marches - memoirs and accounts

Donat, Alexander. **The Holocaust Kingdom: A Memoir** (New York: Holt, Reinhart & Winston, 1965; Holocaust Library pb., 1978).

——————— (ed.), **The Death Camp at Treblinka** (New York: Holocaust Library, 1980).

Levi, Primo. **Survival in Auschwitz: The Nazi Assault on Humanity** (orig. title, **If This Be a Man**) (New York: Orion, 1959; Collier pb., 1973).

Wells, Leon W. **The Death Brigade** (orig. title, **The Janowska Road**) (New York: Macmillan, 1963; Holocaust Library, 1978).

Wiesel, Elie. **Night** (New York: Hill & Wang, 1960; Avon pb., 1972).

Borzykowski, Tuvia. **Between Tumbling Walls** (Israel: Kibbutz Lohamei Haghettaot [Ghetto Fighters' House], 1972).

Goldstein, Bernard. **The Stars Bear Witness** (New York: Viking, 1949).

Lubetkin, Zivia. **In the Days of Destruction and Revolt** (S. Tubin, trans., Y. Yanai, ed.) (Tel Aviv: Hakibbutz Hameuchad Publishing House and Ghetto Fighters' House Publishers in cooperation with Am Oved Publishers, 1981).

Meed, Vladka. **On Both Sides of the Wall: Memoirs from the Warsaw Ghetto** (New York: Holocaust Library, 1979).

C. Resistance in the concentration and death camps

Garlinski, Jossef. **Fighting Auschwitz** (New York: Fawcett, 1971).

Gruber, Samuel. **I Chose Life** (G. Hirschler ed.) (New York: Shengold, 1978).

Kohn, Nathan & Roiter, Howard. **A Voice from the Forest** (New York: Holocaust Library, 1980).

Senesh, Hannah. **Hannah Senesh: Her Life and Diary** (New York: Schocken, 1972).

D. Jews in hiding or otherwise protected

Frank, Anne. **The Diary of a Young Girl** (New York: Pocket Books, 1965).

Friedlander, Saul. **When Memory Comes** (New York: Farrar, Straus & Giroux, 1978; Avon pb., 1980).

E. Jewish partisans

Arad, Yitzhak. **Partisan: From the Valley of Death to Mount Zion** (New York: Holocaust Library pb., 1978).

Examples of Study Questions

Identify the following and briefly indicate their significance:

1.	Blood libel	1.	Walter Rathenau
2.	Dreyfus case	2.	Franz Rosenzweig
3.	Weimar Republic	3.	Leo Baeck
4.	Mein Kampf	4.	Martin Buber
5.	Treaty of Versailles	5.	Adolf Eichmann
6.	Balfour Declaration	6.	Reinhardt Heydrich
7.	Bund	7.	I.G. Farben
8.	S.A. & S.S.	8.	Stephen Wise
9.	Nuremberg Laws	9.	Adam Czerniakow
10.	Evian Conference	10.	Mordechai Anielewicz
11.	Kristallnacht	11.	Emanuel Ringelblum
12.	Munich Pact	12.	Shmuel Szygelboim
13.	British White Paper of 1939	13.	Hirsh Glik
14.	Judenrat		
15.	Einsatzgruppen		
16.	Babi Yar		
17.	Wannsee Conference		

1. In the 1870s, amidst newly developing ideas of racism, a new term was coined: antisemitism. Did antisemitism represent merely a continuation of the age-old hostility to Jews, or was it a new phenomenon? What elements were continuous? What new elements were introduced?

2. Shmuel Ettinger has written in **The Origins of Modern Anti-Semitism**: "Anti-Semitism sleeps in the conciousness of ordinary man, ready to be awakened at the touch of crisis or social stress or by daily competition with Jews." Comment in agreement or disagreement, citing historical examples for whatever position you choose to maintain.

3. J. L. Talmon in "The Universal Significance of Modern Anti-Semitism," writes: "The 'stab in the back' explanation of Germany's defeat in 1918 was seized upon with the greatest avidity as conclusive proof of the correctness of racial

theory." What is the background of this statement? What is its relevance for an explanation of the rise of Hitler?

4.   Some historians stress the importance of Volkish ideology in Weimar Germany in preparing the ground for the rise of Nazism. Comment in agreement or disagreement. What was this ideology? Was it crucial? If yes, how? If no, what factors were more significant in explaining Hitler's accession to power?

5.   Some historians maintain that the Holocaust was the product of "German national character," with antecedents reaching back in history to Martin Luther. Comment in agreement or disagreement, and present evidence to support your point of view.

6.   Prior to 1938, most German Jews chose to remain in Germany. What factors contributed to their behavior? Discuss the relative importance of the gradual changes in Nazi policy, the world view of the Jews themselves, the difficulty of emigration, etc. How would you characterize the response of German Jewry to Nazism before 1938 and thereafter?

7.   Some historians assert that Hitler's antisemitism was the essential element in his program and that therefore World War II was primarily a "war against the Jews." In your view, what were the German war aims? How did antisemitism contribute to the fulfilling of these aims?

8.   When did the Holocaust begin? In January 1933? In September 1935? In November 1938? In September 1939? In June 1941? In January 1942? Each of these dates represents a change in Nazi treatment of the Jews. What were the changes? Was there one pre-determined policy with changes representing shifts in tactics or did basic Nazi aims and goals change? What accounts for the changes? Is it possible to designate a single moment as the beginning of the Holocaust?

9.   As late as 1940, the Nazi leadership was preparing plans for the deportation of European Jews to the Island of Madagascar. What was the purpose of such plans? Why were they considered? What events changed Nazi thinking on this subject? What, if anything, does the existence of the "Madagascar Plan" tell us about the Nazi decision to exterminate the Jewish people?

10. Once the extermination policy began, it was difficult to convince anyone - even the victims themselves - that it was really happening. How do you explain this behavior? How important was the Nazi policy of concealment and falsification? What other factors contributed to the inability to believe?

11. Hannah Arendt speaks of the Jews as having been driven into the "storm center of events" in Europe. What does this mean? What were some of its consequences?

12. Saul Friedlander has written: "Nobody could have foreseen the Final Solution itself... Most Jews remained unaware of the fact that the time of radical changes had come." Can Lucy Dawidowicz's point of view be reconciled with this statement? In your judgment, was the Nazi extermination policy the inevitable outcome of long-held goals or a decision arrived at as a result of pragmatic wartime calculations? Cite evidence to support your view.

13. In the autumn of 1944, David Ben Gurion wrote: "What have you done to us, you freedom-loving people, guardians of justice, defenders of the high principles of democracy and the brotherhood of man? What have you allowed to be perpetrated against a defenseless people while you stood aside...". In the light of the actions of the 'bystanders' - including the government of the U.S.A. - is the indictment justified?

14. How would you describe the behavior of American Jewry? How can one understand or explain this behavior?

15. It is often stated that the truth about the Nazi extermination was not known until the camps were liberated. Is this accurate? When were the facts known? How is it possible to explain the response or lack of it?

16. In May 1944 the deportation of Hungarian Jewry began. This action is often cited as an example of the irrationality of Nazi policy. How can the actions be explained? To what extent does the element of "irration- ality" enter into the formulation of Nazi policy?

17. Following the end of the war, what were the circumstances of the survivors? What actions - if any - were taken to alleviate their problems? How and when was the problem of "displaced persons" ultimately resolved?

18. Mordechai Rumkowski's policy in the Lodz ghetto stressed "survival through work." What was the point of this policy? To what extent was it succesful? How would you describe Rumkowski's role? How did it compare to the behavior of leaders of other ghettos?

V. CONCEPTUAL FRAMEWORK OF THE COURSE

The purpose of the course is to attempt, in so far as possible, to achieve a better understanding of the events in all their ramifications. In pursuing this goal it is necessary to provide some background in both Jewish and general European history - how the Jews came to be living where they were and with the special baggage of attributes and burdens which they possessed. A second essential is some awareness of the circumstances in Central and Eastern Europe - especially in post World War I Germany - which paved the way for the rise of Nazism. An examination of the seizure of power by the Nazis and the gradual intensification of their antisemitic policy reveals the extent to which this policy was unanticipated and misunderstood. Lack of understanding limited the possible response by the bewildered victims.

The course stresses the relationship of Nazi policies and actions regarding Jews to their broader aims of domination, conquest and subjugation of the whole of Europe. It traces the changes in policy from 1933-35, 1935-38, 1938-39, 1939-41 and the ultimate inauguration of the practice of total annihilation after the invasion of the Soviet Union in June 1941. The course attempts to provide some insight into how and why these changes occurred when they did, and why those who were victimized by the unfolding disaster were caught unaware.

In dealing with the wartime period, the behavior of three constituent elements is examined: the perpetrators, the victims, and the bystanders. An attempt is made to analyze the action or inaction of all three groups in the light of knowledge available to them at the time, rather than to pass judgment with the benefit of post-Holocaust hindsight. Special attention is given to the varieties of resistance manifested by the victims despite the desperate circumstances in which they found themselves.

The final segment of the course deals with the revival of the surviving remnant, the struggle for the establishment of the State of Israel, and the elimination of the condition of Jewish powerlessness and total vulnerability.

Two basic textbooks are used; they have varying strengths and present alternative points of view on a variety of issues: **A History of the Holocaust** by Yehuda Bauer & N. Keren, and **The War Against the Jews** by Lucy Dawidowicz. Articles from a variety of sources supplement the texts. Four films are shown during the semester. The number of films produced in recent years makes the choice difficult. In the past year, the films selected were: 1) *Genocide*, a BBC film which gives a visual sense of the rise of Nazism as well as an overview of the period; 2) *Partisans of Vilna*, an excellent documentary on resistance; 3) *Rumkowski and the Lodz Ghetto*, a film which illuminates the dilemmas of the Judenraete; 4) *The Liberation of Auschwitz*, a confrontation with the reality of the extermination camps.

In addition, a number of survivors with varied experiences are invited to meet with the class. The most significant interaction is with members of the university faculty who are known to the students and who discuss their experience.

My major purpose is to enable students to understand the experience of the Jewish people in this century - the unspeakable tragedy and the ineffable resurrection. Students are expected to understand how European Jews in the nineteenth and twentieth centuries were "driven into the storm center of events", how they became the scapegoats *par excellence* for every ache and ill of European societies rocked by turbulence, and how they fell victim to the malevolent Nazi regime. I emphasize the fact that the ultimate goal of Nazism was world domination, and that anti-semitism became a useful device in achieving this goal.

Horrible and unprecedented as the fate of the Jews under the Nazis was, the Holocaust and the disasters which accompanied it lead to the realization that in the face of totalitarian tyranny, Jews are the ones who suffer first and worst, but they are never the only ones.

Issues which are considered include: the role of antisemitism in modern society and its relationship to classical Jew hatred; the willingness of other groups and nations to acquiesce in persecution as long as only the Jews are affected; the variety of responses and forms of resistance to Nazism; the problems and price of powerlessness; the extraordinary significance of Jewish history even in its darkest hour, but especially in its renaissance after the disaster.

I. THE COURSE

THE HOLOCAUST IN HISTORICAL CONTEXT

Steven T. Katz
Department of Near Eastern Studies, Cornell University

II. ACADEMIC CONTEXT OF THE COURSE

This course was taught at Cornell University, a large, distinguished, private university. The selective nature of the admission process ensures good students, and expectations regarding work levels are high. The course is taught in a large lecture format, supplemented by discussion sections. It meets for three hours a week, over a 14-week semester. The average number of students is 250. Students come from all religious and ethnic backgrounds, and the course is presented in a manner that makes the material equally available to all.

The objectives of the course are: a) to situate the Holocaust in its historical context; b) to explore, in detail, what the Holocaust was; and c) to consider briefly some of the intellectual, moral and religious issues that the Holocaust raises.

III. OUTLINE OF THE COURSE

Required Texts

Eliezer Berkovits, **Faith After the Holocaust** (New York: Ktav Publishing House, 1973).

Jacob Katz, **From Prejudice to Destruction** (Cambridge, Mass.: Harvard University Press, 1980).

Lucy Dawidowicz, **The War Against the Jews** (New York: Hall, 1975).

——————————, **A Holocaust Reader** (New York: Behrman House, 1976).

128

Emil Fackenheim, **God's Presence in History: Jewish Affirmations and Philosophical Reflections** (New York: Harper & Row, 1972).

Richard Rubenstein, **The Cunning of History** (New York: Harper & Row, 1975).

Steven Katz, **Post-Holocaust Dialogues** (New York: New York University Press, 1983).

Films
Several films are shown in connection with the course.

Week 1: The European context and the rise of modern antisemitism

Required reading
L. Schwartz, **Great Ages and Ideas of the Jewish People** (New York: Modern Library, 1956), Chap. on "The Modern Period" (on reserve).

H.M. Sachar, **The Course of Modern Jewish History** (New York: Dell, 1977), Chaps. 11 &12 (on reserve).

J. Katz, **From Prejudice to Destruction,** *loc. cit.* (entire) (on reserve).

Week 2: Nazi antisemitism up to 1939

Required reading
L. Dawidowicz, **The War Against the Jews,** Pt. I, *loc. cit.*, pp. 3-168 (on reserve).

Weeks 3, 4, 5: The Holocaust 1939-1941

Required reading
L. Dawidowicz, **Reader,** *loc. cit.*, pp. 55-130, 171-234.

——————————, **War,** Pt. II, *loc. cit.*, pp. 169 to end of book (on reserve).

A. Morse, **While Six Million Died** (entire) (on reserve).

Weeks 6, 7, 8: The Holocaust 1941-1945

Required reading
L. Dawidowicz, **War**, Pt. II, *loc. cit.*, pp. 169 to end of book.

A. Morse, **While Six Million Died**, *loc. cit.* (entire).

Weeks 9, 10: Questions of technology, bureaucracy and totalitarianism

Required reading
R. Rubenstein, **The Cunning of History**, *loc. cit.* (entire).

H. Buchheim, **Totalitarian Rule** (entire) (on reserve).

H. Arendt, **Eichmann in Jerusalem**, Chaps. 2, 6, 7, 8 (on reserve).

Weeks 11, 12: The Aftermath, Philosophical and Theological Questions

Required reading
L. Dawidowicz, **Reader**, *loc. cit.*, pp. 235-280.

R. Rubenstein, **After Auschwitz**, Chaps. 1 & 2 (on reserve).

E. Fackenheim, **God's Presence of God in History**, *loc. cit.* (entire) (on reserve).

E. Berkovits, **Faith After the Holocaust**, *loc. cit.*, Chaps. 3, 4, 5, (on reserve).

S. Katz, **Post-Holocaust Dialogues**, *loc. cit.*, Chap. 3 to end of book (on reserve).

IV. REQUIREMENTS OF THE COURSE FOR GRADING
Students are required to submit one written paper, and to take a final examination.

V. CONCEPTUAL FRAMEWORK OF THE COURSE
Part I: The course assumes no prior knowledge of either modern Jewish history, the history of antisemitism, or the Holocaust. Rather, it sets out to provide an in-

troductory historical understanding of these issues, obviously concentrating on the last of the three, the *Shoah* itself. The first section of the course attempts to sketch a brief but intelligible picture of pre-modern antisemitism, its nature and limits, and to situate this analysis in the wider context of the pre-modern Christian and Muslim world. The second segment of this opening unit then explains what the coming of modernity meant for Jews and Judaism and how it left in its wake the unresolved "problem of the Jews," leading finally, but not inevitably, to modern racial and political antisemitism at the end of the nineteenth century. Here we attempt to explain how this modern legacy contributed to the eventual rise of Nazism, and how it was not yet genocidal.

Part II, 1918-1933: In the second unit we discuss the meaning of World War I for European history and the repercussions of the German defeat for German (and Jewish) history. The objective of the discussion is to indicate the nature of the response to the defeat in certain German circles and what impact this had on the nature of growing German antisemitism, especially among members of the far Right and the emerging Nazi Party. Secondly, we discuss in some detail the nature of the Weimar Republic and its inherent weaknesses which led eventually, though not inevitably, to its decline and overthrow.

Part III, 1933-1937: In this segment we consider Hitler's coming to power and the implementation of the Nazi program of "disemancipation." The treatment is essentially historical, and the lectures review the major stages in the escalation of Nazi anti-Jewish policy and practice.

Part IV, 1938-1941: Here we consider the background and first stages of World War II, how these affected the Jews of Europe, especially of Poland after 1939, and the institution of the Nazi policy of ghettoization. The details of events, as well as the ambiguities in the situation, are analyzed. Particular attention is paid to the question of whether or not the Nazis already had a genocidal plan to destroy European Jewry.

Part V, 1941-1945: The history of the Holocaust is retold. The emphasis again is descriptive, taking the students step by step from the invasion of Russia and the deadly work of the *Einsatzgruppen*, through the construction of the death camps and their actual functioning.

Part VI, Technology, Bureaucracy, Ideology: Here we ask the students to consider how such an event as the *Shoah* was possible. In trying to answer this question we make a close analysis of the logic and ontological character of technology and bureaucracy and, very importantly, indicate how technology and bureaucracy, even though they have a dynamic of their own, are ultimately subject to ideological direction; thus, the ideological superstructure directing the technology and bureaucracy is of prime importance. This then allows us to decipher in detail Hitler's view of "the Jew," and the role "Jews" played in his *Weltanschauung*. As a consequence of this analysis students can begin to understand how Hitler's peculiar form of racist thought led to Auschwitz and required the "Final Solution." In this connection we discuss Hitler's intent to make the world *Judenrein* and introduce the heated debate among scholars whether the *Shoah* was the result of a particular "intention" (genocide), or rather of "non-intentional" functionalist *realia* and concerns. My own position favors the "intentionalist" argument; the alternative seems to me finally unable to explain what happened.

Part VIII, Philosophical and Theological Issues: The *Shoah* obviously generates enormous philosophical and theological dilemmas. By reading some of the main thinkers who have wrestled with these   issues over the past four decades, e.g., Hannah Arendt, Emil Fackenheim, Richard Rubenstein, and Eliezer Berkovits, students are introduced to the questions the *Shoah* raises, while pointing out that answers, if there can ever be "answers," still elude us.

I. THE COURSE

JEWISH AND CHRISTIAN RESPONSES TO THE HOLOCAUST

Richard Libowitz
Department of Theology, Saint Joseph's University, Philadelphia

II. ACADEMIC CONTEXT OF THE COURSE

This single-semester course is the first offering in what may be called Holocaust Studies at Saint Joseph's University, a Catholic university founded and directed by the Society of Jesus (Jesuits). The course is given within the University College division of the University. The University College is an evening, degree-granting program, attractive to many students beyond traditional college age. The students admitted to this course will range in age from mid-twenties to sixties. The overwhelming majority of students are Christian; most are Roman Catholic.

No previous knowledge is assumed on the part of the students.

In developing this course, it was necessary to recognize that students would be coming to class after a full day of work. Reading and research assignments would have to be scaled to reflect the realistic time which students could devote to the materials. This also mandated a greater emphasis upon detailed discussion within class. While the history of the *Shoah* occupied much of the early portions of the semester, primary emphasis was placed on the effects of those events on subsequent religious thought, both Jewish and Christian.

III. OUTLINE OF THE COURSE

1. Course introduction

    Development of working definitions for key terms: Religion, Race, Genocide, Holocaust. Background to Judaism.

2. Introduction II - Judaism and Christianity

    Definitions and comparisons. Who is a Jew? Status in medieval Europe. Emancipation and Assimilation. Evolution of modern antisemitism.

Reading

John Kleiner, "The Attitudes of Martin Bucer and Langrave Philipp Toward the Jews of Hesse (1538-1539)," in **Faith and Freedom**, Richard Libowitz (ed.), (Oxford, 1987).

Elie Wiesel, "And Rabbi Ishmael Did Not Weep," in Libowitz, *ibid.*

3. Germany at the end of World War I
   Rise and fall of the Weimar Republic. The world in the 1920s. Adolf Hitler and the National Socialist Workers Party. Anti-Jewish legislation. What is "law"?

Reading

F. Burton Nelson, "The Holocaust and the *Oikumene*: An Episode for Remembrance," in Libowitz, *loc. cit.*

4. Kristallnacht

Reading

Elie Wiesel, **Night** (New York, 1970).

5. Holocaust

Film: *Night and Fog*, by Alan Resnais.

6. Judgment at Nuremberg

7. Memory I

Film: Selections from *Shoah* by Claude Lanzmann.

8. Memory II

Film: Selections from *Shoah* by Claude Lanzmann.

9. The beginnings of Jewish response
   Richard Rubenstein and the world "after Auschwitz".

   <u>Reading</u>
   Steven Katz, **Post-Holocaust Dialogues** (New York, 1985).

10. Emil Fackenheim, the 614th commandment and the "Commanding Voice" at Auschwitz

    <u>Reading</u>
    Steven Katz, *ibid*.

11. Other Jewish responses: Ignaz Maybaum and Eliezer Berkovits

    <u>Reading</u>
    Steven Katz, *ibid*.

12. Other Jewish responses: Irving Greenberg and Arthur Cohen

    <u>Reading</u>
    Steven Katz, *ibid*.

13. Christian responses to the Holocaust I

    <u>Reading</u>
    Michael Ryan, "Religious Affirmation After Auschwitz," in Libowitz, *loc. cit.*

    Alice L. Eckardt, "The Holocaust, the Church Struggle and Some Christian Reflections," *ibid*.

14. Christian responses II: Church struggle

    <u>Reading</u>
    Hubert Locke, "Church Struggle and the Holocaust: Reflections of a By-Stander," *ibid*.

    Martin Stoehr, "Anti-Semitism as an Ideology," *ibid*.

15. Rethinking Christianity I

Reading
Heinz Kremers, "The Contribution of the New Testament to a Christology within the Jewish-Christian Dialogue," *ibid.*

Leonard Swidler, "Can One Gain Salvation Only Through Yeshua The Christ?" *ibid.*

16. Rethinking Christianity II

Reading
Ruth Zerner, "Men of Faith; 'Hearing the Music'," *ibid.*

17. Christians who chose to make a difference I

Reading
Mordecai Paldiel, "Sparks of Light," *ibid.*

18. Christians who chose to make a difference II

Film: *The Courage to Care.*

19. Neo-Nazism in America

Film: *California Reich.*

20. Confrontation with religious prejudice I

Reading
Franklin H. Littell, **The Crucifixion of the Jews** (Macon, Ga., 1986).

21. Confrontation II

22. Confrontation III

Guest speaker: Franklin H. Littell.

23. Jews and Christians: Living together or merely alongside?

Reading
Paul M. van Buren, "Ecclesia Semper Reformanda: The Challenge of Israel," in Libowitz, *loc. cit.*

24. Approaches to the teaching of the Holocaust in the university

25. The perspective of a survivor

Guest speaker

26. Simon Wiesenthal, **The Sunflower** (New York, 1976).

IV. REQUIREMENTS OF THE COURSE FOR GRADING
Students are expected to keep up with reading assignments, attend class and participate in discussions, maintain a journal of responses to their studies, complete a research project, and submit several writing assignments, in lieu of examinations.

V. CONCEPTUAL FRAMEWORK OF THE COURSE
The purpose of this course is to provide an introduction to the effects of the Holocaust upon the subsequent religious thought of Jews and Christians. It is also intended to assist other teachers in preparing their own courses on the Holocaust. The course has been cross-listed as an upper-level under-graduate course in Theology and a graduate course in Education. Within the the classroom, this results in additional assignments for graduate students, as well as additional discussion sessions, during which time I analyze the purposes and methods which are being used in class.

In this, the first Holocaust course offered within a Catholic college or university in Philadelphia, I decided to focus upon post-Holocaust religious thought as a means of opening the subject to a student body having little knowledge of Jews, Judaism or the *Shoah* itself. Emphasis upon Christian responses is significant for the realization that the Holocaust was not purely a "Jewish event" of little concern to the Gentile world, but a matter of great importance to Christianity as well.

The students tend to be adults, working men and women who continue their formal education while raising families and pursuing full-time jobs. They often lack the time to read the lengthier assignments I would present to day students and, as noted, secondary source compilations are often used in place of primary documents. On the other hand, the students bring a greater desire for education as well as a trove of life experiences to their academic efforts.

The course is conducted in a relatively informal manner, relying upon a flexible lecture/discussion format which encourages questions and allows for digressions. This requires a firm knowledge of the subject, since one never knows when a discussion might require "pulling back" to a planned theme without cutting off class involvement. Readings and discussions are enhanced by the use of guest speakers, film and video tape. The presence of a survivor in class never fails to lend a special aura to the discussion.

Because I wish the students to grasp the enormity of evil that is called *Shoah*, I avoid a dependence upon quantified data. I believe too many place names, numbers and dates merely allow the student to avoid confrontation with the event itself. Thus, after a reading of *Night* and the viewing of a film such as *Night and Fog*, students are required to write a *subjective* paper about what they have seen and read. While subjective work may not be graded in the usual manner, the paper is in itself a mandatory assignment. The goal is to personalize study, leading students to a post-classroom concern about the Holocaust and its significance for them, nearly fifty years after Liberation. This in no way demeans traditional objective study, or rigorous research; I consider, however, that traditional research in this case is insufficient for human understanding.

I. THE COURSE

THE HOLOCAUST: THE NAZIS, OCCUPIED EUROPE, AND THE JEWS

Michael R. Marrus
Department of History, University of Toronto

II. ACADEMIC CONTEXT OF THE COURSE

This is a third-year undergraduate course offered at the University of Toronto - a large, urban "multiversity" with several professional faculties, a large School of Graduate Studies, and a widely diverse undergraduate student body. The enrollment in this course ranges between fifty and seventy-five students, about half of whom are Jewish. The course regularly attracts a small number of senior citizens who either audit the course or take it for university credit; some of these are Holocaust survivors. The recommended preparation for this course is one other course in European history. Most of the students will have completed a one-semester undergraduate survey of Europe since 1890.

The course surveys the destruction of two-thirds of European Jewry by the Nazis during the Second World War. The first term explores Nazi policy toward the Jews in the context of anti-Jewish ideology, bureaucratic structures, and the varying conditions of occupation and domination in Europe under the Third Reich. The second term continues the latter theme, but emphasizes the world outside - reactions of Jews, European populations and governments, the Allies, churches, and political movements.

Until recently, the course involved two hours of lectures and a mandatory, hour-long discussion group per week. Because of budgetary constraints the discussion group is now optional, and has a smaller attendance. Students may attend a weekly tutorial group to raise questions about material discussed in lectures and assigned readings. Occasionally, films are presented in conjunction with the course.

III. OUTLINE OF THE COURSE

Note: Weekly readings marked with an asterisk address specific themes, but are not necessarily intended to cover material discussed in the lectures. For most weeks

139

there is an assigned reading from books used as texts in the course. In addition, there is a list of alternate readings from which students make choices according to their own time and interest. When there is no specifically assigned reading, students are asked to choose from among the alternate selections. These lists of alternate readings are also the basis for the essays in the second term. The library has copies of much of the syllabus material, including photocopied articles, available on short-term loan.

It is suggested that students purchase copies of the following, which are available in the book store:

Raul Hilberg, **Destruction of the European Jews** (Student Edition, Holmes & Meir).

Lucy Dawidowicz, **A Holocaust Reader** (Behrman House).

Eberhard Jaeckel, **Hitler's World View** (Harvard).

Primo Levi, **Survival in Auschwitz** (Collier), <u>or</u> Terrence Des Pres, **The Survivor** (Oxford).

David Wyman, **The Abandonment of the Jews** (Pantheon).

Students may also wish to purchase the following:

Michael Marrus, **The Holocaust in History** (Lester & Orpen Dennys).

FIRST TERM: THE DESTRUCTION PROCESS

Week 1. Antecedents (1): The Jews and Modern Europeans

Salo Baron, "European Jewry Before and After Hitler," **American Jewish Yearbook** 63 (1962), pp. 3-49.

Yehuda Bauer, "The Place of the Holocaust in Contemporary History," **Studies in Contemporary Jewry** I (1984), pp. 201-224.

Shmuel Ettinger, "The Origins of Modern Anti-Semitism," in Yisrael Gutman and Livia Rothkirchen, eds., **The Catastrophe of European Jewry**, pp. 3-39.

Jacob Katz, **From Prejudice to Destruction: Anti-Semitism, 1700-1933**.

—————, "Was the Holocaust Predictable?" **Commentary** (May 1975), pp. 41-48.

Michael Marrus, "The Theory and Practice of Antisemitism," **Commentary** (August 1982), pp. 38-42.

George Mosse, "European History: The Seedbed of the Holocaust," **Midstream** (May 1973), pp. 3-25.

Shulamit Volkov, "Antisemitism as a Cultural Code - Reflections on the History and Historiography of Antisemitism in Imperial Germany," **Leo Baeck Institute Year Book XXIII** (1978), pp. 25-46.

Meyer Weinberg, **Because They Were Jews: A History of Antisemitism**.

Week 2. Antecedents (2): The Jews and the Germans

*Raul Hilberg, **Destruction of the European Jews**, Ch. 1.

*Lucy Dawidowicz, **Holocaust Reader**, Introduction, pp. 28-29.

Werner Angress, "The German Jews 1933-1939," in Henry Friedlander & Sybil Milton, (eds.), **The Holocaust: Ideology, Bureaucracy, and Genocide**.

Sarah Gordon, **Hitler, Germans, and the "Jewish Question"**.

Michael Kater, "Everyday Anti-Semitism in Pre-War Nazi Germany: The Popular Basis," **Yad Vashem Studies XVI** (1984), pp. 129-159.

George Kren & Leon Rappaport, **The Holocaust and the Crisis of Human Behavior**.

George L. Mosse, **The Crisis of German Ideology**.

——————————, **Germans and Jews.**

——————————, **German Jews Beyond Judaism.**

Donald Niewyk, **The Jews in Weimar Germany.**

Peter Pulzer, "Why Was There a Jewish Question in Imperial Germany?" **Leo Baeck Institute Yearbook** XXV (1980), pp. 133-146.

Week 3. Antecedents (3): The Jews and the Nazis

   *Eberhard Jaeckel, **Hitler's World View** (entire book).

   *Lucy Dawidowicz, **Holocaust Reader,** pp. 30-33.

   Yehuda Bauer, "Genocide; Was it the Nazis' Original Plan?" **Annals of the American Academy of Political and Social Science** 45 (July 1980), pp. 35-45.

   Sarah Gordon, **Hitler, Germans, and the "Jewish Question".**

   Adolf Hitler, **Mein Kampf.**

   Peter Merkl, **Political Violence Under the Swastika.**

   George Mosse, **Germans and Jews.**

   Ernst Nolte, **Three Faces of Fascism.**

   Karl Schleunes, **The Twisted Road to Auschwitz.**

Week 4. Persecution of the Jews in Germany, 1933-1941

   *Raul Hilberg, **Destruction of the European Jews,** pp. 27-64.

   *Lucy Dawidowicz, **Holocaust Reader,** Chs. 2, 5.

Helmut Krausnick, "The Persecution of the Jews," in Helmut Krausnick et al., **Anatomy of the SS State.**

Michael Marrus, **The Unwanted: European Refugees in the Twentieth Century.**

Karl Schleunes, **The Twisted Road to Auschwitz.**

Herbert A. Strauss, "Jewish Emigration from Germany: Nazi Policies and Jewish Response," **Leo Baeck Institute Yearbook** XXV (1980), pp. 313-363, and *ibid.*, XXVI (1981).

Jacob Toury, "From Forced Emigration to Expulsion - The Jewish Exodus over the Non-Slavic Borders of the Reich as a Prelude to the 'Final Solution'," **Yad Vashem Studies** XVII (1986), pp. 51-91.

Week 5. The Jews and the East Europeans

*Lucy Dawidowicz, **Holocaust Reader,** Ch. 3 (in preparation for the next week).

Stanislav Andreski, "An Economic Interpretation of Antisemitism in Eastern Europe," **Jewish Journal of Sociology** (December 1963), pp. 201-213.

Celia Heller, **On the Edge of Destruction: Jews of Poland Between the Two World Wars.**

Pawel Korzec, **Juifs en Pologne.**

Ezra Mendelsohn, **The Jews of East Central Europe Between the World Wars.**

——————————, "Interwar Poland: Good for the Jews or Bad for the Jews?" in Chimen Abramsky, Maciej Jachimczyk & Antony Polonsky (eds.), **The Jews in Poland.**

——————————, "Jewish Reactions to Antisemitism in East Central Europe," in Jehuda Reinharz (ed.), **Living With Antisemitism,** pp. 296-310.

Hugh Seton-Watson, "Government Policies Towards the Jews in Pre-Communist Eastern Europe," **Soviet Jewish Affairs** (December 1969), pp. 20-25.

Week 6. Evolution of the "Final Solution"

*Raul Hilberg, **Destruction of the European Jews**, Ch. 4, pp. 157-186.

Martin Broszat, "Hitler and the Genesis of the 'Final Solution': An Assessment of David Irving's Theses," **Yad Vashem Studies** XIII (1979), pp. 73-125.

Christopher Browning, **The Final Solution and the German Foreign Office**.

―――――――――――, **Fateful Months: Essays on the Emergence of the Final Solution.**

―――――――――――, "Nazi Resettlement Policy and the Search for a Solution to the Jewish Question 1939-1941," **German Studies Review** IX (1986), pp. 497-517.

Gerald Fleming, **Hitler and the Final Solution.**

Saul Friedlander, "From Anti-Semitism to Extermination: A Historiographical Study of Nazi Policies Toward the Jews and an Essay in Interpretation," **Yad Vashem Studies** XVI (1984), pp. 1-50.

Eberhard Jaeckel, **Hitler in History**.

Lothar Kettenacker, "Hitler's Final Solution and its Rationalization," in Gerhard Hirschfeld, ed., **The Policies of Genocide**, pp. 73-92.

Michael Marrus, **The Unwanted: European Refugees in the Twentieth Century**.

―――――――――――, "The History of the Holocaust: A Survey of Recent Literature," **Journal of Modern History** 59 (1987), pp. 114-160.

Hans Mommsen, "The Realization of the Unthinkable: The 'Final Solution of the Jewish Question' in the Third Reich," in Gerhard Hirschfeld, *loc. cit.*, pp. 93-144.

Norman Rich, **Hitler's War Aims**, 2 vols.

Karl Schleunes, **The Twisted Road to Auschwitz.**

Week 7. The machinery of destruction: Party, SS, bureaucracy

*Raul Hilberg, **Destruction of the European Jews**, 187-221, 263-293.

*Lucy Dawidowicz, **Holocaust Reader**, Ch. 4.

Uwe Dietrich Adam, "Persecution of the Jews, Bureaucracy and Authority in the Totalitarian State," **Leo Baeck Institute Yearbook** XXIII (1978), pp. 139-148.

Heinz Hoehne, **The Order of the Death's Head.**

Fred Katz, "Implementation of the Holocaust: The Behavior of Nazi Officials," **Comparative Studies in Society and History** 24 (1982), pp. 510-529.

Robert Koehl, **RKFDV: German Resettlement and Population Policy.**

————————————, **The Black Corps: The Structure and Power Struggles of the SS.**

Helmut Krausnick et al., **Anatomy of the SS State.**

Jochen von Lang & C. Sybill (eds.), **Eichmann Interrogated: Transcripts from the Archives of the Israeli Police.**

Robert Jay Lifton, **The Nazi Doctors: Medical Killing and the Psychology of Genocide.**

Week 8. Ghettoization in the East (1): Concentration

*Raul Hilberg, **Destruction of the European Jews**, pp. 64-96.

Yitzhak Arad, **Ghetto in Flames: The Struggle and Destruction of the Jews in Vilna in the Holocaust.**

Solomon Bloom, "Dictator of the Lodz Ghetto; the Strange History of Mordechai Chaim Rumkowski," **Commentary** 7 (1949), pp. 111-122.

Lucjan Dobroszycki, ed., **The Chronicle of the Lodz Ghetto.**

Philip Friedman, "Two 'Saviors' Who Failed: Moses Merin of Sosnowiec and Jacob Gens of Vilna," **Commentary** 26 (1958), pp. 479-491.

Yisrael Gutman, **The Jews of Warsaw 1939-1943: Ghetto, Underground, Revolt.**

Yisrael Gutman & Cynthia J. Haft (eds.), **Patterns of Jewish Leadership in Nazi Europe 1933-1945.**

Raul Hilberg, "The Ghetto as a Form of Government: An Analysis of Isaiah Trunk's Judenrat," in Yehuda Bauer & Nathan Rotenstreich (eds.), **The Holocaust as an Historical Experience**, pp. 155-171.

Raul Hilberg et al. (eds.), **The Warsaw Diary of Adam Czerniakow: Prelude to Doom.**

Shmuel Huppert, "King of the Ghetto - Mordechai Haim Rumkowski, the Elder of the Lodz Ghetto," **Yad Vashem Studies** XV (1983), pp. 125-157.

Chaim Kaplan, **The Warsaw Diary of Chaim A. Kaplan.**

Joseph Kermish, ed., **To Live With Honor and Die With Honor.**

Emanuel Ringelblum, **Notes from the Warsaw Ghetto.**

Isaiah Trunk, **Judenrat: The Jewish Councils in Eastern Europe under Nazi Occupation.**

Leonard Tushnet, **Pavement of Hell.**

Week 9. Ghettoization in the East (2): Deportation

*Lucy Dawidowicz, **Holocaust Reader**, Chs. 6-8.

Yitzhak Arad, "'Operation Reinhard': Extermination Camps of Belzec, Sobibor and Treblinka," **Yad Vashem Studies** XVI (1984), pp. 205-239.

——————————, **Belzec, Sobibor, Treblinka: The Operation Reinhard Death Camps**.

Jurgen Forster, "The Wehrmacht and the War of Extermination Against the Soviet Union," **Yad Vashem Studies** XIV (1981), pp. 7-34, and Gerhard Hirschfeld (ed.), **The Policies of Genocide**.

Heinz Hoehne, **The Order of the Death's Head**.

Jochen von Lang & C. Sybill (eds.), **Eichmann Interrogated: Transcripts from the Archives of the Israeli Police**.

Wolfgang Scheffler, "The Forgotten Part of the 'Final Solution': The Liquidation of the Ghettos," **Simon Wiesenthal Center Annual** 2 (1985), pp. 31-51.

Week 10. Jewish Resistance in Eastern Europe

*Lucy Dawidowicz, **Holocaust Reader**, Ch. 9.

*Raul Hilberg, **Destruction of the European Jews**, pp. 293-305.

Reuben Ainsztein, **Jewish Resistance in Nazi-Occupied Europe**.

Yitzhak Arad, **Ghetto in Flames: The Struggle and Destruction of the Jews in Vilna in the Holocaust**.

Yehuda Bauer, **They Chose Life: Jewish Resistance in the Holocaust**.

David Engel, **In the Shadow of Auschwitz: The Polish Government in Exile and the Jews.**

Yisrael Gutman, **The Jews of Warsaw, 1939-1943: Ghetto, Underground, Revolt.**

——————————, "Polish Responses to the Liquidation of Warsaw Jewry," **Jerusalem Quarterly** 17 (Fall 1980), pp. 40-55.

Oscar Handlin, "Jewish Resistance to the Nazis," **Commentary** 34 (1962), pp. 398-405.

Richard Lukas, **Forgotten Holocaust: The Poles Under German Occupation.**

Shmuel Krakowski, **The War of the Doomed: Jewish Armed Resistance in Poland.**

Dov Levin, **Fighting Back: Lithuanian Jewry's Armed Resistance to the Nazis 1941-1945.**

Henri Michel, "Jewish Resistance and the European Resistance Movement," **Yad Vashem Studies** VII (1968), pp. 7-16.

Yuri Suhl, ed., **They Fought Back: The Story of Jewish Resistance in Nazi Europe.**

Isaiah Trunk, "Note: Why Was There No Armed Resistance Against the Nazis in the Lodz Ghetto?" **Jewish Social Studies** 43 (Summer-Fall 1981), pp. 329-334.

——————————, **Jewish Responses to Nazi Persecution.**

Week 11. Death camps in the East (1): Machinery of destruction

   *Raul Hilberg, **Destruction of the European Jews**, Ch. 6.

   *Lucy Dawidowicz, **Holocaust Reader**, pp. 104-120.

   Yitzhak Arad, **Belzec, Sobibor, Treblinka: The Operation Reinhard Death Camps.**

Bruno Bettelheim, **The Informed Heart.**

————————————, **Surviving and Other Essays.**

Tadeuz Borowski, **This Way to the Gas, Ladies and Gentlemen.**

Terrence Des Pres, **The Survivor.**

Alexander Donat, ed., **The Death Camp at Treblinka.**

W. Glicksman, "Social Differentiation in the German Concentration Camps," in Joshua A. Fishman (ed.), **Studies in Modern Jewish History.**

Yisrael Gutman & Avital Saf (eds.), **The Nazi Concentration Camps.**

Eugene Heimler, **Concentration Camp.**

Eugen Kogon, **The Theory and Practice of Hell.**

Miklos Nyiszli, **Auschwitz: A Doctor's Eyewitness Account.**

Miriam Novitch, **Sobibor: Martyrdom and Revolt.**

Anna Pawelzynska, **Values and Violence in Auschwitz.**

Falk Pingel, "Resistance and Resignation in Nazi Concentration Camps," in Gerhard Hirschfeld (ed.), **The Policies of Genocide.**

Rudolf Vrba & Alan Bestic, **I Cannot Forgive.**

Leon W. Wells, **The Janowska Road.**

Week 12. Death camps in the East (2): The SS empire

*Primo Levi, **Survival in Auschwitz.**

Yitzhak Arad, **Belzec, Sobibor, Treblinka: The Operation Reinhard Death Camps.**

Yisrael Gutman & Avital Saf (eds.), **The Nazi Concentration Camps.**

Rodolf Hoess, **Commandant of Auschwitz.**

Robert Koehl, **The Black Corps: The Structure and Power Struggles of the SS.**

Helmut Krausnick et al., **Anatomy of the SS State.**

Gita Sereny, **Into That Darkness.**

Albert Speer, **Infiltration.**

Week 13. Counting the Victims: A Balance Sheet

*Primo Levi, **Survival in Auschwitz.**

SECOND TERM: REACTIONS

Week 14. Who knew what? When? Where? How?

*David Wyman, **The Abandonment of the Jews**, Parts 1 and 2.

Yehuda Bauer, "When Did They Know?" **Midstream** (April 1968), pp. 51-58.

Sarah Gordon, **Hitler, Germans and the "Jewish Question".**

Alex Grobman, "What Did They Know? The American Jewish Press and the Holocaust," **American Jewish History** LXVIII (1979), pp. 327-352.

Ian Kershaw, **Popular Opinion and Political Dissent in the Third Reich.**

——————————, "The Persecution of the Jews and German Popular Opinion in the Third Reich," **Leo Baeck Institute Yearbook** XXVI (1981), pp. 261-289.

Otto Dov Kulka, "'Public Opinion' in Nazi Germany and the 'Jewish Question'," **Jerusalem Quarterly** 25 (1982), pp. 121-144 and 26 (1983), pp. 34-45.

Walter Laqueur, "Hitler's Holocaust: Who Knew What, When, Where?" **Encounter** (July 1980), pp. 6-25.

——————————, **The Terrible Secret.**

——————————, "Jewish Denial and the Holocaust," **Commentary** (December 1979), pp. 44-55.

Detlev Peukert, **Inside Nazi Germany: Conformity, Opposition, and Racism in Everyday Life.**

Deborah Lipstadt, **Beyond Belief: The American Press and the Coming of the Holocaust 1933-1945.**

Lawrence Stokes, "The German People and the Destruction of the European Jews," **Central European History** 6 (1973), pp. 167-191.

Hans-Heinrich Wilhelm, "The Holocaust in National Socialist Rhetoric and Writings - Some Evidence against the Thesis that before 1945 Nothing Was Known About the 'Final Solution'," **Yad Vashem Studies** XVI (1984), pp. 95-127.

Week 15. Allied refugee policy, 1933-1943

*David Wyman, **The Abandonment of the Jews**, Part 3.

Haim Avni, **Spain, The Jews, and Franco.**

Irving Abella and Harold Troper, **None is Too Many: Canada and the Jews of Europe.**

Henry Feingold, **The Politics of Rescue.**

Saul Friedman, **No Haven for the Oppressed.**

Martin Gilbert, **Auschwitz and the Allies**.

Michael Marrus, **The Unwanted: European Refugees in the Twentieth Century**.

Monty Penkower, **The Jews Were Expendable: Free World Diplomacy and the Holocaust**.

Jacob Toury, "From Forced Emigration to Expulsion - The Jewish Exodus over the Non-Slavic Borders of the Reich as a Prelude to the 'Final Solution'," **Yad Vashem Studies** XVII (1986), pp. 51-91.

Bernard Wasserstein, **Britain and the Jews of Europe 1939-1945**.

Week 16. Occupied states in the West: Holland and Denmark

Louis De Jong, "Jews and Non-Jews in Occupied Holland," in Max Beloff, ed., **On the Track of Tyranny**, pp. 345-381.

Harold Flender, **Rescue in Denmark**.

Michael Marrus & Robert Paxton, "The Nazis and the Jews in Occupied Western Europe," **Journal of Modern History** 54 (1982), pp. 687-714.

Jacob Presser, **The Destruction of the Dutch Jews**.

B.A. Sijes, "Several Observations Concerning the Position of the Jews in Occupied Holland during World War II," in Yisrael Gutman & Efraim Zuroff (eds.), **Rescue Attempts during the Holocaust**.

Hugo Valentin, "Rescue and Relief Activities on Behalf of Jewish Victims of Nazism in Scandinavia," **YIVO Annual of Jewish Social Science** VIII (1953), pp. 224-251.

Leni Yahil, "Methods of Persecution: A Comparison of the 'Final Solution' in Holland and Denmark," **Scripta Hierosolymitana** 23 (1972), pp. 279-300.

————————————, **The Rescue of Danish Jewry**.

Week 17. Satellites of the Reich (1): Vichy France

Jacques Adler, **The Jews of Paris and the Final Solution.**

Richard Cohen, **The Burden of Conscience: French Jewry's Response to the Holocaust.**

———————————, "The Jewish Community of France in the Face of Vichy-German Persecution, 1940-1944," in Frances Malino & Bernard Wasserstein (eds.), **The Jews in Modern France.**

———————————, "A Jewish Leader in Vichy France 1940-1943: The Diary of Raymond-Raoul Lambert," **Jewish Social Studies** 43 (1981), pp. 291-310.

Michael Marrus and Robert Paxton, **Vichy France and the Jews.**

Leni Yahil, "The Jewish Leadership of France," in Yisrael Gutman & Cynthia Haft (eds.), **Patterns of Jewish Leadership in Nazi Europe 1933-1945.**

Week 18. Half-hearted Allies: Italy and Bulgaria

Daniel Carpi, "The Catholic Church and Italian Jewry under the Fascists," **Yad Vashem Studies** IV (1960), pp. 43-54.

———————————, "The Rescue of Jews in the Italian Zone of Occupied Croatia," in Yisrael Gutman and Cynthia Haft, eds., **Patterns of Jewish Leadership in Nazi Europe 1933-1945.**

Frederick Chary, **The Bulgarian Jews and the Final Solution 1940-1944.**

Liliana Picciotto Fargion, "The Anti-Jewish Policy of the Italian Social Republic," **Yad Vashem Studies** XVII (1986), pp. 17-49.

Michael Marrus and Robert Paxton, **Vichy France and the Jews.**

Meir Michaelis, **Mussolini and the Jews.**

Nissan Oren, "The Bulgarian Exception: A Reassessment of the Salvation of the Jewish Community," **Yad Vashem Studies** VII (1968), pp. 83-106.

Vicki Tamir, **Bulgaria and Her Jews.**

Susan Zuccotti, **The Italians and the Holocaust: Persecution, Rescue, Survival.**

Week 19. Satellites (2): Rumania and Hungary

Randolf Braham, **The Politics of Genocide: The Holocaust in Hungary** (2 vols.).

——————————, "The Jewish Question in German-Hungarian Relations during the Kallay Era," **Jewish Social Studies** 39 (1977), pp. 183-208.

Mario Fenyo, **Hitler, Horthy, and Hungary; German-Hungarian Relations 1941-44.**

Andrew Handler, ed., **The Holocaust in Hungary.**

Nicholas Nagy-Talavera, **The Green Shirts and the Others.**

Week 20. Reading Week

Week 21. The churches and the Holocaust

Owen Chadwick, "Weizsaecker, the Vatican, and the Jews of Rome," **Journal of Ecclesiastical History** 28 (1977), pp. 179-199.

——————————, **Britain and the Vatican during the Second World War.**

John Conway, "Records and Documents of the Holy See Relating to the Second World War," **Yad Vashem Studies** XV (1983), pp. 327-345.

Helen Fein, **Accounting for Genocide.**

Saul Friedlander, **Pius XII and the Third Reich.**

Judah Graubart, "The Vatican and the Jews: Cynicism and Indifference," **Judaism** 24 (Spring 1975), pp. 168-180.

Leonidas Hill, "History and Rolf Hochhuth's 'The Deputy'," in R.G. Collins (ed.), **From an Ancient to a Modern Theatre,** pp. 145-157.

Otto Dov Kulka and Paul R. Mendes-Flohr, **Judaism and Christianity under the Impact of National Socialism 1919-1945.**

John Morley, **Vatican Diplomacy and the Jews during the Holocaust.**

Anthony Rhodes, **The Vatican in the Age of the Dictators 1922-1945.**

Week 22. The politics of rescue (1): Bargaining with the Nazis

*David Wyman, **The Abandonment of the Jews,** pp. 209-287.

Yehuda Bauer, **The Jewish Emergence from Powerlessness.**

——————————, **The Holocaust in Historical Perspective.**

——————————, **American Jewry and the Holocaust.**

——————————, "Jewish Foreign Policy during the Holocaust," **Midstream** (December 1984), pp. 22-25.

Randolf Braham, **The Politics of Genocide: the Holocaust in Hungary** (2 vols.).

John Conway, "Between Apprehension and Indifference: Allied Attitudes to the Destruction of Hungarian Jewry," **Wiener Library Bulletin** XXVII (1973/74), pp. 37-48.

Amos Elon, **Timetable.**

Yisrael Gutman & Efraim Zuroff (eds.), **Rescue Attempts during the Holocaust.**

Alex Weissberg, **Desperate Mission: Joel Brand's Story.**

Week 23. The politics of rescue (2): Military proposals

*Dino Brugioni & Robert Poirer, "The Holocaust Revisited," **U.S. Central Intelligence Agency Report.**

*David Wyman, **The Abandonment of the Jews,** pp. 228-307, Conclusion.

Martin Gilbert, **Auschwitz and the Allies.**

——————————, "The Question of Bombing Auschwitz," in Yisrael Gutman & Avital Saf (eds.), **The Nazi Concentration Camps.**

Week 24. Reaching judgment at Nuremberg

Tom Bauer, **The Pledge Betrayed: America and Britain and the Denazification of Postwar Germany.**

Joseph Borkin, **The Crime and Punishment of I.G. Farben.**

Robert Conot, **Justice at Nuremberg.**

Benjamin Ferencz, **Less Than Slaves: Jewish Forced Labor and the Quest for Compensation.**

Peter Hayes, **Industry and Ideology: I.G. Farben in the Nazi Era.**

Werner Maser, **Nuremberg: A Nation on Trial.**

Bradley Smith, **Reaching Judgment at Nuremberg.**

Week 25. Survivors: The end of the Holocaust

Robert Abzug, **Inside the Vicious Heart.**

Yehuda Bauer, "The Death Marches," **Modern Judaism** 3 (1983), pp. 1-21.

——————————, "Jewish Survivors in DP Camps and Sh'erith Hapletah," in Yisrael Gutman & Avital Saf (eds.), **The Nazi Concentration Camps.**

Leonard Dinnerstein, **America and the Survivors of the Holocaust.**

Michael Marrus, **The Unwanted: European Refugees in the Twentieth Century.**

Michael Selzer, **Deliverance Day: The Last Hours at Dachau.**

Week 26. Summary and Conclusions

IV. REQUIREMENTS OF THE COURSE FOR GRADING
A test (given at the end of the first term); an essay (due at the end of the second term); and a final examination.

   The final grade is computed on the basis of 25% for the term test, and 75% for the average of the essay and the final examination.

V. CONCEPTUAL FRAMEWORK OF THE COURSE
This course provides a broad survey of the events of the Holocaust as a review of my weekly topics will suggest. While I refer from time to time to social scientific or other approaches to the topic, I keep fairly strictly to problems of historical interpretation. Within the latter approach, however, I try to cast my net as widely as possible.

   I have tried to present my general orientation to the study of the history of the Holocaust in my recent book, **The Holocaust in History** (1987). Essentially, I am concerned to integrate the study of the Holocaust into the broad framework of modern historical study, and therefore to "normalize" its place in the curriculum as well as in the general stream of historical consciousness. I am very attentive to the unique and singular aspects of the destruction of European Jewry, but I believe that the Holocaust must nevertheless find its place in the course of study in the same manner as do other great issues that are defined by historians.

Because of this concern, I devote special attention to questions of context - the events of the Holocaust within the framework of the Second World War, and their broader historical environment. I am constantly looking for the contextual reference points that will help explain Nazi Jewish policies and responses to them. I thus approach the subject less from the standpoint of Jewish history than from the general perspective of twentieth century Europe and North America. I try to avoid moral judgments and seek to adopt a "professional" posture to the extent that this is possible. My lectures often stress historiographical disputes, and I make it clear that scholarly opinion is divided on important issues.

Each year I try to arrange a visit of at least one academic who has done some scholarly work in the field. While I have special showings of some films (*Chaim Rumkowski and the Jews of Lodz*, *The Wannsee Conference*, and others), and refer the students to other films and to works of fiction, I try to keep the work in the course rather "bookish" and structurally similar to other courses that students take.

I. THE COURSE

JEWISH LEADERSHIP UNDER NAZI DOMINATION

Dan Michman
Department of Jewish History, Bar-Ilan University

II. ACADEMIC CONTEXT OF THE COURSE

Bar-Ilan is a medium-sized university by Israeli standards (c. 11,500 students in 1988). It is officially a religious university, requiring its students to take at least a basic number of courses in Jewish Studies (Bible, Talmud, Jewish History, Jewish Thought); however, about 50 per cent of the students are not religious. The average number enrolled annually in the Department of Jewish History is about 320. A basic introductory course on the Holocaust is required from every student in the department, irrespective of his main period of interest.

This course was given twice during recent years. It took the form of a 28-week seminar, meeting each week for 90 minutes. About 30 students enrolled each academic year. Most of the participants were second and third-year students (within a required 3-year B.A. program); a quarter or third of them were first-year and second-year students of the M.A. program. Most of them were Jewish History department students; some were students of the Department of General (mainly European) History. Each year one or two of the older participants is a Holocaust survivor.

Previous knowledge required: two introductory courses in modern Jewish history; one introductory course on antisemitism and the Holocaust. Students are required to purchase an anthology of selected sources.

III. OUTLINE OF THE COURSE

Part I (first semester): A combination of source readings in class, and discussions based on required reading between the sessions;

Part II (second semester): Each student must present the outline and sources of a research paper in class, and defend his thesis; in each session (of 90 minutes) two students present their work. The last session of the year is dedicated to a summary of the topic.

PART I

1. General introduction (one session); The meaning, characteristics and purposes of leadership in general (2 sessions)

    Required reading
    "Manhigut" (Leadership) **Entziklopedia lemada-ei ha-hevra** (Encyclopaedia of the Social Sciences; in Hebrew) vol. 3 (Tel Aviv, 1967), pp. 578-582.

    "Leadership," **International Encyclopaedia of the Social Sciences** vol. IX (New York, 1968), pp. 91-112.

    Gibb, C.A., "Leadership," **The Handbook of Social Psychology,** Second edition (G. Lindzey & E. Aronson, eds.), vol. 4. (Reading, Mass., Menlo Park, Cal., London, Don Mills, Ont. 1969), pp. 212-213.

2. The general situation of Jewish leadership on the eve of the Holocaust (2 sessions)

    Required reading
    Toury, Y., "Irgunim yehudiyim ve-hanhagoteihem be-artzot ha-emantzipatziya" (Jewish Organizations and their Leadership in the Countries of the Emancipation) **Yalkut Moreshet** 4 (July 1965), pp. 118-129.

    Mendelsohn, E., "Ha-hanhaga ha-yehudit be-mizrah europa ba-tkufa she-bein shtei milhamot ha-olam" (Jewish Leadership in Eastern Europe between the two World Wars) **Dmut ha-hanhaga ha-yehudit be-artzot ha-shlita ha-natzit,** Y. Gutman (ed.) (Jerusalem, 1979), pp. 1-10. (An English version was published as **Patterns of Jewish Leadership in Nazi Europe 1933-1945,** Y. Gutman [ed.] [Jerusalem, 1979], pp. 1-12).

3. Nazi policies towards Jewish leadership in Germany, 1933-1935 (1 session)

<u>Source reading in class</u>
Draft of a law for the regulation of the position of the Jews 1933 (English translation was published by U.D. Adam in **Yad Vashem Studies**, vol. II. 1976.)

Opinion of Dr. Achim Gercke concerning this draft, 1933, in **Nationalsozialistische Monatschrifte**, no. 38, (1933).

Some clauses from a circular of the SD concerning the composition of "Lageberichte", 1934, in G.C. Browder, "Die Anfang des SD. Dokumente aus der Organisations berichte des Reichsfuehrer SS," **Vierteljahreshefte fuer Zeitgeschichte** vol. 27, no.2 (1979), p. 311 ff.

Excerpts from the paragraph on the Jews in the "Lagebericht" of the SD, May-June 1934; published by O.D. Kulka, **Ha-megamot be-fitron ha-ba'aya ha-yehudit ba-reich ha-shlishi** (Diverse Trends in the Attempt to Solve "the Jewish Problem" in the Third Reich), Collection of Sources, The Hebrew University (Jerusalem, 1972), p. 48.

4. Jewish efforts to centralize and reorganize community life in Germany (1 session)

<u>Source reading in class</u>
The establishment of the Central Committee of German Jews for Relief and Construction (English translation of proclamation in **Documents on the Holocaust**, Y. Arad, Y. Gutman, A. Margaliot [eds.] [Jerusalem, 1981], pp. 47-50).

The establishment of the *Reichsvertretung*, September 1933, *ibid.*, pp. 57-59.

Abolition of the legal status of the Jewish communities, March 1938, *ibid.*, p. 91).

<u>Required reading</u>
Kulka, O.D., "Ha-hitahdut ha-artzit shel ha-yehudim be-germania 1938/9-1943" (The Reich Association of the Jews in Germany 1938/9-1943), **Dmut ha-hanhaga**

ha-yehudit be-artzot ha-shlita ha-natzit, pp. 37-48 (English transl. in Patterns of Jewish Leadership in Nazi Europe 1933-1945), pp. 45-58).

5. The emergence of the concept of Jewish Councils among Nazi authorities (2 sessions)

Source reading in class
A document of the Jewish section of the SD (II 112), December 7, 1937 (published in Hebrew by Kulka, Ha-megamot), pp. 77-78.

Eichmann takes control of Jewish life in Austria (English transl. in Documents on the Holocaust), pp. 93-95.

Excerpts from the meeting at Goering's office, November 12, 1938, *ibid.*, pp. 108-115)

The Establishment of the Reich Central Office for Jewish Emigration, January 24, 1939, *ibid.*, p. 125.

The establishment of the *Reichsvereinigung*, July 1939, *ibid.*, pp. 139-143.

Required reading
Rosenkranz, H., "Yahadut ostria bein hagira kefuya le-vein geirush" (Austrian Jewry between Forced Emigration and Deportation), Dmut ha-hanhaga ha-yehudit be-artzot ha-shlita ha-natzit, pp. 56-62 (English translation in Patterns of Jewish Leadership in Nazi Europe 1933-1945), pp. 65-74.

Esh, Sh., "Hakamat ha-ihud ha-artzi shel yehudei Germania u-feulotav ha-ikkariyot" (The establishment of the Reich Association of Jews in Germany and its Main Activities), Iyunim be-heker ha-shoah ve-yahadut zemaneinu (Studies in the Holocaust and Contemporary Jewry), Jerusalem, 1973, pp. 275-291.

6. The two patterns: Jewish councils and Jewish associations (2 sessions)

Source readings
Heydrich's urgent letter to the commanders of the *Einsatzgruppen*, September 21, 1939 (Documents on the Holocaust), pp. 173-178.

The establishment of Jewish Councils in the General Government, November 28, 1939, *ibid.*, p. 191.

The establishment of the Association of Jews in Belgium, November 25, 1941 (translation by the lecturer).

The establishment of the General Union of French Jews, November 29, 1941 (French original in Adler, J., **Face a la persecution**, Paris, 1985, pp. 277-278); transl. by lecturer.

Required reading
Trunk, I., **Judenrat** (New York, 1972), pp. 1-35.

7. Other forms of Jewish leadership during the Holocaust: underground leaders; social and communal organizations and leaders; rabbis (3 sessions)

Required reading
Gutman, Y., **Ba-alata u-va-ma'avak** (Fighters Among the Ruins) (Tel-Aviv, 1985), pp. 202-214, 245-262.

Bauer, Y., **American Jewry and the Holocaust** (Detroit, 1981), pp. 67-92.

Cohen, Y., "Dat u-moledet: le-darka shel ha-konsistoriya ha-merkazit be-tzarfat bi-tkufat milhemet ha-olam ha-sheniya" (Religion and Fatherland: The Central Consistory in France During the Second World War), **Bein yisrael la-umot** (Israel and the Nations, Essays Presented in Honor of Shmuel Ettinger) (Jerusalem, 1987), pp. 307-334.

Katz, Y. **Massoret u-mashber** (Tradition and Crisis: Jewish Society at the End of the Middle Ages) (Jerusalem, 1963), pp. 196-200.

Katz, Y., **Goy shel shabbat** (The Sabbath Gentile) (Jerusalem, 1983), pp. 180-182.

Bacon, G., "Da'at Tora ve-hevlei mashiah" ("Da'at Tora" and Pre-messianic Tribulations), **Tarbiz** vol. 52, no. 3 (1983), pp. 499-501.

"Rabbanut," **Entziklopedia Ivrit** (Encyclopaedia Hebraica), vol. 30, pp. 477-478.

Walk, J., "Ha-hanhaga ha-datit bi-tkufat ha-shoa" (Religious Leadership during the Holocaust Period) **Dmut ha-hanhaga ha-yehudit be-artzot ha-shlita ha-natzit,** pp. 325-335 (English translation in **Patterns of Jewish Leadership,** pp. 377-392).

IV. REQUIREMENTS OF THE COURSE FOR GRADING

1. A mid-term examination (30%) requiring familiarity with the following bibliography:

Arendt, H., **Eichmann in Jerusalem: A Report of the Banality of Evil** (New York, 1963), pp. 102-112.

Bauer, Y., "Tguvoteha shel ha-manhigut ha-yehudit li-mediniyut ha-natzim" (Reactions of the Jewish Leadership to Nazi Policies), **Yalkut Moreshet** no. 20 (December 1975), pp. 109-125.

Hilberg, R., **The Destruction of the European Jews** (London 1961), pp. 144-146, 662-664.

Robinson, J., **And the Crooked Shall be Made Straight** (Philadelphia, 1965).

—————————, "Ha-getto ke-tzurat mimshal" (The Ghetto as a Form of Government), **Yalkut Moreshet** no. 20 (December 1975), pp. 89-103.

Trunk, I., **Judenrat,** pp. XXV - XXX (article by J. Robinson), pp. 570-575.

Weiss, A., "Le-ha'arakhatam shel ha-yudenratim" (Evaluating the *Judenraete*), **Yalkut Moreshet** no. 11 (November 1969), pp. 108-111.

—————————, "Beirurim bi-sheilat ma'amada ve-emdoteha shel ha-hanhaga ha-yehudit be-polin ha-kevusha" (Some Considerations Concerning the Status and Policies of the Jewish Leadership in Occupied Poland), **Kovetz Yad Vashem XII** (1978), pp. 243-266. (English translation in **Yad Vashem** Studies vol. XII).

——————————, "Ha-mahloket ba-historiografia al dmutam shel ha-yudenratim vetafkideihem" (The Historiographical Controversy on the Jewish Councils and their Role), **Ha-shoa ba-historiografia**, Y. Gutman & G. Greiff (eds.) (Jerusalem, 1987), pp. 555-569. (English translation in **The Historiography of the Holocaust Period**, Jerusalem, 1989).

Y. Gutman (ed.), **Dmut ha-hanhaga ha-yehudit be-artzot ha-shlita ha-natzit**, articles of Trunk, Hilberg, Bauer (English translation in **Patterns of Jewish Leadership**).

2. A research paper (60%). The students may choose a topic, but suggestions are offered, such as: The Jewish leaderships of Warsaw; Leo Baeck; The underground leaderships in Warsaw and Bialystok; The "Yiddische Sotsiale Aleinhilf" in Poland - another form of leadership during the Holocaust?; A comparison of three "Jewish Associations" - Germany, Belgium, France; Jewish leadership in France in the 1930s and during the Holocaust; Rumkowski and the Lodz *Altestenrat*; Attitudes of Jewish leaders in Germany to the ascendance of Nazism, 1932-1935; The leadership of the German Jews in the Lodz Ghetto; The Jewish leadership of Budapest in the 1940s.

3. Class presentation of outline of research paper, and participation in discussions (10%).

V. CONCEPTUAL FRAMEWORK OF THE COURSE

This is an advanced course in the history of the Holocaust, and deals with one of the major problematic themes of this period. As all students are assumed to be acquainted with the general outlines of modern Jewish history and the framework of Nazi antisemitic policies, the course focuses on the specific problems of the Jewish leadership during the most critical period for Jewish society. It is assumed that 1) most of the students have only a vague knowledge of the sociological, psychological, and political aspects of leadership; and 2) there is general agreement that the "Jewish Councils" were *the* Jewish leadership of the Holocaust period.

As leadership is one of the most important factors in the functioning of any society, this theme can be used to focus upon the special problematics of the period (such as, to what extent the goals of the Nazis were understood by the Jews), as well as on the impact of modern Jewish historical developments (such as emancipation) on Jewish behavior and action, and on the continuity of traditional concepts (among rabbis, for example). Thus the student acquires deeper historical insight into the period.

The term *Judenrat*, has become very loaded and negative. Therefore another goal of this course is to understand the development of that concept and the Germans' expectations of it; to see how Jews tried to use the body; to analyze local influence on the formation of various councils; and to remove the natural inclination to start immediately with value judgment.

In most Holocaust literature, the Jewish Councils are viewed as the only Jewish leadership of the period. The course tries to counter this stereotype by introducing examples of other kinds of Jewish leadership.

Since this is an advanced course, methodological approaches are of the utmost importance. Students are therefore required to consult basic psychological and sociological literature in order to clarify concepts (in our case: the differentiation between "leadership" and "headship") with the aid of other social- scientific disciplines.

Finally, the course encourages scholarly writing of research papers on specific problems. The outlines and sources of each paper are examined both by the class and by the professor before the final version is delivered.

Note: The lecturer has written an academic study unit on the subject within a broader course on the Holocaust at the Open University of Israel: **Bi-mei shoah u-fkuda** (In Days of Holocaust and Reckoning), unit 10: "Ha-hanhaga ha-yehudit" (Jewish leadership), Everyman's University, Tel-Aviv, 1987, 192 pp.

This unit was also translated into Spanish: **El Holocausto, Un estudio historico**, unidad 5 (capitulo X: "El liderazgo comunitario judio antes del Holocausto"; capitulo XI: "La conduccion central de las comunidades judias durante el Holocausto"; capitulo XII: "Otros centros de liderazgo") Universidad Abierta de Israel, Tel-Aviv, 1987, 175 pp.

I. THE COURSE

HOLOCAUST THEOLOGY

James F. Moore
Department of Theology, Valparaiso University, Indiana

II. ACADEMIC CONTEXT OF THE COURSE

This is an undergraduate course offered within the Department of Theology. Valparaiso is an independently operated Lutheran university with a high percentage of students from a Lutheran background. Students in any area of the university are required to take three courses from the department, one of which must be an upper-level course such as this one. Most students in the course are Christian and have a minimal background both in Jewish studies and in the historical context of the Holocaust. They are assumed to have taken two lower-level courses in the Department of Theology.

The course is conducted over one semester (14 weeks), meeting for two 75 minute sessions each week.

III. OUTLINE OF THE COURSE

1. Historical Context of the Holocaust (6 sessions; 3 weeks)

   Required reading
   Cargas, Harry James, **A Christian Response to the Holocaust** (Denver, 1981), Parts I-III.

   Recommended reading
   Hilberg, Raul, **The Destruction of the European Jews** (New York, 1961).

   Levin, Nora, **The Holocaust** (New York, 1968).

   Fleischner, Eva, ed., **Auschwitz: Beginning of a New Era?** (New York, 1974), Part II.

2. The impact of the Holocaust on European Jewry (8 sessions; 4 weeks)

Required reading
Wiesel, Elie, **Night,** (New York, 1960).

Hillesum, Etty, **An Interrupted Life** (New York, 1981).

Recommended reading
Grobman, Alex & Daniel Landes, eds., **Genocide** (Los Angeles, 1983).

Gilbert, Martin, **Atlas of the Holocaust** (London, 1982).

Sherwin, Byron & Susan Ament, eds., **Encountering the Holocaust** (Chicago, 1979).

Bettelheim, Bruno, **The Informed Heart** (Glencoe, Ill, 1960).

Levi, Primo, **If This is a Man,** (New York, 1959).

Donat, Alexander, **The Holocaust Kingdom: A Memoir** (New York, 1965).

3. A Jewish response to the Holocaust (6 sessions; 3 weeks)

Required reading
Fackenheim, Emil, **God's Presence in History** (New York, 1970).

Recommended reading
Roskies, David, **Against the Apocalypse** (Cambridge, Mass, 1984).

Berkovits, Eliezer, **With God in Hell** (New York, 1979).

Rubenstein, Richard, **After Auschwitz** (Indianapolis, 1965).

Rubenstein, Richard & John Roth, **Approaches to Auschwitz** (Atlanta, 1987).

Katz, Steven, **Post-Holocaust Dialogues** (New York, 1985).

4. A Christian response to the Holocaust (8 sessions; 4 weeks)

Required reading
Eckardt, Roy & Alice Eckardt, **Long Night's Journey into Day** (Detroit, 1982).

Recommended reading
Ruether, Rosemary Radford, **Faith and Fratricide** (New York, 1974).

Fiorenza, Elizabeth & David Tracey, **The Holocaust as Interruption** (Edinburgh, 1984).

Peck A.J. (ed.), **Jews and Christians After the Holocaust** (Philadelphia, 1982).

Fleischner, Eva (ed.), **Auschwitz: Beginning of a New Era?** (New York, 1974).

Petuchowski, Jacob (ed.), **When Jews and Christians Meet** (Albany, NY, 1988).

IV. REQUIREMENTS OF THE COURSE FOR GRADING

1. Two examinations: a mid-term and a final. Both are single question essay examinations focusing   in the mid-term on the events of the Holocaust, and in the final on possible responses. In each case, students are evaluated on their ability to organize, and to reflect on, the materials of the course; their willingness to show openness to a variety of issues and views; their evident struggle with the difficult issues raised in the course; and their sensitivity to the Jewish viewpoint and lifestyle. 60% of the grade.

2. A personal journal of daily entries that represent reflections on the readings, class discussions, etc. Entries should be short, reflect creativity of style (prose, poetry, sketches or cartoons, for example), and show the ongoing struggle to understand and respond to the questions raised in this course. These journals are checked twice during the semester. 30% of the grade.

3. Class attendance and participation 10% of the grade.

V. CONCEPTUAL FRAMEWORK OF THE COURSE

This course is a systematic study of the many issues stemming from the events of the Nazi Holocaust, and of how those events have affected both Jews and Christians. The course is challenging and course materials, at times, shock our sensibilities because they confront us with the horrors of the Holocaust. The objective of the course is not only to acquaint students with the facts but also to engage them in the process of trying to shape a religious and moral response to the evil of the Holocaust.

This course intends to expand the horizons of students so that they will be more adequately equipped to identify the importance of the Holocaust as an event of radical proportions; be more fully sensitive to the feelings, outlook and questions of many (if not most) contemporary Jews, and be more completely understanding of the necessity for adequate human and theological response to the Holocaust by both Christians and Jews.

There are four basic areas of concern that define the structure of this course. First, it is designed as an introductory course in Jewish studies and must have a component that introduces non-Jewish students to the history and character of Judaism. Second, it is a course on the Holocaust and must treat the historical and political factors contributing to that event with as much care and thoroughness as possible. Third, it is a course in theology and relates especially to the theological perspective unique to Judaism, both pre- and post-Holocaust. Finally, the course aims to survey the impact of the Holocaust upon Christianity, primarily upon Christian theology as perceived by leading Christian thinkers. Each of these four components raises central questions, as follows:

1. *A history of Judaism*

a) What were the factors that led to the composition and condition of the European Jewish communities immediately prior to the Second World War? Many non-Jewish students have only a vague perception of the history of Judaism and certainly little understanding of the nature of Jewish life in those areas of Europe especially affected by the Holocaust. Thus, a full development of this question provides the student with a clearer picture of Judaism in general and of the Judaism and Jews of Eastern Europe in particular.

b) What was the ongoing relationship between Judaism, Jews, and the surrounding world (particularly the Christian world)? Non-Jewish students will have paid little attention to the role of Judaism in their culture, and to prevailing attitudes toward Jews. This question leads us to examine both the history of the relations between Jews and non-Jews (especially Christians), with particular attention given to the rise of antisemitism. Because of the nature of this course, this question also leads us to a discussion of the role of antisemitism in Christian belief and theology (both the real presence of antisemitism, and the question of its necessity for Christian belief).

2. *The Holocaust as event*

a) What were the factors that produced National Socialism and Hitler's peculiar ideology? In exploring this question we endeavor to be as historically accurate as possible, in order to assess the causes for the rise of Nazism. This leads not only to the Christian roots of antisemitism but also to the rise of nationalism in the nineteenth century and to the odd sort of "scientific" racism that emerged in the latter half of that century. Naturally, this exploration also follows the path of the Nazis' rise to power as well as to their formulation of the plan for genocide.

b) Why was there so little opposition to the Nazi plan? An investigation of this question leads to an assessment of the political and moral reaction of non-Jews, and the reaction of various Jewish groups (including the victims) to the enormity of the planned genocide. The aim is to assess the validity of the claim that there was little reaction and opposition to the Nazis. This, in turn, will be of central importance for understanding various post-Holocaust responses.

c) What were the various psychological and social factors affecting both victims and perpetrators? An investigation of this question requires a full range of supporting material that explores both the ideological and political structure of the death camps as well as the various patterns of psycho-social response to the constant presence, and fear, of death and torture. The point of this investigation is as much to provide perspective on responses to the Holocaust as it is to understand the complex psychological profile of the camps.

3. *Jewish responses to the Holocaust*

a) What types of response to this tragedy have come from the Jewish community? The course provides a wide range of responses (literary, philosophical, analytical, religious) and of contents of response (traditional religious, anti-religious, coolly detached, emotionally charged, revisionist). The point of the investigation is to provide the student with a proper perspective on the range of responses that have appeared, as well as ample resources for forming his own response.

b) What is the impact upon the post-Holocaust Jewish community? Responding to this question requires an investigation into the impact upon both the survivors and the Jewish community in general. Any adequate description of responses must take account of various views expressed by survivors as well as major post-Holocaust developments in the Jewish community (such as the establishment of the State of Israel).

c) How has the community responded to the question of the surviving war criminals? This question has both a practical/historical and a moral dimension. Any full response requires consideration of contrasting views within the Jewish community, and of the complex nature of the moral/political questions involved.

4. *Christian responses to the Holocaust*

a) How have Christians responded to the Holocaust? Christian response to the Holocaust is different from Jewish response since the Christian faces questions about his/her faith community that the Jew does not (e.g., why did Christians fail to respond during the Holocaust more than they did?). Answering this question requires an examination of which Christians (or church bodies) have made responses and for what reasons.

b) How have various Christian thinkers approached the question of the history of Christian antisemitism? This is a broad question that allows not only recognition of Christian complicity but also some constructive attempts to re-think the Christian theological tradition. Again, various options are presented, to give both perspective and resources to the student. The course integrates the instructor's own attempt to develop a Christian response on the basis of scriptural and traditional resources. This may provide the students with a model for forming their own response to the Holocaust.

I. THE COURSE

THE HOLOCAUST: GENOCIDE IN EUROPE, 1933-1945

Aubrey Newman
Department of History, University of Leicester, U.K.

II. ACADEMIC CONTEXT OF THE COURSE

Leicester University has now incorporated, almost by chance, a strong element of Jewish history into its mainstream history courses. A course on **Europe and the Jews, 1648-1948** is part of the normal range of options open to second-year students studying history as a "specialist" subject, as a "major" within "Combined Studies", or as part of a joint History/Politics degree. In consequence, this course is in competition with other options and students choose whichever courses they think fit. Since the course first began it has been chosen by some 16 to 24 students each year.

As a result of a demand for the provision of a specialist course (in our terms a "Special Subject"), which allowed for the detailed analysis of textual documentary material, a third-year course on **The Holocaust** was provided for the History specialists. It is a one-year course, comprising thirty lectures plus additional seminar sessions for the class as a whole; twenty sessions specifically to discuss documentary materials; regular essay work in smaller groups of three or four; and audio-visual sessions as arranged with the class.

The students have an unfettered choice among a number of options. In each of the first two years eight students enrolled for the course; at one time seventeen had requested enrolment but it was not possible for that number to be accommodated within the framework either of the department or of the teaching methods used. Since there are virtually no Jewish students enrolled for History at this university, none of these students had any preliminary Jewish background and they all had to be introduced to a number of concepts which might have been taken for granted by Jewish students.

III. OUTLINE OF THE COURSE

This list represents the basic lecture themes covered during the course. The size of the group enables the themes to be varied at will and by request of the class.

1. Introduction: the nature of the Holocaust
2. Growth of antisemitism in 19th century Germany, I
3. Growth of antisemitism in 19th century Germany, II
4. Demographic changes in Jewish communities in Europe
5. Relations between host country and Jewish communities, I
6. Relations between host country and Jewish communities, II
7. Growth of antisemitism in post-Versailles Europe, I
8. Growth of antisemitism in post-Versailles Europe, II
9. Growth of antisemitism in post-Versailles Europe, III
10. Weimar Germany and the growth of the Nazi party
11. Germany and German Jewry 1933-1939, I
12. Germany and German Jewry 1933-1939, II
13. The reactions of the Great Powers to refugees
14. The outbreak of war and its implications, 1939-1941
15. The "ghettoization" of Poland 1939-1941, I
16. The "ghettoization" of Poland 1939-1941, II
17. Life in the ghettos: Warsaw
18. Life in the ghettos: Lodz
19. The invasion of Russia: The *Wehrmacht* and the *Einsatzkommando*
20. The move in policy; the path to Wannsee
21. Wannsee and its implementation; the place of the S.S.
22. "Survival and Resistance"
23. Resistance in the ghettos - Warsaw
24. Resistance in the ghettos - Bialystok, Vilna, Kovno
25. Life in the camps; Sobibor, Treblinka, Auschwitz
26. The Germans and Western Europe (France and Belgium)
27. The Germans and Western Europe (Netherlands and Denmark)
28. Germany and its satellites
29. The literature of the Holocaust
30. The impact of the Holocaust; "5000 communities"

A growing list of films, tape-recordings, etc. have been made available, and a number of additional sessions are arranged to introduce members of the class to this material.

IV. REQUIREMENTS OF THE COURSE FOR GRADING

Students are expected to write essays at appropriate intervals, to produce a least one major seminar paper, and to participate in a regular series of tutorials involving detailed study of texts. The essays are intended to show students how to use the textual material, and have a general pedagogic aim of teaching the use of evidence. They are also used as an opportunity to introduce students to particularly contentious issues, and they afford students the chance of raising issues on their own account. There is no element of "assessment" from these essays in their final degree results. On the other hand there is an understanding that substantial topics which have been worked on for the "seminar papers" will be reflected in the questions set in the final examination paper on this subject.

At the end of the course there is a final examination covering all the work of the previous two years. This subject is examined by two written papers. The first of these is devoted entirely to textual comments, and each student has to write on a total of nine such extracts (chosen out of eighteen specimens on the paper). The second involves the writing of three essays chosen from a total of ten questions.

Set Texts

As part of their examination, students are expected to show a close and detailed acquaintance with documents illustrating the events from 1933 to 1945. In conformity with the pattern within the Department for "Special Subjects" there is one paper devoted to such textual analysis. As a result, students have to be thoroughly acquainted with Arad, Margolit, and Gutman, and with the Dawidowicz Reader cited in the bibliography, as well as with other documents as may, from time to time, be prescribed.

See the attached appendices:

A: List of Books
B: Specimen essay titles and seminar paper titles
C: Example of examination paper requiring essay answers
D: Example of examination paper requiring documentary textual analysis

V.   CONCEPTUAL FRAMEWORK OF THE COURSE

The course has till now been taken entirely by non-Jewish students, who have had an introduction to the nature of the "Jewish presence" in Europe. Taking its place in a "mainstream" history syllabus, the course has to be relevant to Jewish history as well as European history. Those enrolled can be presumed to have knowledge of historical processes and to be able to cope with the detailed analysis of documentary materials. Since the course is classed as a "Special Subject", it has to include a complete paper of commentary on certain "set texts", and this does entail a very close acquaintance with these documents. It must be emphasized that the course is not intended to dwell upon the actual mechanics of destruction, though care is taken to remind students of what was involved: the death of six million Jews as well as of millions of non-Jews.

The course opens with an analysis of antisemitism in Europe - Central, Western, and Eastern - beginning in the mid-nineteenth century and then developing through the post-Versailles structure of Europe. A detailed discussion of Weimar Germany leads into the rise of the Nazi party to power and the detailed steps taken by the Nazis from 1933 to 1939 (the invasion of Poland) to remove the Jews from the economic life of Germany. The reactions of the Jews in Germany and outside, and of the Western powers (Evian), fall into this section.

The second section details the growth of Nazi military power in Europe up till the invasion of Russia. It includes an analysis of the various steps taken in Poland to concentrate Jews into ghettos, and the various attempts by the Jews in the ghettos to establish a "normal" life.

Section three discusses the destruction of the Jews and involves examination of the steps towards (and the significance of) the Wannsee conference and the successive stages by which the Nazi policy was implemented. An important part of this section is an analysis of the ways in which each of those states which formed part of Hitler's "New Order" reacted and either saved or surrendered "their" Jews. Significant attention is paid to the particular case of Hungary and to the possibilities of reaction by the Western Allies to pleas for the destruction of the Auschwitz complex.

Appendix A: List of Books for Essays and Seminar Papers

This bibliography is rather wider than might have been anticipated, but its purpose is to have titles available for the students to refer to for the purpose of writing their essays or seminar papers. Individual guidance is made available at the appropriate stage to help undergraduates select the most suitable titles for their particular work.

The bibliography is confined to works in English although there is, obviously, a vast literature in other languages. There are normally no references to periodical literature, but see the review article by Geoffrey Eley, "Holocaust History," in **London Review of Books**, 3-16 March 1983. See also the series, **Yad Vashem Studies** published by Yad Vashem (the premier institute for the study of the Holocaust in Israel); volume XV has a complete index of volumes I to XV.

General

I.   S. Dubnow, **Nationalism & History** (Philadelphia, 1959).

   A. Ruppin, **The Jew in the Modern World** (London, 1934).

II. R. Chazan & M.L. Raphael, **Modern Jewish History: A Jewish Reader** (New York, 1974).

   P.R. Mendes-Flohr & J. Reinharz, **The Jew in the Modern World,** (New York, 1980).

III. A.J. Davies, **Anti-Semitism and the Foundations of Christianity** (New York, 1979).

   J. Katz, **From Prejudice to Destruction,** (Harvard, 1980).

   L. Poliakov, **The History of Antisemitism**, Volume 4 (Oxford, 1985).

IV. Y. Bauer & N. Keren, **A History of the Holocaust** (New York, 1982).

   L. Dawidowicz, **The War Against the Jews** (New York, 1976).

   N. Levin, **The Holocaust** (New York, 1973).

A. Grobman & D. Landes (eds.), **Genocide** (New York, 1983).

S. Milgram, **Obedience to Authority** (New York, 1973).

L. Poliakov, **Harvest of Hate** (Syracuse, 1954).

V. Y. Arad, A. Margolit & Y. Gutman, **Documents on the Holocaust,** (Jerusalem, 1981).

L. Dawidowicz, **A Holocaust Reader,** (New York, 1976).

R. Hilberg, **Documents of Destruction** (New York, 1981).

C.C. Aronsfeld, **The Text of the Holocaust,** (Marblehead Mass., 1985).

G e r m a n y

I.   H. Arendt, **The Origins of Totalitarianism** (New York, 1958, 1966).

N. Cohn, **Warrant for Genocide** (New York, 1967).

P. Gay, **Freud, Jews and other Germans** (New York, 1978).

R.S. Levy, **The Downfall of the Anti-Semitic Political Parties in Imperial Germany** (New Haven, 1975).

P. Massing, **Rehearsal for Destruction** (New York, 1949).

G.L. Mosse, **Germans and Jews** (New York, 1970).

G.L. Mosse, **The Nationalization of the Masses** (New York, 1975).

S. Poppel, **Zionism in Germany 1897-1933** (Philadelphia, 1977).

P. Pulzer, **The Rise of Political Antisemitism in Germany and Austria** (New York, 1964).

J. Reinharz, **Fatherland or Promised Land: The Dilemma of the German Jews 1893-1914** (Ann Arbor, 1975).

I. Schorsch, **Jewish Reactions to German Anti-Semitism, 1893-1914** (New York, 1972).

U. Tal, **Christians and Jews in Germany** (New York, 1975).

II. D. Abraham, **The Collapse of the Weimar Republic** (Princeton, 1981).

S.M. Bolkovsky, **The Distorted Image** (New York, 1975).

F.L. Carsten, **Revolution in Central Europe 1918-19** (London, 1977).

Y.N. Dubkowski & I. Wallman, **Towards the Holocaust: The Social and Economic Collapse of the Weimar Republic** (Westpoint, 1983).

P. Gay, **Weimar Culture** (New York, 1968).

P. Gay, **The Berlin Jewish Spirit** (New York, 1972).

R.N. Hunt, **Germany's Social Democracy 1918-33** (New Haven, 1976).

D.L. Niewyk, **The Jews in Weimar Germany** (Baton Rouge, Louisiana, 1980).

D.L. Niewyk, **Socialist, Anti-Semite and Jew** (Baton Rouge, Louisiana, 1971).

J. Noakes, **The Nazi Party in Lower Saxony 1921-1933** (London, 1971).

S. Volkow, **The Rise of Popular Anti-Modernism in Germany** (Princeton, 1978).

III. W.S. Allen, **The Nazi Seizure of Power** (Chicago, 1965).

R.C. Baum, **The Holocaust and the German Elite** (New York, 1981).

A. Beyerchein, **Scientists under Hitler** (New Haven, 1977).

K.D. Bracher, **The German Dictatorship** (New York, 1970).

C.R. Browning, **The Final Solution and the German Foreign Office** (New York, 1979).

C.R. Browning, **Fateful Months: Essays on the Emergence of the Final Solution** (New York, 1985).

A. Bullock, **Hitler** (London, 1962).

S. Gordon, **Hitler, Germans, and the "Jewish Question"** (Princeton, 1985).

J. Hidden & J. Farquharson (eds.), **Explaining Hitler's Germany** (London, 1983).

D. Irving, **Hitler's War** (London, 1971), see also C.W. Snyder, "The Selling of Adolf Hitler," **Central European History** XII, 1979.

A.R. Manvell & H. Fraenkel, **The Incomparable Crime** (London, 1967).

G.L. Mosse, **The Crisis of German Ideology: Intellectual Origins of the Third Reich** (New York, 1968).

G.L. Mosse, **Toward the Final Solution** (New York, 1978).

A. Schweitzer, **Big Business in the Third Reich** (London, 1968).

W.L. Shirer, **The Rise and Fall of the Third Reich** (New York, 1960).

R. Wistrich, **Hitler's Apocalypse** (London, 1985).

F. Weinstein, **The Dynamics of Nazism: Leadership, Ideology, and the Holocaust** (New York, 1980).

Outside   Germany

I.   L. Dawidowicz, **The Golden Tradition** (New York, 1967).

S. Dubnow, **History of the Jews in Russia and Poland** (edn. of New York, 1975).

C.S. Heller, **On the Edge of Destruction** (New York, 1979).

B. Vago & G.L. Mosse, **Jews and Non-Jews in Eastern Europe 1918-45** (Jerusalem, 1974).

II. R. Ainsztein, **Jewish Resistance in Nazi-Occupied Eastern Europe** (London, 1974).

Y. Bauer, **They Chose Life: Jewish Resistance in the Holocaust** (New York, 1973).

B. Bettelheim, **The Informed Heart**, (New York, 1971).

Joel Brand, **Desperate Mission** (New York, 1958).

A. Donat, **The Holocaust Kingdom: A Memoir** (New York, 1965).

H. Druks, **Jewish Resistance during the Holocaust** (Jerusalem, 1971).

H. Fein, **Accounting for Genocide** (New York, 1979).

P. Friedman, **Their Brother's Keepers** (New York, 1957).

M. Gilbert, **The Holocaust** (London, 1985).

Y. Gutman & L. Rothkirchen, **The Catastrophe of European Jewry** (Jerusalem, 1976).

Y. Gutman & E. Zuroff, **Rescue Attempts during the Holocaust** (Jerusalem, 1979).

Y. Suhl, **They Fought Back** (New York, 1967).

I. Trunk, **Judenrat** (New York, 1972).

I. Trunk, **Jewish Responses to Nazi Persecution** (New York, 1980).

A. Wirth (ed.), **The Stroop Report: "The Warsaw Ghetto Is No More"** (New York, 1980).

III. R. Braham, **The Politics of Genocide: The Holocaust in Hungary** (2 volumes) (New York, 1980).

F. Chary, **The Bulgarian Jews and the Final Solution** (Pittsburgh, 1972).

H. Flender, **Rescue In Denmark** (New York, 1963).

L. Yahil, **The Rescue of Danish Jewry** (Philadelphia, 1969).

M.R. Marrus & R.O. Paxton, **Vichy France and the Jews** (New York, 1981).

M. Michaelis, **Mussolini and the Jews** (New York, 1978).

J. Presser, **The Destruction of the Dutch Jews** (New York, 1965).

S t r u c t u r e   o f   t h e   H o l o c a u s t   S t a t e

J. Borken, **The Crime and Punishment of I.G. Farben** (New York, 1978).

E. Crankshaw, **The Gestapo** (New York, 1956).

H.V. Dicks, **Licensed Mass Murder** (New York, 1972).

G. Fleming, **Hitler and the Final Solution** (Los Angeles, 1984).

E. Fromm, **The Anatomy of Human Destruction** (New York, 1978).

R. Hilberg, **The Destruction of the European Jews** (3 volumes) (New York, 1985 edition); see also the student edition (New York, 1987).

R. Hoess, **Commandant of Auschwitz** (New York, 1960).

H. Hoehne, **The Order of the Death's Head** (New York, 1960).

I. Kershaw, **The Nazi Dictatorship** (London, 1987).

H. Krausnick et al. (eds.), **Anatomy of the S.S. State** (London, 1973).

A.R. Manvell & H. Fraenkel, **Heinrich Himmler** (New York, 1965).

G. Reitlinger, **S.S.: Alibi of the Nation** (New York, 1957).

G. Reitlinger, **The Final Solution** (New York, 1961).

K.A. Schleunes, **The Twisted Road to Auschwitz** (London, 1972).

F. Stangl, **Into that Darkness** (New York, 1974).

T h e   C a m p s   a n d   G h e t t o s
There is a very wide and growing literature on the camps, and it is impossible to mention more than a small portion of it.

R. Ainsztein, **The Warsaw Ghetto Revolt** (New York, 1979).

Y. Arad, **Ghetto in Flames** (Jerusalem, 1980).

J. Blatter & S. Milton, **Art of the Holocaust** (New York, 1981).

L. Dobroszycki (ed.), **The Chronicle of the Lodz Ghetto** (New Haven, 1984).

A. Donat, **The Death Camp at Treblinka** (New York, 1980).

K.G. Feig, **Hitler's Death Camps** (New York, 1981).

R. Hilberg (ed.), **The Warsaw Diary of Adam Czerniakow** (New York, 1979).

A.I. Kutsch (ed.), **Scroll of Agony: The Warsaw Diary of Chaim Kaplan** (New York, 1982).

P. Levi, **Survival in Auschwitz** (New York, 1959).

B. Mark, **Uprising in the Warsaw Ghetto** (New York, 1975).

M. Novitch, **Sobibor** (New York, 1980).

J. Slan (ed.), **Notes from the Warsaw Ghetto: The Journal of Emmanuel Ringelblum** (New York, 1958).

T h e   A l l i e s

H. Feingold, **The Politics of Rescue** (New Brunswick, 1970).

M. Gilbert, **Auschwitz and the Allies** (New York, 1981).

W. Laqueur, **The Terrible Secret** (New York, 1981).

A.D. Morse, **While Six Million Died** (New York, 1967).

A.J. Sherman, **Island Refuge** (Oxford, 1973).

B. Wasserstein, **Britain and the Jews of Europe, 1939-1945** (Oxford, 1979).

D. Wyman, **Paper Walls** (Amherst, Mass., 1968).

D. Wyman, **The Abandonment of the Jews** (New York, 1984).

T h e   P a p a c y

S. Friedlander, **Pius XII and the Third Reich** (New York, 1966).

G. Lewy, **The Catholic Church and Nazi Germany** (New York, 1964).

J.F. Morley, **Vatican Diplomacy and the Jews during the Holocaust** (New York, 1981).

R. Hochhuth, **The Deputy** (New York, 1968).

E. Bentley (ed.), **The Storm Over "The Deputy"** (New York, 1964).

Responses

H. Arendt, **Eichmann in Jerusalem** (New York, 1965).

Y. Bauer, **The Jewish Emergence from Powerlessness** (Toronto, 1979).

Y. Bauer & N. Rotenstreich, **The Holocaust as Historical Experience** (New York, 1981).

H. Friedlander & S. Milton (eds.), **The Holocaust: Ideology, Bureaucracy, and Genocide** (New York, 1980).

P. Friedman, **Roads to Extermination: Essays on the Holocaust** (Philadelphia, 1980).

G. Hausner, **Justice in Jerusalem** (New York, 1966).

Von Lang & C. Sibyll, **Eichmann Interrogated** (New York, 1983).

M. Ryan, **Human Responses to the Holocaust** (New York, 1981).

T. Keneally, **Schindler's Ark** (London, 1981).

Atlases

M. Gilbert, **The Holocaust** [An Atlas; as distinct from his much larger description] (London, 1978).

M. Gilbert, **Altlas of the Holocaust** (London, 1982).

M. Gilbert, **The Final Journey** (London, 1979).

Miscellaneous

L. Dawidowicz, **The Holocaust and the Historians** (Cambridge, Mass., 1981).

S. Friedlander, **When Memory Comes** (New York, 1980).

R. Rubenstein, **The Cunning of History** (New York, 1975).

R. Rubenstein, **After Auschwitz** (New York, 1966).

Appendix B: Specimen Essay Titles and Seminar Paper Titles

Essays

Would the Final Solution have been possible without the acquiescence of the local population?

"Without Hitler antisemitism would never have become extermination." Discuss.
Assess the part played in the ghettos of Eastern Europe by Rumkowski/Gens/Czerniakow.

"There was only one aspect of the European problem missing from Evian - the Jew." Discuss.

Seminar Papers

The role of the Papacy between 1933 and 1945.
The extent and the nature of Jewish resistance in Eastern Europe.
The character of Eichmann.
The fate of the Jews in Denmark/Italy/Bulgaria.
The nature of antisemitism in Germany before 1933.
Life in the camps.

Appendix C: Example of Examination Paper Requiring Essay Answers

Answer THREE Questions: (Time allowed: 3 hours)

1.   "Hitler did not create racism and antisemitism in Germany: he merely used for his own ends the forces which were already there." Discuss.
2.   To what extent were German Jews after 1933 able to adapt to their changing ways of life?
3.   "To stay alive was in itself an act of resistance," How far does this explain Jewish reactions to German rule?
4.   "The Allies could have done more to assist the Jews of Europe." Do you agree?
5.   How reliable are our sources for the development of "The Final Solution"?
6.   How far could life in the major ghettos of Eastern Europe between 1939 and 1942 be described as "normalized"?
7.   To what extent does the operation of the "Final Solution" throw light upon Hitler's creation in Europe of a uniform "New Order"?
8.   "The Pope was caught in an appalling dilemma between his duty to defend individual members of the Church and his need to defend the Church in general." Comment.
9.   To what extent was there a "Dilemma of Hungarian Jewry"?
10. "For the historian of European Jewry, more striking than the destruction of so many individuals was the destruction of so many communities and traditions." Discuss.

Appendix D: Example of Examination Paper Requiring Documentary Textual Analysis

Comment on THREE of the following.   (Time allowed: 3 hours)

(a)   The Ostjuden must be got rid of without delay, and ruthless measures must be taken immediately against all other Jews... In order that the unemployed Semites cannot secretly undermine us... they should be placed in collecting camps.
       (**Volkischer Beobachter**, 10 March, 1920)

(b)   The bitterest struggle for the victory of Jewry at the present time is being waged in Germany. Here it is the National Socialist movement which alone has taken upon itself the struggle against this execrable crime against mankind.
       (Adolf Hitler, **Zweites Buch**, 1928)

(c)   If a Civil Servant did not already have civil-service status on 1 August 1914, he must prove that he is of Aryan descent, or that he fought at the front, or that he is the son or father of a man killed in action during the World War.
       (First decree for the Implementation of the Law for the Restoration of the Professional Civil Service, 11 April, 1933)

(d)   The laws passed by the Reichstag at Nuremberg have affected the Jews in Germany most severely. They are nonetheless intended to create a basis on which a tolerable relationship between the German and Jewish peoples will be possible... A prerequisite for a tolerable relationship is the hope that the Jews and the Jewish communities of Germany will be allowed the moral and economic means of existence by the halting of defamation and boycott.
       (Statement by the **Central Representation of German Jews**, 24 September, 1935)

(e)   I demanded an emigration figure of 20,000 Jews without means for the period from 1 April 1938 to 1 May 1939 of the Jewish community and the Zionist organization for Austria and they promised me that they would keep to this... They are completely in my hands here, they do not dare take a step without checking with me first.
       (Letter from Adolf Eichmann, Vienna, 8 May, 1938)

(f)   The hostile attitude of Jewry towards the German People and Reich, which does not shrink even from cowardly murder, calls for determined resistance and severe expiation... I therefore order the following: The totality of Jews who are German subjects will pay a fine of 1,000,000,000 (one billion) Reichsmarks to the German Reich.

(Order by Hermann Goering, 12 November, 1938)

(The above questions constitute one-third of the questions in the examination paper. They are provided by way of illustration of this type of examination.)

I. THE COURSE

LITERATURE OF THE HOLOCAUST

Anita Norich
Department of English Language and Literature, University of Michigan

II. ACADEMIC CONTEXT OF THE COURSE

This course has been offered as an undergraduate senior seminar, and in a graduate lecture/discussion framework. In the former case, it met three times a week, for 50 minutes each session; in the latter, twice a week for 80 minutes each session. In both cases the course was offered to a relatively small group of students, 12 to 20 in number, within a very large university. Prerequisites for the course included upper level English literature courses, but no prior exposure to Holocaust literature or history. The undergraduates were largely, but not exclusively Jewish. The graduate students, on the other hand, were primarily Gentiles from various departments: English, Comparative Literature, American Culture, History.

I have resisted offering this course in the large lecture format preferred by my university, because I want to encourage the kind of open discussion and response that the material demands. The course relates to texts written in several languages and countries (all read in English translation, although students with reading comprehension in other languages are encouraged to read and discuss the originals). Films are also viewed, and frequent reference is made to the secondary critical works on the Holocaust.

III. OUTLINE OF THE COURSE

1st week: Introduction: Paul Celan "Todesfuge";
            Anthony Hecht, "More Light! More Light!"
            Kadia Molodowsky, "God of Mercy"
            Nelly Sachs, selected poems

2nd week: Elie Wiesel, **Gates of the Forest** and **Night**

3rd week: Abba Kovner, **My Little Sister**

4th week: Primo Levi, **If Not Now, When?**

5th week: Tadeusz Borowski, **This way to the Gas, Ladies and Gentlemen**

6th week: Yankev Glatshteyn, selected poetry

7th week: Avrom Sutskever, selected poetry

8th week: Aharon Appelfeld, **The Age of Wonders**

9th week: Andre Schwarz-Bart, **Last of the Just**

10th week: Ilona Karmel, **An Estate of Memory**

11th week: D.M. Thomas, **The White Hotel**

12th week: Jerzy Kosinski, **The Painted Bird**

13th week: Jurek Becker, **Jacob the Liar**

Depending on the University calendar, the class usually views two or three films chosen from the following:
Night and Fog, Image Before My Eyes, Little Shop on Main Street, Jacob the Liar, The Fifth Horseman Is Fear.

IV. REQUIREMENTS OF THE COURSE FOR GRADING
Students are expected to complete all assignments and engage in active classroom participation. Undergraduates are required to submit three papers (4-6 pp.), an in-class examination, and a final take-home examination. In the graduate class, students present an oral report which is submitted as a short essay of 3-4 pp. and one longer paper of 15-20 pp. The oral reports are determined in consultation with

each student and are based on critical, theoretical or historical readings depending on the student's individual interests.

V. CONCEPTUAL FRAMEWORK OF THE COURSE

The course is designed to address questions about the imaginative responses to the Holocaust in various cultures and languages. It addresses the problem of responses to catastrophe within Jewish culture and Hebrew and Yiddish texts, within the American English context, in Poland, Germany and elsewhere in Western Europe. Similarities in these responses, as well as cultural specificities, are examined. Works written by Jewish and non-Jewish survivors, as well as those more removed from the immediate events are discussed, as are the depictions of victims and oppressors. Particular attention is also devoted to the ways in which the Holocaust has become a metaphor for various private and public tragedies within contemporary culture.

One major focus of the course is an examination of the often-repeated insistence that silence is the only proper response to the horror of World War II. We challenge this myth of silence by discussing the ways in which authors themselves undermine the silence they claim as their privilege. The roles of poetic language (particularly metaphor), realism, the depiction of violence, literary tradition, and subversive literary voices are examined in the attempt to articulate a language of what has come to be called *l'univers concentrationnaire*.

The material read requires a methodologically complex negotiation of the demands of history, memory, and literary analysis. We seek to answer the question of how literature, which creates order out of events and ideas, can express the chaos with which we are confronted in the Holocaust. Does the Holocaust radically alter the literary pursuit of order? Does it inaugurate the "post-modernist" stage of contemporary culture?

Students are exposed to a wide range of responses to the Holocaust and the the literary challenge it poses. The course emphasizes the range of such responses rather than focusing on definitive answers to the inescapable existential questions raised by the material.

I. THE COURSE

MAJOR ISSUES IN THE HISTORY OF THE HOLOCAUST

Dalia Ofer
Institute of Contemporary Jewry, The Hebrew University of Jerusalem

II. ACADEMIC CONTEXT OF THE COURSE

The course is offered to undergraduate students as an elective at the Hebrew University of Jerusalem. It is a four-credit course and meets two hours weekly for two semesters, or four hours weekly for one semester. Undergraduates in a General Studies B.A. program may take this course as part of a unit of courses in Contemporary Jewry, and students of the Humanities, Social Sciences, Law and Science faculties may take it as a one-course elective. Students from the first to third year of studies are eligible to participate. Most of the students who choose the course are from the Humanities, some majoring in history. Most students are attracted to the course out of interest; having been exposed in high school to the history of the Holocaust, they want to learn more. Some come with a good background in Jewish and general history. For most students the subject is loaded with emotion and many harbor "mystified" notions in regard to the Holocaust. One should remember that Israelis are exposed to information and images of the Holocaust from an early age, particularly through the media and the educational system, in connection with the annual "Day of Commemoration for the Holocaust and the Heroism of its Victims" (*Yom ha-shoah ve-ha-gevura*).

Since most students are reluctant to read English, and do not have mastery of other foreign languages, the reading is mostly in Hebrew. Reading is required for each session. Although the course is conducted as a lecture, questions are posed for discussion and the students are eager to participate.

III. OUTLINE OF THE COURSE

1. Defining the problem - studying the Holocaust in the context of Jewish and European history of the 20th century

193

Reading
Yehuda Bauer, "Against Mystification," in **The Holocaust in Historical Perspective** (Henceforth Bauer, **Perspective**), Tel Aviv, 1982 (Heb.).

Shaul Friedlander, "The Historical Meaning of the Holocaust," **Molad** 1 (1975):
33-34 (Heb.)

2. From "hatred of Jews" (*sin'at yisrael*) to racial antisemitism

Reading
Jacob Katz, **Mi-sin'at yisrael le-shlilat ha-geza**, (English edition: **From
Prejudice to Destruction**) Tel Aviv, 1979, pp. 215-258.

Moshe Zimmermann, "From Radicalism to Antisemitism," in Almog Shmuel (ed.),
Sin'at yisrael le-doroteha (**Antisemitism throughout the Ages**), Jerusalem,
1983, pp. 263-279.

Israel Gutman **Be-alata u-ve-ma'avak**, (**Fighters among the Ruins**), Tel Aviv,
1985, (Henceforth, Gutman, **Be-alata**) pp. 11-47.

Paul Massing, **Rehearsal for Destruction**, N.Y., 1949.

3. Jews and Germans in the Weimar Republic

Reading
L. Snyder, **The Weimar Republic**, N.Y., 1966, pp. 11-98.

George L. Mosse, **Germans and Jews: The Right and Left in the Search for a
"Third Force" in Pre-Nazi Germany**, N.Y., 1970, Chapter 1.

——————————, **The Crisis of German Ideology**, N.Y. 1964, chapters 16, 17.

4. Nazi ideology and the Jewish problem

Reading
Norman Cohn, **Warrant for Genocide**, N.Y., 1967, Chapters 1-3, 6-9.

George L. Mosse, **Nazism - A Historical and Comparative Analysis of National Socialism**, Oxford, 1977.

5. Nazi policy towards the Jews from the seizure of power to the beginning of World War II

Reading
Lucy Dawidowicz, **The War Against the Jews 1938-1945**, N.Y., 1975, Chapters 3, 9. (Henceforth, Dawidowicz, **The War**).

Yitzhak Arad, Israel Gutman, Avraham Margaliot, eds., **Documents on the Holocaust**, Jerusalem, 1976, (Heb.) (English: N.Y., 1980), Documents nos: 7, 10, 31-35, 41, 45, 46, 48. (Henceforth, **Documents**).

6. German Jews and the Holocaust

Reading
Avraham Margaliot, "The Jews of Germany in the Last One Hundred Years before the Destruction," **Molad**, April-May 1968 (Heb.).

——————————, "The Reaction of German Jewry to the Nuremberg Laws," **Yad Vashem Studies** XII, 1978.

——————————, "The Dispute over the Leadership of German Jewry, 1933-1938," **Yad Vashem Studies** X, 1974, pp. 129-148.

——————————, "The Reasons for the Late Emigration of German Jews," in Israel Gutman & Efraim Zuroff (eds.), **Rescue during the Holocaust**, Yad Vashem 2nd International Historical Conference, Jerusalem, 1978.

7. The Jewish policy of the Nazis - Stages and development

Reading
Raul Hilberg, **The Destruction of European Jewry**, N.Y., Introduction, Chapter 1.

Heinz Hoehne, **The Order of the Death's Head**, London, 1969, Chapters 12, 13.

Martin Broszat, "Hitler and the Genesis of the 'Final Solution': An Assessment of David Irving's Theses," in **Yad Vashem Studies XIII**, 1979, pp. 73-125.

Documents, Nos: 65, 66, 76, 88-90, 106-108, 113-115, 160-164, 168, 178

8. The Jews of Europe on the Eve of the War

Reading
Salo Baron, "The Jews of Europe Between the World Wars," in **The Catastrophe of European Jewry: Antecedents, History, Reflections: Selected Papers**, Israel Gutman, Livia Rothkirchen (eds.), Jerusalem: Yad Vashem, 1976 (Heb.) (English: 1978) (Henceforth, **Catastrophe**).

9. Jewish self-organization under Nazi rule

Reading
Shaul Esh, "Holiness of Life in the Destruction," in **Catastrophe**.

Israel Gutman, **Be-alata**.

——————————, **The Jews of Warsaw, 1939-1943**, Indiana, 1980, Chapter 3.

10. Jewish leadership during the Holocaust - Dilemma of public responsibility (a): Judenrat

Reading
Isaiah Trunk, **Judenrat**, N.Y., 1972, Introduction, Chapters 3, 14, 16, 17.

Israel Gutman, ed., **Jewish Leadership under Nazi Occupation**, Yad Vashem Third International Historical Conference, Jerusalem, 1980.

Yitzhak Arad, **Ghetto in Flames: the Struggle and Destruction of the Jews in Vilna in the Holocaust**, Tel Aviv, 1976 (Heb.) (English: N.Y., 1984), pp. 229-289 (Henceforth, Arad, **Vilna**).

Documents, Nos: 74, 75, 78-83, 91-96, 100, 101, 105, 109-112, 120, 121, 165, 173, 187-195.

11. Jewish leadership (b): Forms and definition of Jewish resistance

Reading
Philip Friedman, "Jewish Resistance during the Holocaust, Forms and Aspects," in **Catastrophe**, pp. 361-373.

Yizhak Arad, "Jewish Armed Resistance in Eastern Europe - Its Characteristics and Problems," in **Catastrophe**, pp. 374-388.

12. Jewish leadership (c): Youth movements and the resistance

Reading
Gutman, **Be-alata**, pp. 167-215.

Tennenboim Tammaroff, **Dapim min ha-dleka**, Tel Aviv, 1985.

Nachman Blumenthal, **Darko shel Judenrat: Documents from the Bialystok Ghetto**, Jerusalem, 1962, Introduction (Heb.).

Arad, **Vilna**, pp. 189-229.

13. Jewish resistance in the forests and camps

Reading
Samuel Krakowski, **Lehima yehudit be-polin neged ha-natzim**, Jerusalem, 1977, Chapters 1, 8, 12.

14. Concluding remarks on Jewish leadership and Jewish resistance during the Holocaust

Reading
Gutman, **Be-alata**, pp. 215-281.

Bauer, **Perspective**, pp. 118-133.

Dawidowicz, **The War**, Chapter 16.

15. The fate of the Jews in Western Europe - The case of France

Reading
Dawidowicz, **The War**, Appendix: Western Europe.

Michael Marrus and Robert Paxton, **Vichy France and the Jews**, Chapters 3, 8, and Conclusion.

16. The Jews of Western and Eastern Europe during the Holocaust - A comparison

17. The free world and the fate of the Jews during the Holocaust: a. The Evian Era   b. When did the Final Solution become known? c. The Bermuda Conference

Reading
Walter Laqueur, **The Terrible Secret**, N.Y., 1980, Chapters 4, 5, and Appendix.

David Wyman, **Paper Walls: America and the Refugee Crisis 1938-1941**, N.Y., 1968, p. 43-67, 155-217.

——————————, **The Abandonment of the Jews**, N.Y., 1984, pp. 209-235, 288-311.

18. Conclusion

Reading
Uriel Tal, "On the Study of the Holocaust and Genocide," in **Yad Vashem Studies** XIII, pp. 7-52.

Students are required to view privately two of the following films. They are available in the University library.

1. Genocide (a general history of the Holocaust) - BBC
2. Adolf Hitler, a biography
3. The Itinerary (Elie Wiesel)
4. The Sorrow and the Pity (Life in France during the Holocaust)
5. Rumkowski, King of the Jews
6. Auschwitz and the Allies

7. Memo of Eichmann (The Eichmann Trial)
8. Heritage, Part 8

IV. REQUIREMENTS OF THE COURSE FOR GRADING

Students are given a final examination, which requires analysis of a primary source, and an essay. They are expected to demonstrate ability to analyze the document textually and place it in historical context. The essay calls for the ability to examine a broader issue that was referred to in class and treated in more detail in the readings.

V. CONCEPTUAL FRAMEWORK OF THE COURSE

Teaching about the Holocaust in Israel, with its large population of survivors, and in the evocative atmosphere of contemporary political events, demands special considerations and sensitivities.

The course attempts to provide the student not only with knowledge, but also with some critical tools that will enable him/her to comprehend, to compare, and to draw personal conclusions. This requires the student to gain some familiarity with the main works on the subject and the various types of writing on the Holocaust period. It also necessitates a comparative perspective that will indicate why the Holocaust is considered by so many as an "epoch-making event."

The method of study combines general examination of the European context, with a detailed follow-up of particular case studies. The case studies serve as models of the process by which the researcher analyzes and arrives at conclusions. The students are confronted with the specific decision- making dilemmas that the protagonists faced during the Holocaust period, so that they may attempt to reconstruct in their imagination the considerations, deliberations, and anxieties involved in the decision-making process, and thereby sense some of the feelings and frustrations experienced by individuals and leaders in various critical situations. At the same time, an attempt is made to steer between excessive intellectualization which may lead to indifference, and over-emotional reaction that may interfere with intellectual understanding and analysis. We aim at a critical approach, combined with deep human respect for the victims.

The following are the main organizing ideas around which the course is built:

A. *The uniqueness or universality of the Holocaust* is discussed in relation to other catastrophes in the twentieth century, such as the case of the Armenians prior to the Holocaust, the Gypsies during the Holocaust, the mass massacres in Biafra or Bangladesh, or the events connected with the Vietnam war.

B. *Relations between Jews and non-Jews* are dealt with in historical perspective. In order to explain the Holocaust within a broader historical context, emancipation, integration-assimilation, and antisemitism are explored. A brief discussion is also devoted to the Jewish and general history of Europe, touching upon the main political, social and economic developments of the twentieth century. This is illustrated with more detail in the special case of the Weimar Republic - the role of Jews in it and the German reaction to this.

C. *Relations between ideology and policy.* Nazi ideology is examined in this regard, considering fascism, racism, the *fuehrer* principle, antisemitism, and attitudes to religion. The course traces the connections between ideological principles and actual Nazi policy toward the Jews after 1933. Various historical approaches are illustrated through examination of the treatment of German Jews before the war, and the political dynamics that contributed to the shaping of the "Final Solution" during the various stages of the war.

This issue is also discussed in relation to the Allies' rescue policy, and the treatment of the Jews in Italy and other satellites of Germany.

D. *Considering the alternatives.* By raising various issues, the students have to make an effort to reenact how Jews understood reality under Nazi rule and made decisions; the frame of mind of Jewish leaders, youth organizations, and other political movements; and how they used historical experience to guide their evaluations and behavior. What were the means at the disposal of ordinary people enabling them to grasp the singular reality that the Nazis created, and on which historical experiences were they relying?

E. *Unravelling the information of the "Final Solution."* The questions raised relate to the problems and limitations of human understanding, the way the mind is a captive of the precedents of human experience, and how this influences perceptions of new situations and information. These considerations relate to the Jews under Nazi occupation, to the Jews in the free world, to the non-Jewish population, and to governments.

The methodology of the course attempts to reconstruct the history of the Holocaust through these organizing ideas, while keeping to the main chronological thread. Topics are selected and examined in a comparative manner, as illustrated in the course outline given above. Finally, an attempt is made to suggest a typology of human, social, and political behavior as revealed in the study of the Holocaust period. Throughout, primary sources are used to illustrate methodology of historical research and analysis, and to examine conflicting interpretations of major issues in the history of the Holocaust.

I. THE COURSE

JEWISH RESPONSES TO CATASTROPHE

David G. Roskies
List College of Jewish Studies, The Jewish Theological Seminary of America

II. ACADEMIC CONTEXT OF THE COURSE

This course is an interdisciplinary undergraduate honors seminar, meeting 2 hours per week for one semester. Geared to freshmen and sophomore students of exceptional ability and with a substantial Judaic background, it covers the whole expanse of recorded Jewish history. Since these students already have some grounding in the biblical and rabbinic periods, this course proceeds rather quickly to its main focus - Jewish life and letters in Central and Eastern Europe from the 1840s to the present. Unlike most seminary courses, however, all the readings in this one are in English. Rather than dwell on the stylistic differences between one period and another, one literary genre and the next, the course deals with the larger theological and thematic issues.

III. OUTLINE OF THE COURSE

The curricular backbone of the course is provided by the instructor's two books, **Against the Apocalypse: Responses to Catastrophe in Modern Jewish Culture** (1984), and the companion volume, **The Literature of Destruction: Jewish Responses to Catastrophe** (1989). In the latter book, which serves as the basic text, the primary sources are laid out in chronological order with copious notes and bibliographical material. By means of the text's annotation of scriptural and rabbinic sources, students are able to gauge the continuity and revolution in the Jewish response to catastrophe down through the ages. Thus, even students with no Judaic background can achieve a fairly sophisticated "intertextual" reading. The weekly 2-page writing assignments are designed to anticipate the actual discussions in the classroom.

Insisting throughout the semester on the precise historical context of each literary response, I encourage the students, in the last assignment, to violate the canons of historicity and textual criticism: to create their own "liturgical" response to a catastrophic event of their own choice.

Texts

Anthology - **The Literature of Destruction: Jewish Responses to Catastrophe**, David G. Roskies (ed.) (Philadelphia: Jewish Publication Society, 1989).

Chazan - Robert Chazan, **European Jewry and the First Crusade** (University of California Press, 1987).

Gopnik - Adam Gopnik, "Comics and Catastrophe," **The New Republic**, 22 June 1987.

Halkin - **Crisis and Leadership: Epistles of Maimonides**, David Hartman & Abraham Halkin (eds.), discussions by David Hartman (Philadelphia: Jewish Publication Society, 1985).

Kantor - **The Book of Alfred Kantor** (New York: McGraw-Hill, 1971; Schocken, 1988).

Mintz - Alan Mintz, **Hurban: Responses to Catastrophe in Hebrew Literature** (New York: Columbia University Press, 1984).

Ostow - Mortimer Ostow, "The Jewish Response to Crisis," in **Judaism and Psychoanalysis** (New York: Ktav, 1982).

Roskies - David G. Roskies, **Against the Apocalypse: Responses to Catastrophe in Modern Jewish Culture** (Harvard University Press, 1984).

Scholem - Gershom Scholem, **The Messianic Idea in Judaism and Other Essays on Jewish Spirituality** (New York: Schocken, 1971).

Spiegelman - Art Spiegelman, **Maus: A Survivor's Tale** (Pantheon, 1986).

Yerushalmi - Yosef Hayim Yerushalmi, **Zakhor: Jewish History and Jewish Memory** (University of Washington Press, 1982).

1. Liturgy and memory

   Primary Sources: Anthology, secs. 1-3, 24-28, 34, 38-39, 78, 94, 98, 100.

   Secondary Sources: Yerushalmi, chs. 1-2, Roskies, ch. 1.

2. Women, God and history

   Primary Sources: Anthology, secs. 4-21.

   Secondary Sources: Mintz, pp. 22-41, ch. 2.

   Writing Assignment: How and why are women privileged in these ancient texts?

3. The politics of Jewish survival

   Primary Sources: Anthology, secs. 22-23, 29-33, 35-37.

   Secondary Sources: Halkin-Hartman, pp. 47-51, 67-83; Chazan, ch. 4.

   Writing Assignment: Compare the politics of Jewish survival in the medieval Sephardic and Ashkenazi communities.

4. The rhetoric of modern prophecy

   Primary Sources: Anthology, secs. 40-47.

   Secondary Sources: Roskies, ch. 3; Mintz, pp. 141-154.

   Writing Assignment: What rhetorical means are used by Mendele, the Bund, the Hebrew Writers' Union, and the speaker in Bialik's poem to move their respective audiences to action?

5. Speech and the psychology of violence

Primary Sources: Anthology, secs. 49-60.

Secondary Sources: Roskies, chs. 6-7; Ostow, "The Jewish Response to Crisis".

Writing Assignment: How do the survivors of catastrophe use speech to "work through" the trauma?

6. The *shtetl* as *kehillah kedoshah*

Primary Sources: Anthology, secs. 48, 61-63.

Secondary Sources: Roskies, ch. 5.

Writing Assignment: How does the new communal covenant replace the one of old?

7. The poetics of violence

Primary Sources: Anthology, secs. 64-70.

Secondary Sources: Roskies, ch. 4.

Writing Assignment: What role do sacred mountains play in the apocalyptic response to catastrophe?

8. The Nazi ghetto as *kehillah kedoshah*

Primary Sources: Anthology, secs. 71-77.

Secondary Sources: Roskies, ch. 8.

Classroom debate: Resolved that the Nazi Ghetto Was a Conducive Setting for Jewish Autonomy.

9. Holocaust: Birth of an archetype

Primary Sources: Anthology, chs. XVI, XVIII.

Secondary Sources: Roskies, ch. 9.

Writing Assignment: What are the parts that stand for the whole, and when does that whole defy analogy?

10. Messianism as a response to catastrophe

Primary Sources: Anthology, secs. 89-90, 95-97.

Secondary Sources: Scholem, "Toward an Understanding of the Messianic Idea in Judaism"; "The Messianic Idea in Kabbalism".

Writing Assignment: How is messianism related to catastrophe in the modern era?

11. Iconography

Primary Sources: **The Book of Alfred Kantor**; Spiegelman, **Maus: A Survivor's Tale**.

Secondary Sources: Roskies, ch. 10; Adam Gopnik, "Comics and Catastrophe".

Writing Assignment: Is representational art commensurate with the Holocaust?

12. Student Presentations

IV. REQUIREMENTS OF THE COURSE FOR GRADING

Ten 2-page writing assignments due, one per week. At the end of the course the students are given a final assignment: Compose a liturgy for *Yom Hashoah* or *Yom Hazikkaron*, or create a "Third Seder" incorporating new sounds and images of catastrophe.

V.   CONCEPTUAL FRAMEWORK OF THE COURSE

The larger purpose of the course is to retrieve the Jewish hermeneutic of history; to restore conceptually - if not in actual practice - the process of Jewish collective memory. In this sense the subject of recurrent national disaster is incidental, for the same goal could be achieved through the study of other historical themes, such as messianism or apostasy. Yet the cumulative, self-regulating, and self- referential process of Jewish collective memory has never met a greater challenge than the calamitous events of the present century.

This course, then, sets out to explore the aboveground, normative traditions of Jewish response to catastrophe that - until the nineteenth century - were "coded" primarily into the liturgy. The key word is "normative," despite its having been discredited in the writings of Gershom Scholem. For what we are following is the attempt of a religious and intellectual elite to govern the way the Jewish "masses" remember the past and respond to future calamities. It is within the Jewish community, furthermore, that the success of this rabbinic strategy can most fruitfully be gauged, whether this community still views itself as a *Kehilla Kedosha*, a Holy Congregation bearing witness to God's presence in exile, or whether it is being wracked by dissension from within and threatened by forces from without, as in the East European shtetl and its demonic counterpart, the Nazi ghetto.

Liturgy, community, and memory, are the forces of continuity; secularism, emancipation, and violence are the countervailing forces of change. In Eastern Europe, where the course of true emancipation never did run smoothly, collective behavior remained the norm until the Holocaust, and the rise of a secular literature in Hebrew, Yiddish, Polish, and Russian did much to revive the archetypal reading of history. One way, indeed, that the secular ideologies of socialism, Zionism and self-determination came to replace the old theology of sin-retribution-and-restoration was by adopting and subverting the language of Scripture and the liturgy.

How far, then, could one stretch the old ways of coding, recording, and commemorating Jewish catastrophe without tearing the web apart? Could such watershed events as World War I and the Bolshevik revolution still be disassembled into the old archetypes of exile, destruction, and redemption - however modern their reinterpretation? By following a strict chronology one can see how the growing cycles of violence were translated into ever more subversive forms of response: psychological fiction in which the solitary individual was exposed to the naked force of mob violence; apocalyptic poems that blasphemed against all the sancta, Jewish and Christian.

Even as these centrifugal forces were gaining momentum, however, there was significant movement in the opposite direction, as Jewish prose writers and poets began to perceive the possibility of total destruction. Shtetl novellas of the 1920s, and "prophetic" oracles of the 1930s, rehearsed in microcosm and metaphor what was soon to become historical reality.

With this methodology and material in place, it is now possible to study the precise impact of the Holocaust on Jewish collective memory. Moving from genre to genre, from year to year, from ghetto to death camp, one discovers how the Jews under Nazi occupation tried to make sense of the unfolding disaster in terms of the old and old-new archetypes of destruction; how even the most subversive texts of the twentieth century were pressed into action as sources of consolation; how a new archetype of destruction gradually took shape, even before it had its own name. Students for whom the Holocaust is a disembodied event standing outside of human culture and historical causality will themselves discover that a normative Jewish response was, and indeed, is, still possible so long as one continues to disassemble the vast and unknowable horror in terms of what has already occurred. And if, in the end, this hermeneutic is accessible only to those schooled in a classical curriculum, it may yet survive in the universal language of the graphic arts.

I.   THE COURSE

THE HOLOCAUST: HISTORY AND PERSPECTIVES

Karl A. Schleunes
Department of History, University of North Carolina at Greensboro

II.   ACADEMIC CONTEXT OF THE COURSE

The University of North Carolina at Greensboro is a public university with about 11,000 students. Until 1962 it was the women's college of the state university system. Sixty percent of its students are female. It is currently one of the state system's three doctoral degree-granting institutions.

The course will be offered in the history department which is located administratively in a College of Arts and Sciences. Many students in the course will be junior and senior history majors, although the course is designed to attract students with other majors as well. A majority of students are from the American South and are of the first generation in their family to attend college.

No previous knowledge of the Holocaust is required and very little knowledge of it will be assumed. The College of Arts and Sciences does require a two-semester survey course in Western Civilization, and some understanding of the Western cultural tradition can be assumed. A majority of students will come to the course with a world view, even if it is largely secular, that has been shaped by various Protestant versions of Christianity. They will bring with them the attendant assumptions about human nature, good and evil, and the course of human destiny. This examination of the Holocaust will force them to look at these assumptions critically.

III.   OUTLINE OF THE COURSE

1.   Introducing the Holocaust

    A.   The view from inside
         Elie Wiesel, **Night** (New York, 1960).

Film: Night and Fog

Otto Friedrich, "The Kingdom of Auschwitz," **The Atlantic** (September 1981), pp. 30-60.

B.   "Silence" or analysis
Yehuda Bauer, "Against Mystification; The Holocaust as Historical Phenomenon," in **The Holocaust in Historical Perspective** (Seattle, 1978).

Raymond Aron, "Is There a Nazi Mystery?" **Commentary** (June 1980), pp. 29-41.

2.   Antisemitism in history: Why the Jews?

A.   General works on antisemitism
Shmuel Ettinger, "The Origins of Modern Antisemitism," in Yisrael Gutman and Livia Rothkirchen (eds.), **The Catastrophe of European Jewry** (Jerusalem, 1976), pp. 3-39.

Michael Marrus, "Theory and Practice of Anti-Semitism," **Commentary** 74 (August 1982), pp. 38-42.

Jacob Katz, **From Prejudice to Destruction: Anti-Semitism 1700-1933** (Cambridge, Mass., 1980).

B.   The "continuity" thesis: is there an "eternal antisemitism?"
Rosemary Radford Ruether, **Faith and Fratricide; The Theological Roots of Antisemitism** (New York, 1974).

Norman Ravitch, "The Problem of Christian Anti-Semitism," **Commentary** 73 (April, 1982), pp. 41-52.

Franklin Littell, **The Crucifixion of the Jews** (New York, 1975).

Joshua Trachtenberg, **The Devil and the Jews; The Medieval Conception of the Jews and its Relation to Modern Antisemitism** (New Haven, 1943).

The New Testament Gospel accounts of the crucifixion: Matthew, Chs. 26-27; Mark, Chs. 14-15; Luke, Chs. 22-23; John, Chs. 29-31.

C. The discontinuity thesis of antisemitism
Hannah Arendt, "Antisemitism," Section One of **The Origins of Totalitarianism** (new ed.) (New York, 1973).

3. Nineteenth-Century Racism and Antisemitism

A. Europe in general
Count Arthur de Gobineau, **The Inequality of the Races** (1854) (trans. A. Collins) (Los Angeles, 1966).

Allan Chase, **The Legacy of Malthus**, esp. Chs. 4 & 15 (New York, 1975).

B. Racism in Germany
George L. Mosse, **Toward the Final Solution: A History of European Racism**, (New York, 1978).

Benno Mueller-Hill, **Murderous Science: Elimination by Scientific Selection of Jews, Gypsies, and Others; Germany 1933-1945** (Oxford, 1988)

Jacob Katz, "Was the Holocaust Predictable?" **Commentary** (May 1975).

4. The situation in Germany after World War I to 1933

A. Nazi ideology
The NSDAP's Twenty-Five Point Program of 1920.

Adolf Hitler, **Mein Kampf**, Ch. XI "Nation and Race" (New York, 1939).

The Protocols of the Elders of Zion.

G.L. Mosse, **The Crisis of German Ideology; Intellectual Origins of the Third Reich** (New York, 1964 .

B. Hitler's rise to power
K.D. Bracher, **The German Dictatorship**, Chs. II and III (New York, 1970).

Film: Mein Kampf (by Erwin Leiser).

5. The Nazis and the Holocaust

A. The Third Reich from 1933 to 1945
K.A. Schleunes, **The Twisted Road to Auschwitz**, Chs. 3-7 (Chicago, 1970).

David Bankier, "Hitler and the Policy-Making Process on the Jewish Question," **Holocaust and Genocide Studies** 3 (1988), pp. 1-20.

Sarah Gordon, **Hitler, Germans and the "Jewish Question,"** Chs. 4-6, (Princeton, N.J., 1984).

B. World War II and the making of the Holocaust
K.D. Bracher, **The German Dictatorship**, Ch. VIII (New York, 1970).

Raul Hilberg, **The Destruction of the European Jews**, Student edition, Chs. 1-5 (New York, 1985).

Christopher Browning, **Fateful Months; Essays on the Final Solution** (New York, 1985).

Gerald Fleming, **Hitler and the Final Solution** (Berkeley, 1982).

6. The death camps

A. The camps
Konnilyn Feig, **Hitler's Death Camps; The Sanity of Madness** (New York, 1981).

Yitzhak Arad, **Belzec, Sobibor, Treblinka; The Operation Reinhard Camps**, (Bloomington, Indiana, 1987).

Martin Broszat, "The Concentration Camps 1933-1945," in Helmut Krausnick et al. (eds.), **Anatomy of the S.S. State** (New York, 1965).

B. Life in the camps
Primo Levi, **Suvival in Auschwitz** (New York, 1961).

Rudolf Hoess, **Commandant at Auschwitz** (Cleveland, 1960).

Portions of the film Shoah.

Raul Hilberg, **The Destruction of the European Jews**, Student edition, Chs. 6-7.

7. Perspectives on the Holocaust: Topics proposed for individual student reports and papers

A. Perspectives from psychology
Stanley Milgram, **Obedience to Authority: An Experimental View** (New York, 1974).

Hannah Arendt, **Eichmann in Jerusalem: A Report of the Banality of Evil** revised edition (New York, 1964).

Michael Selzer and Florence Miale, **The Nuremberg Mind** (New York, 1975).

Bruno Bettelheim, **The Informed Heart** (Glencoe, Ill., 1960).

George Kren & Leon Rappoport, **The Holocaust and the Crisis of Human Behavior** (New York, 1980).

B. Perspective of theology
1. Jewish theology
Eugene Borowitz, "Confronting the Holocaust," Ch. 9, **Choices in Modern Jewish Thought** (New York, 1983).

Irving Greenberg, "Cloud of Smoke, Pillar of Fire; Judaism, Christianity and Modernity after the Holocaust," in Eva Fleischner (ed.), **Auschwitz; Beginning of a New Era?** (New York, 1977).

Richard Rubenstein, **After Auschwitz: Radical Theology and Contemporary Judaism** (Indianapolis, 1966).

2. Christian theology
Gregory Baum, **Christian Theology after Auschwitz** (New York, 1976).

Vatican Council II, **Nostra Aetate** (1965).

Juergen Moltmann, **The Crucified God** (New York, 1974).

Roy Eckardt, **For Righteousness Sake: Contemporary Moral Philosophies** (New York, 1987).

C. Literature, film, art
Sidra Ezrahi, **By Words Alone: The Holocaust in Literature** (Chicago, 1980).

Alvin H. Rosenfeld, **A Double Dying: Reflections on Holocaust Literature** (Bloomington, Ind., 1980).

Lawrence L. Langer, **The Holocaust and the Literary Imagination** (New Haven, 1975).

Judith E. Doneson, **The Holocaust in American Film** (Philadelphia, 1987).

Ilan Avisar, **Screening the Holocaust** (Bloomington, Ind., 1988).

Janet Blatter and Sybil Milton, **Art of the Holocaust** (New York, 1981).

D. Other areas or topics bearing investigation
War crimes trials; Deniers of the Holocaust; Bystanders to the Holocaust: countries, institutions, people; The rescue of Jews; The "uniqueness" or "universality" of the Holocaust

8. A final reflection

Reading and Discussion of George Steiner, "A Season in Hell," **In Bluebeard's Castle** (New Haven, 1971).

IV. REQUIREMENTS OF THE COURSE FOR GRADING

Students will be expected to take a mid-term and a final examination, both of which will contain primarily essay questions. Each student will also be asked to write a 5-7 page paper on a topic suggested by the syllabus in Section 7, or on a topic selected by the student and approved by the instructor. This paper is also to be the basis for a 15-minute oral report to the class.

V. CONCEPTUAL FRAMEWORK OF THE COURSE

1. The student will be introduced to the Holocaust by looking first at its horrors. This will be done by way of watching a film and reading a novel and an essay, each of which forces a direct confrontation with the horror and with some of its possible implications. This insistence that the student look directly at the images of the horror will be brief. Thereafter, the course will focus upon analysis, the objective being to fit the horrors of Auschwitz into an understanding of the Western cultural and historical experience. Students will almost inevitably find this fit to be uncomfortable and only partial.

2. The attempt to fit Auschwitz into the student's understanding of his or her own culture requires a storehouse of information about the history of that culture. Only from that storehouse can the pieces that need to be fitted together be drawn. A study of antisemitism in this sense serves a dual purpose. The lengthy examination of this phenomenon proposed in the syllabus serves not merely to acquaint students with centuries of anti-Jewish prejudice, but also to review historically the religious, social and political settings in which this prejudice was born, flourished and, at times, failed to flourish. The Roman Empire, early Christianity, the Church Fathers, The Middle Ages, the Reformation, the Enlightenment, the Industrial Revolution, and the twentieth century, are all illuminated by examining their relationship to Jews as a people and to Judaism as a religion. Any useful thinking about the Holocaust, to my mind, must rest upon this foundation.

3. Racism in the late nineteenth century became an all- embracing doctrine for explaining human behavior, whether it was religious, political, cultural or economic. Racists divided the peoples of the world into superior and inferior groups, assigning to some the positive powers of creation, and to others the

negative status of parasites. Racism came to justify the rule of certain peoples over others and to legitimize inequalities of social, economic, and ethnic or national status. One stream of this racism appropriated the ancient prejudices against the Jews and mixed them with the pseudo- scientific biological conceptions then flourishing to produce the new racially-based prejudice for which the term antisemitism was invented. Racist assumptions also undergirded the new "science" of eugenics which had as its implicitly logical goal the breeding of a master race. Under the Nazis a generation later, the new antisemitism and eugenics were combined into the doctrine of race that underlay both Nazi territorial expansionism and the mass murder of supposedly inferior and parasitic peoples.

4.   This section of the course might also be titled "Why Germany?" because it investigates - though only briefly - why the racism of the nineteenth century in its antisemitic and eugenic versions proved so appealing to many Germans in the decade after their defeat in World War I. The purpose of this section is to provide the student with a rudimentary understanding of how and why Hitler came to power, and of the role that racism played in the Nazis' understanding of how the world worked.

5.   Section 5 deals with the Holocaust proper and is concerned with the problem of the process of Nazi decision-making that eventually led to Auschwitz. The outbreak of war in September 1939 is seen as a decisive turning point in the Nazis' expanded ambitions to reshape the world according to their racial conceptualizations. Eugenics as well as antisemitism led to mass murder. Considerable attention is paid to events in 1941, in order to examine the connection between the Nazis' invasion of the Soviet Union and their decision to produce a "Final Solution to the Jewish Problem." Auschwitz and the five other death camps were all established during the last months of 1941 and the early months of 1942.

6.   This section on the death camps focuses once again upon the horrors of the Holocaust. The objective is to arrive at an understanding of how these camps functioned and how, for at least a few people, survival in them was possible. Rudolf Hoess's memoir is assigned to provide a look at a murderer; Primo Levi's to provide a look at a survivor.

7.   This section of the course will be shaped in large part by the students themselves. Each student is required to investigate an area of the Holocaust. Recommendations for topics are listed in the syllabus itself, although other topics, if approved by the instructor, will also be acceptable. The student

will be required to submit a 5-7 page paper on his or her topic and to report to the class on findings presented in the paper. This part of the course is designed to allow students to define for themselves the perspectives they find most interesting and useful in explaining the Holocaust, and to subject those perspectives to general class discussion and possible refinement.

8. The final week of the class, or at least two sessions, is to be devoted to a consideration of George Steiner's provocative essay on the cultural continuities that he believes made the Holocaust possible. He reaches back in the Western cultural tradition to the ancient Hebrew prophets and forward to Karl Marx to construct a social and moral universe in which the Holocaust became possible. Students will be asked to respond to Steiner's essay and to measure their own understandings against it. I hasten to say that students are not required to agree with Steiner on any point; at this point in the course they should, however, have the intellectual resources to subject his argument to critical analysis.

I. THE COURSE

THE POLITICS OF GENOCIDE

Colin Tatz
Department of Politics, Macquarie University, Sydney, Australia

II. ACADEMIC CONTEXT OF THE COURSE

Macquarie is one of Sydney's four metropolitan universities. It has 8,000 students based in 11 Schools (excluding the medical/dental/engineering disciplines). It is not the university chosen by the majority of Jewish students. They attend Sydney, the University of New South Wales, and the University of Technology.

The course was taught for the first time in 1988, for one semester - two/three hours per week for 13 weeks. The initial enrolment of 42 students for this third-year level course was quite beyond expectation. As a result, the course will be taught annually. There are prerequisites for acceptance in the course: either earlier courses in race politics, Aboriginal politics, or modern German or European history.

III. OUTLINE OF THE COURSE

Essential reading
Helen Fein, **Accounting for Genocide** (New York, 1983).

I. Walliman & M. Dobkowski (eds.), **Genocide and the Modern Age: Etiology and Case Studies in Mass Death** (New York, 1987).

Gerhard Hirschfield (ed.), **The Policies of Genocide: Jews and Soviet Prisoners of War in Nazi Germany** (London, 1986).

Irving Louis Horowitz, **Taking Lives: Genocide and State Power** (New Brunswick, 1981).

Richard Hovannisian (ed.), **The Armenian Genocide in Perspective** (New Brunswick, 1986).

Encyclopaedia Judaica, Article on "The Holocaust".

David Lang & Christopher Walker, **The Armenians,** London: Minority Rights Group, Report No. 32 (1987), revised edition.

Leo Kuper, **The Prevention of Genocide** (1985).

Essential References
David Szonyi, **The Holocaust: An Annotated Bibliography and Resource Guide** (New York, 1985).

Richard Hovannisian, **The Armenian Holocaust: A Bibliography Relating to the Deportations, Massacres, and Dispersion of the Armenian People, 1915-1923** (Cambridge, Mass., 1978).

Students are asked to consult David Szonyi's bibliography, and to meet with the lecturer for guidance on references relevant to their major essay topic.

The best guide to the content of the course is the set of assignment topics listed below.

IV. REQUIREMENTS OF THE COURSE FOR GRADING
Students are required to write two essays: one, for 65%, of 3,500 to 4,000 words on the Holocaust (and/or the Armenian Genocide); a second, for 35%, of 2,000 words on one of 40 case studies in genocide.

FIRST ESSAY (The following are 3 examples out of 7 given to the class. Students may choose one)

1. "In order to understand a particular genocidal event better, it is imperative that one examine other instances of mass annihilation... In contrast to the massacres of earlier historical epochs, twentieth-century genocidal phenomena have been conditioned by the... capabilities of supernaturalist elites, who possess unique instrumentalities of mass extermination. These distinctive

features include (1) organizational specificity; (2) planning, programming, and timing; (3) bureaucratic efficiency and comprehensiveness; (4) technological capability; and (5) the ideological imperative."

R. Hrair Dekemjian in **The Armenian Genocide in Perspective**. Discuss the Holocaust and the Armenian Genocide in his terms.

2. "What makes the Holocaust unique is the existence of two elements: planned total annihilation of a national or ethnic group, and the quasi-religious, apocalyptic ideology that motivated the murder."

Prof. Yehuda Bauer in "Whose Holocaust?" **Midstream**, November 1980, p. 45. Bauer argues that the Holocaust was both universal and unique. Discuss that seeming contradiction. At the same time, discuss the implications of universalizing genocidal acts, of "flattening out" and "normalizing" such events.

3. In August 1939, while discussing the forthcoming invasion of Poland with his High Command, Hitler - in responding to a suggestion that the Poles and Jews could not be massacred - asked the question: "Who, after all, speaks today of the annihilation of the Armenians?"

Discuss world reaction to the Turkish and German killings: who knew what and when, who said what and when, and to what effect?

SECOND ESSAY

With reference to:
1. The ideological basis for the genocide;
2. The socio-political basis for the genocide;
3. The techniques/technologies used;
4. The question of legal/moral responsibility, especially the role of the state;
5. The interest or indifference of neighbors and nations during the events;
6. The nature of the genocide (its "classification," scale, dimension);
7. The punishment (if any) for it; world reaction to it.

Discuss **ONE**:
1. The treatment of gypsies (the Roma or Romany people) in World War II.
2. Mass killings of Communists in Indonesia 1965-66.
3. Mass killings in Cambodia (Kampuchea) 1976-1981.

4. Selective genocide in Rwanda and Burundi.
5. The fate of the San (Bushmen) in Southern Africa.
6. The "wreckers" and "the enemies of the Soviet Union" during Stalin's purges.
7. The secession of Biafra from Nigeria.
8. The creation of Bangladesh, involving 3 million dead, 1971.
9. The Ache Indians in Paraguay.
10. South Africa: is apartheid genocide?
11. The case of Brazil's Indians.
12. Australia's Aborigines: what aspects amount to genocide?
13. The annihilation of Aborigines in Tasmania.
14. The liquidation of Kulaks in Russia, 1930s.

V. CONCEPTUAL FRAMEWORK OF THE COURSE

The purpose of the course is to study the systematic extermination of national, racial, religious or ethnic (or tribal) groups. Objectives include:

* Analyzing the motives for such killings;
* examining the socio-political conditions under which such mass killings occur;
* attempting to pinpoint legal and moral/personal responsibility for their occurrence;
* attempting to understand the indifference of bystanders;
* assessing gradations of genocide - from destroying cultural institutions, to forcibly transferring children from one group to another, to the planned total annihilation of an entire race/group;
* reviewing what safeguards there are against repetitions of genocide.

A primary purpose is to demonstrate the uniqueness (and universality) of the Jewish Holocaust, and to locate and define other genocidal killings by comparison. Here the Armenian genocide forms the second major case study.

The essence of this course is to come to terms with the use and abuse of the language that deals with the Holocaust in particular and genocidal killings in general. The Holocaust is both universal and unique: and this dialectic must be demonstrated to students. There is a need to show that there are gradations of genocidal killing, and that there are dangers in classifying all such killings as one and the same phenomenon.

The UN's definition of genocide is seriously deficient.The attempts at prevention of this crime are dismal in their achievement. The course examines possible alternatives, including secondary and tertiary education as a method of highlighting genocide. In this context, the course draws a distinction between the art of forgiving and the improbability of forgetting such events on the part of victim communities.

I. THE COURSE

THE NAZI TOTALITARIAN STATE AND THE HOLOCAUST

Nechama Tec
Department of Sociology, University of Connecticut at Stanford

II ACADEMIC CONTEXT OF THE COURSE

This is a one-semester course that began as a cooperative venture of two historians and a sociologist: Joel Blatt, Lucjan Dobroszycki and Nechama Tec. After several years, because of special commitments, Lucjan Dobroszycki's participation is limited to only occasional lectures.

It is a regular undergraduate course but geared toward more advanced undergraduates and assumes some prior knowledge of European history. About 50 students usually take the course, less than half of them Jewish.

III. OUTLINE OF THE COURSE

Required reading
Lucy Dawidowicz, **A Holocaust Reader** (New York: Behrman House Inc., 1976).

Gerald Fleming, **Hitler and the Final Solution** (Los Angeles: University of California Press, 1982).

Raul Hilberg, **The Destruction of the European Jews** (New York: Holmes and Meier, 1985).

Walter Laqueur, **The Terrible Secret** (Boston: Little Brown, 1980).

Primo Levi, **Survival in Auschwitz** (New York: Collier Books, 1961).

Nechama Tec, **Dry Tears** (New York: Oxford University Press, 1984).

Nechama Tec, **When Light Pierced the Darkness** (New York: Oxford University Press, 1987).

1. Introduction and overview (Tec)

    Dawidowicz - "Introduction", pp. 1-21; "The Final Solution", pp. 25-82.

    Hilberg - "Precedents" and "Definition by Decree", pp. 5-38.

    Tec - **Dry Tears** - "The Approaching Shadow" and "My World Before", pp. 1-66.

    Tec - **When Light...** - "Introduction", pp. 3-23.

2. Antisemitism: Historical background (Blatt)

    Hilberg - pp. 5-24.

    Fleming - pp. 1-31.

    Tec - **When Light...** - Chapters 6 and 9 (also pp. 59-63).

    Dawidowicz - pp. 25-33.

3. Rise of Fascism and rise of Nazism in Germany (Blatt)

    No assigned reading.

4. Hitler (Blatt)

    Fleming - entire book.

5. The Nazi totalitarian state and the Holocaust (Dobroszycki)

    Hilberg - pp. 27-292.

    Dawidowicz - pp. 25-82; particularly 73-82.

6. The Nazi totalitarian state, the Holocaust and the German people (Blatt, Tec)

   Hilberg - pp. 27-292; especially "Mobile Killing Operations," pp. 99-153.

7. Mid-term examination & discussion thereafter

8. The Ghetto (Tec)

   Dawidowicz - "The Ordeals of the Ghettos in Eastern Europe" and "The Ordeals of the Judenrate," pp. 171-273.

   Hilberg - "Concentration", pp. 41-96.

   Tec - **When Light...** - "The World of the Rescuer and the Rescued," pp. 25-84.

9. Concentration camps (Tec)

   Dawidowicz - "Confronting Death: The Ordeals of Deportation," pp. 289-327.

   Hilberg - "Deportations" and "Killing Center Operations", pp. 157-259.

   Levi - **Survival in Auschwitz** - entire book.

10. Passing and hiding (Tec)

    Tec - **Dry Tears** - entire book.

    Tec - **When Light...** - Chapters 4-10, pp. 70-193.

11. Resistance (Tec)

    Dawidowicz - "Resistance: The Ordeal of Desperation", pp. 329-380.

12.-13. Reactions to the Holocaust (Blatt, Tec)

    Hilberg - "Rescue", pp. 309-331.

Laqueur - **The Terrible Secret** - entire book.

14. Concluding discussion (Blatt, Tec)

No assigned reading

IV. REQUIREMENTS OF THE COURSE FOR GRADING
A mid-term examination (20%); a final examination (35%); a term-paper (35%) and class participation (10%).

V. CONCEPTUAL FRAMEWORK OF THE COURSE
As a sociologist I had been guided by the idea that there was a certain disaffinity between the inductive method, on the one hand, and the quantitative approach, on the other. Therefore, in my own research and classrooms, I leaned towards the inductive method and towards quantitative analysis.

However, when I began to take interest in study and teaching about the Holocaust, I came to realize that an understanding of this complex subject could, at best, be partial. I also noticed that the difficulties in grasping the meanings and implications of Holocaust materials became more pronounced when I tried to generalize and quantify.

These experiences led me to the conclusion that in the study of the Holocaust abstract generalizations and quantitative analysis of data tend to interfere with the meanings and interpretations of these sensitive materials. I also had to recognize that generalizations and statistical analyses, when applied to Holocaust data, often promise something they cannot deliver. This, for example, is due to the fact that in this area of research representative samples do not seem possible. By definition, Holocaust events are extraordinary and difficult to grasp. Only concrete examples and illustrations help make them more comprehensible.

Difficulties and limitations of generalizations and quantitative presentations suggest a greater reliance on qualitative analysis. The use of qualitative data, in turn, points to the advantages of the inductive method. In short, in the study of the Holocaust, instead of proceeding from the general to the specific, it seems more advisable to move from the specific to the general. In line with these assumptions, when teaching this subject I start with qualitative case histories and keep the available quantitative data in the background. I use whatever figures and abstract principles are available only as additional evidence and for clarification.

As for the content of this course, the historians concentrate on fascism, anti-semitism, and the Nazi totalitarian state machinery, while I focus on the victims and on the ways in which they lived, struggled, and perished in different contexts: the ghetto, the concentration camps, the forests, and the forbidden Christian world, the so-called "Aryan side".

When examining the victims in these different settings, I am guided by such basic sociological concepts as stratification, social control, deviancy, and socialization. For example, when discussing the ghetto, I show how the entire stratification system changed, what happened to the leadership positions, how members of the pre-war upper class became beggars, and how some pre-war underworld characters, because of their Nazi collaboration, were assigned to the most powerful positions.

As I deal with these issues, I am guided by the idea that, during World War II, life for European Jews was reduced to its bare essentials and was deprived of its conventional trimmings. This gives an uncluttered view of the human condition. Precisely because during the Holocaust life was reduced to its bare essentials, the study of this period provides the opportunity to see and understand better the meanings and implications of basic human conditions. And so, I am convinced that in addition to offering important lessons for the future, and in addition to providing historical descriptions of unprecedented events, the study of the Holocaust contains unlimited possibilities for the discovery of significant sociological principles.

More specifically, too, we know that extreme situations create extreme reactions of evil and goodness. When I deal with this period I pay special attention to human decency and goodness as represented by compassion, altruism, survival, and rescue. To be sure, these positive features were atypical, and were overshadowed by the enormity of the Nazi crimes. Nevertheless, they continue to be an important part of my classroom presentations. Thus, for example, when I lecture about concentration camps, I talk about bonding that existed among concentration camp inmates. I show that within this sea of cruelty there was compassion, mutual help, and self-sacrifice. Indeed, most concentration camp diaries show that all inmates who stayed alive had benefited from these positive forces. Extreme deprivational conditions, if they are to be overcome, require cooperation.

It is, of course, a matter of historical record that the overwhelming majority of concentration camp inmates could not overcome the evil forces and perished. Still, when I deal with the destructive processes in different European countries, I emphasize that in each of them there were some who tried to rescue Jews. I discuss the meaning and implications of their rescue. We must know that some people had risked their lives to save Jews and that some of them lost their lives in the process. Here I agree with Jan Karski, who feels that it is important for all of us to realize, that though abandoned by all governments, Jews were not abandoned by all people.

Joel Blatt's participation in this course has concentrated on historical background, on Hitler, and on the responses of those outside Nazi control. In a session covering the history of Antisemitism, he looks at the context of Judaism in the time of Jesus and early Christianity. Christian Antisemitism is necessary background for the Holocaust, but is not sufficient as a complete explanation, since Hitler acted as a racial antisemite and not as a Christian; in fact, he was vehemently anti-Christian. Blatt also adds a discussion of 19th and 20th century currents of antisemitism. At the conclusion of the session, he reads brief excerpts from Sartre's **Anti-Semite and Jew**.

In a second background class he examines the rise of fascism in Europe and specifically in Germany. In studying the rise of Nazism to power in Germany, Lucjan Dobroszycki talks of Hitler's "two moments" (1918-1923 and 1929-1933). Blatt discusses five traumas from 1918 to 1933 that brought Hitler close to power: World War I and German defeat; the revolutions in Germany of 1918-1919; The Versailles Treaty of 1919; the German inflation of the early 1920s; The Great Depression (1929-1933).

In the class on Hitler he utilizes some of the psycho-historical insights of Robert Waite and Walter Langer. Antisemitism lay at Hitler's core. Without it, he would have had to confront himself, which he systematically refused to do, radiating self-hatred outward.

When considering the responses of the United States, Great Britain, Canada, the Vatican, and others to the Holocaust, Blatt emphasizes that for each of them the rescue of Jews was a low priority, while for Hitler the murder of Jews was one of his highest priorities. He also   accentuates the ways in which the "lifeboat mentality" aided Hitler's advances, particularly in the period of appeasement.

Two appropriate poems that he reads at different moments in the course are William Butler Yeats "The Second Coming" and W.H. Auden, "Musee des Beaux Arts".

I. THE COURSE

ANALYSIS OF LITERATURE FOR CHILDREN AND YOUNG ADULTS: BOOKS ON THE HOLOCAUST

Jane Vogel Fischman & DayAnn Kennedy
Faculty of Educational Studies, Department of Learning and Instruction, State University of New York at Buffalo

II. ACADEMIC CONTEXT OF THE COURSE

This is a one-semester (14-15 week) graduate elective course offered by the education faculty. It is conducted in one session per week of three hours' duration. The class includes master's and doctoral level students in education, as well as a few members of the library science master's program. Our main purpose is to train and encourage teachers and librarians (most often school librarians) to: 1) analyze critically books for children and young adults (grades 6-13 or first year college), 2) select them carefully, and 3) acquire the confidence, skills and knowledge for teaching and/or including in their curricula, cross-disciplinary elements of controversial or sensitive issues.

The course has a dual organization; it is actually a course within a course. One part focuses on the techniques of critical analysis and book selection; the other uses the Holocaust as a model for teaching and learning about sensitive and controversial subjects. Students become aware, also, of the other media, methods, and materials available for enriching the study of the Holocaust through its literature. Most of the "students" are already employed as teachers or librarians in secondary schools; the majority of them have little prior knowledge of the Holocaust. Our aim, then, is to prepare them to teach sensitive subjects with confidence, using the Holocaust as a model.

Teaching the Holocaust is now mandatory in New York State; it appears as part of the 10th grade World Civilization course and in many 12th grade history electives. Teachers need training to prepare their curricula, not only in history, but also in English, Art, and Music, which lend themselves to a cross-disciplinary approach.

The course was designed as a way to meet this need. (It is an example of what Irving Halperin has called teaching by "indirection;" that is, it teaches by "evoking the Holocaust through the reading of certain writers, even when, in some instances, the central theme and situations in their work are not at all concerned with it." (**Judaism**, Vol. 55, no. 4, p. 441)

III. OUTLINE OF THE COURSE
Asterisks signify required reading.

1. Introduction

   A. Introduction to the principles of criticism: Applications for children's and young adults' literature

   *M.K. Rudman, **Children's Literature: An Issues Approach** (New York, 1984), Introductory chapters.

   *A. Nilsen & K. Donelson, **Literature for Today's Young Adults** (New York, 1985), pp. 244-257.

   B. Introduction to the Holocaust: Methodology and terminology

   *H. Friedlander, "Postscript: Toward a Methodology of Teaching about the Holocaust," in H. Friedlander & S. Milton, **The Holocaust: Ideology, Bureaucracy and Genocide, The San Jose Papers** (Millwood, 1979).

2. Background

   A. Principles of book selection: Application for choosing books on sensitive subjects

   *Rudman, **Children's Literature: An Issues Approach**, chapters on war, the Holocaust, and death.

   B. Historical Background of the Holocaust

   *M. Meltzer, **Never to Forget: The Jews of the Holocaust** (New York, 1976).

*Teaching Guide to **Never to Forget: The Jews of the Holocaust** (New York), (obtainable from Bantam/Dell).

Recommended
D. Altshuler & L. Dawidowicz, **Hitler's War Against the Jews**, (Philadelphia, 1978).

3. Prejudice and antisemitism

   A. Problems in print: Selection and availability

   *Rudman, **Children's Literature: An Issues Approach,** chapters on prejudice, ethnic and religious groups.

   Recommended
   Nilsen & Donelson, **Literature for Today's Young Adults**, readings on the topic.

   B. Examples of young adult literature: Prejudice

   NB. Because children's and young adult books are so often in and out of print, only titles and authors are given. A good resource is D. Szonyi's **The Holocaust: An Annotated Bibliography and Resource Guide.**

   *M. Levoy, **Alan and Naomi.**

   *F. Arrick, **Chernowitz.**

   *B. Greene, **The Summer of My German Soldier.**

   *Guide to **The Summer of My German Soldier** (available, free, from Bantam/ Dell, New York).

4. Obedience

   A. *M. Strom & W. Parsons, **Facing History and Ourselves: Holocaust and Human Behavior** (Watertown, 1982), chapter and readings on Obedience.

B. Examples of young adult literature: Obedience

*H. Richter, **Friedrich.**

*M. Rhue, **The Wave.**

*Guide to **The Wave** (available from Bantam/Dell).

5. Resistance

A. *Strom and Parsons, **Facing History and Ourselves: Holocaust and Human Behavior,** chapter and readings on resistance.

B. Examples of young adult literature: Resistance

*G. Samuels, **Mottele.**

Recommended
N. Benchley, **Bright Candles, A Novel of The Danish Resistance.**

A. Lustig, **A Prayer for Katerina Horovitzova.**

Y. Suhl, **Uncle Misha's Partisans.**

6. Children and young adults in the Holocaust: Decisions and relationships

A. *Rudman, **Children's Literature: An Issues Approach,** chapters on maturity and relationships.

B. Young adults' literature: Decisions and relationships

*A. Holm, **I am David,** (also published as **Passage North**).

*J. Reiss, **The Upstairs Room.**

Recommended
E. Hautzig, **The Endless Steppe.**

J. Kerr, **When Hitler Stole Pink Rabbit.**

——————, **A Small Person Far Away.**

M. Jacot, **The Last Butterfly.**

J. Joffo, **A Bag of Marbles.**

M. Marriette, **I am Rosemarie.**

M. Sachs, **A Pocket Full of Seeds.**

L. Segal, **In Other People's Houses.**

7. Children's and young adult literature: Genre

   A. More principles of criticism

   <u>Recommended</u>
   Selected readings from the works of S. Ezrahi, A. Berger, L. Langer, and A. Rosenfeld.

   B. Genre examples for children and young adults

   Diaries
   *The Diary of Anne Frank.
   *E. Wiesel, Night.

   <u>Recommended</u>
   M. Gray, **For Those I Loved.**

   G. Klein, **All But My Life.**

   Poetry
   *I Never Saw Another Butterfly.

Recommended
Poetry of Sachs, Pagis, Sutzkever, Glatstein.

Novels

Short Stories
*Vignettes from P. Levi, **Moments of Reprieve**.
*Borges, "Deutsches Requiem".
*Spiegel, "A Ghetto Dog".
*Rothberg, "The Animal Trainer".
*Helprin, "Tamar".
(These stories are kept at the reserve desk in the library.)

Anthologies
Students are to choose one of the following for review:
Glatstein and Margoshes, **Anthology of Holocaust Literature**.
Friedlander, **Out of the Whirlwind: A Reader of Holocaust Literature**.
Dawidowicz, **A Holocaust Reader**.
Stadler, **The Holocaust**.

8. Other media

    A. Concepts of enrichment through arts related to literature

    B. Media examples for teaching children and young adults

    Film
    Recommended
    A. Insdorf, **Indelible Shadows: Film and the Holocaust** (New York, 1983).

    *Viewing: Night and Fog

    Art
    Recommended
    M. Costanza, **The Living Witness: Art in the Concentration Camps and Ghettos**.

J. Blatter and S. Milton, **Art of the Holocaust.**

A. Spiegleman, **Maus: A Survivor's Tale.**

Music

Photographs

<u>Recommended</u>

Grossman, **With a Camera in the Ghetto.**

Meier & Hellman, **The Auschwitz Album.**

Schoenberner, **The Yellow Star: The Persecution of the Jews in Europe 1933-1945.**

Newspapers

*The Record - available from the Anti-Defamation League, New York.

IV. REQUIREMENTS OF THE COURSE FOR GRADING

The course requirements include class attendance and participation, readings, the keeping of a response journal, preparation of three short reports (discussion of one poem, one book review, and presentation of one media example - a video tape, movie, phonograph record, filmstrip, artwork, or collection of photos), and the compilation of a term project, to be individually negotiated.

V.   CONCEPTUAL FRAMEWORK OF THE COURSE

1. Introduction

It is difficult enough for teachers to develop a cognition of confidence and experience; they may tend to avoid the recommendation, presentation, and discussion of works of literature which treat controversial or sensitive subjects. In fact, teaching such works requires little more rationale and methodology than teaching the works normally suggested for children and young adults. Indeed, the more sensitive or controversial works offer a challenge to librarians, teachers, and students. Additionally, teaching such works generally results in growth and a sense of accomplishment for all.

The first part of the course consists of an overview of principles of literary criticism as they apply to children's and young adult literature. This includes a review of the theories of such literary critics as Rosenblatt, Holland, and Bleich. Presentation is made of sections of Bruce Miller's **Teaching the Art of Literature** (National Council of Teachers of English). There is discussion of basic terms including plot, setting, and characterization. What are the tools we use in teaching a literary work? What methods help students apply these tools? What subjects are considered sensitive or controversial, and what makes them so?

Using the Holocaust as a model for teaching sensitive material, the introductory section of the course includes the following topics: What methods can be used for teaching the Holocaust through literature? (How do these methods differ from "regular" methodology, and why do they differ?) What are the considerations for teaching literature in translation? What are the problematics of Nazi use of language and euphemism? Reference is made especially to the volume **Documents of the Holocaust,** published by Yad Vashem. Attention is also given to the use of language to "express the inexpressible" and the contrast between the years of survivor silence and the present dedication to preserving survivor testimonies in video archives.

2. Background

The course continues with the presentation and discussion of principles of book selection and how they apply to choosing books on sensitive subjects. The topic of censorship is explored. Chapters from Rudman are read and discussed.

Meltzer's **Never to Forget: The Jews of the Holocaust** is considered both as an example of an American Library Association (ALA) Notable Book and as an introduction to the history of the Holocaust. Comparison is made between Meltzer's book and the book by Altshuler and Dawidowicz, **Hitler's War Against the Jews,** which is an adaptation for young adults of Dawidowicz's book. Members of the history and psychology departments present brief lectures which outline important topics in studying the Holocaust. These "visiting lecturers" also act as resources to help answer such questions as: "What prior knowledge do students have?"; "What questions about the Holocaust will be raised by the students?" and "What do students need to know about the Holocaust?"

3. Prejudice and Antisemitism
   This section of the course is concerned with prejudice and antisemitism as sensitive topics themselves, and as essential elements in teaching about the Holocaust. The problems of book selection and book availability are raised through readings in Rudman and in Nilsen and Donelson; three selections are analyzed as examples of Young Adult Holocaust literature dealing with prejudice and antisemitism that are currently available.

4. Obedience
   The readings from Strom and Parsons are used as the basis for class consideration of the teaching of values and morality. **The Wave** is used as an example of a popular book (made into an "Afterschool Special" television drama) which is concerned with the question "Can it happen again?" **Friedrich** is read and discussed as an example of an outstanding book; one which has been translated into many languages. **Friedrich** illustrates the technique of point of view, and is the first volume in a trilogy. Other Young Adult works on the Holocaust which have sequels are discussed: the issues they raise, including that of the Holocaust's aftermath and its effect upon the second generation, are presented.

5. Resistance
   The subject of resistance follows the topic of obedience. It is presented as a moral issue and a question of survival. Survival as resistance, spiritual resistance, fate, coincidence, and "miracle" are considered.

   Mottele is discussed as an example of a novelized account on the topic of resistance; the book is contrasted with **Uncle Misha's Partisans** as a "docunovel." These books are used for the development of critical tools including analysis of the use of sentimentality and fact in a literary work.

6. Children and young adults in the Holocaust: Decisions and relationships
   The lectures in this section of the course are concerned with how children and young adults relate to, identify with, and learn from, literature containing characters who are their chronological contemporaries. Reiss' **The Upstairs Room** is a Notable Book which provides material for comparison with **The Diary of Anne Frank. I am David** is an example of a book which may be read on both the literal and symbolic levels. Students in the course are asked to offer critical analy-

sis of this award-winning work. They also read at least one of the books from the recommended list and analyze it for class discussion.

7. Children's and young adult literature of the Holocaust by genre
Principles of literary criticism as they apply within the special context of Holocaust literature are presented. The critical works of such analysts of Holocaust literature as Alan Berger, Sidra Ezrahi, Lawrence Langer, and Alvin Rosenfeld are summarized. Discussion occurs in response to the following questions: "Into what genres may works of Holocaust literature be classified?" What works may be said to comprise the canon of Holocaust literature?" **The Diary of Anne Frank** and Elie Wiesel's **Night** are analyzed as components of this canon. Recommended readings in the various genres are presented as student reports.

8. Other Media
This part of the course deals with principles and methods of enrichment through the arts related to literature. The use of the visual and audio arts to broaden and deepen comprehension in sensitive areas is discussed. Students view *Night and Fog*, both to heighten their own understanding of the Holocaust and to consider how they might employ the showing of this film with young adults. Other recommended media examples are presented by the students for analysis and discussion.

The course concludes with the presentation and discussion of the students' projects.

BIBLIOGRAPHY

ABELLA, I. & H. TROPER. **None is Too Many: Canada and the Jews of Europe 1933-1948** (Toronto: Lester & Orpen Dennys, 1982).
——————. "The Line Must be Drawn Somewhere, Canada and the Jewish Refugees 1933-39," **Canadian Historical Review** (June 1979) or in WEINFELD, M., W. SHAFFIR & I. COTTLER (eds.), **The Canadian Jewish Mosaic** (Toronto: University of Toronto, 1981).
ABRAHAM, D. **The Collapse of the Weimar Republic** (Princeton: Princeton University Press, 1981).
ABRAMSKY, C., M. JACHIMCZYK & A. POLONSKY (eds.). **The Jews in Poland** (Oxford: Basil Blackwell, 1986).
ABZUG, R.H. **Inside the Vicious Heart: Americans and the Liberation of the Nazi Concentration Camps** (New York: Oxford University Press, 1985).
ADAM, U.D. "Persecution of the Jews, Bureaucracy and Authority in the Totalitarian State," **Leo Baeck Institute Yearbook** 23 (1978), pp. 139-148.
ADLER, J. **The Jews of Paris and the Final Solution: Communal Response and Internal Conflicts 1940-1944** (New York: Oxford University Press, 1987).
——————. **Face a la Persecution: Les Organisations Juives a Paris de 1940 a 1944** (Paris: Calmann-Levy, 1985).
AGNON, S.Y. "The Sign" (A. Green, transl.), in ROSKIES, D. (ed.), **The Literature of Destruction: Jewish Response to Catastrophe** (Philadelphia: Jewish Publication Society, 1988).
AINSZTEIN, R. **The Warsaw Ghetto Revolt** (New York: Holocaust Library, 1979).
——————. **Jewish Resistance in Nazi-Occupied Europe** (London: P. Elek, 1974).
ALDGATE, A. **Cinema and History: British Newsreels and the Spanish Civil War** (London: Scholar Press, 1979).
ALEXANDER, E. "Stealing the Holocaust," **Midstream** (November 1980), pp. 46-51.
ALLEN, W.S. **The Nazi Seizure of Power: The Experience of a Single German Town 1930-1935** (Chicago: Quadrangle, 1965).
ALLEY, R. **Graham Sutherland** (London: Arts Council, 1982).

ALMOG, S. **Antisemitism Through the Ages** (Oxford: Pergamon Press, 1988). (Hebrew edn.: **Sin'at Israel Le-Doroteha** [Jerusalem: Zalman Shazar Center for Jewish History, 1983]).

ALTER, R. "Deformations of the Holocaust," **Commentary** (February 1981), pp. 48-54.

ALTER, Y.L. "Teshuvah," in HOLTZ, B.W. (ed.), **Back to the Sources: Reading the Classic Jewish Texts** (New York: Summit Books, 1984).

ALTSHULER, D. & L. DAWIDOWICZ. **Hitler's War Against the Jews: The Holocaust** (New York: Behrman House, 1978).

AMISHAI-MAISELS, Z. "Christological Symbolism of the Holocaust," in BAUER, Y. et al, **Remembering for the Future. Volume 2: The Impact of the Holocaust on the Contemporary World** (Oxford: Pergamon Press, 1989).

—————. "The Complexities of Witnessing," **Holocaust and Genocide Studies**, vol. 2, no. 1 (1987), pp. 123-147.

—————. "Ben Shahn and the Problems of Jewish Identity," **Jewish Art** 12/13 (1986-1987), pp. 304-319.

—————. "The Use of Biblical Imagery to Interpret the Holocaust," **Ninth World Congress of Jewish Studies**, vol. 2, Division D (1985), pp. 17-24.

—————. "The Jewish Jesus," **Journal of Jewish Art** 9 (1982), pp. 84-104.

ANDRESKI, S. "An Economic Interpretation of Antisemitism in Eastern Europe," **Jewish Journal of Sociology** (December 1963), pp. 201-213.

ANGRESS, W. "The German Jews 1933-1939," in FRIEDLANDER, H. & S. MILTON (eds.), **The Holocaust: Ideology, Bureaucracy, and Genocide** (New York: Kraus, 1980).

ANONYMOUS. "The Last Song of the Jewish Community of Lublin," in BLUMENTHAL, DAVID R., **Understanding Jewish Mysticism**, vol. 2 (New York: Ktav, 1982), pp. 104-107.

ANTONOVSKY, A. et al. "Twenty Five Years Later: A Limited Study of Sequelae of the Concentration Camp Experience," **Social Psychology**, vol. 6, no. 4 (1971), pp. 186-193.

APPELFELD, A. **The Age of Wonders** (D. Bilu, transl.) (Boston: David A. Godine, 1981).

ARAD, Y. **Belzec, Sobibor, Treblinka: The Operation Reinhard Death Camps** (Bloomington: Indiana University Press, 1987).

—————. "Operation Reinhard: Extermination Camps of Belzec, Sobibor and Treblinka," **Yad Vashem Studies** XVI (1984), pp. 205-239.

—————. **Partisan: From the Valley of Death to Mount Zion** (New York: Holocaust Library, 1978).

—————. **Ghetto in Flames: The Struggle and Destruction of the Jews in Vilna in the Holocaust** (Jerusalem: Yad Vashem, 1976, 1980, 1984).

——————. "Jewish Armed Resistance in Eastern Europe - Its Characteristics and Problems, in GUTMAN, Y. & L. ROTHKIRCHEN (eds.), **The Catastrophe of European Jewry: Antecedents, History, Reflections: Selected Papers** (Jerusalem: Yad Vashem, 1976).

——————, Y. GUTMAN & A. MARGALIOT (eds.), **Documents on the Holocaust: Selected Sources on the Destruction of the Jews of Germany and Austria, Poland and the Soviet Union** (Jerusalem: Yad Vashem, 1976, 1978, 1980, 1981).

ARENDT, H. **Eichmann in Jerusalem: A Report of the Banality of Evil** (New York: Viking Press, 1963).

——————. **The Origins of Totalitarianism** (Cleveland & New York: Meridian Books, 1969).

ARIKHA, A. **Boyhood Drawings Made in Deportation** (Paris: Amis de l'Aliyah des Jeunes, 1971).

ARNHEIM, R. **Visual Thinking** (Berkeley: University of California Press, 1969).

ARON, R. "Is There a Nazi Mystery?" **Commentary** (June 1980), pp. 29-41.

ARONSFELD, C.C. **The Text of the Holocaust** (Marblehead, Mass.: Micah Publications, 1985).

ARRICK, F. **Chernowitz** (Scardale, New York: Bradbury Press, 1981).

Arte e Resistenza in Europa (Bologna: Museum Civico, 1965).

AVISAR, I. **Screening the Holocaust: Cinema's Image of the Unimaginable** (Bloomington: Indiana University Press, 1988).

AVNI, H. **Spain, the Jews, and Franco** (E. Shimoni, transl.) (Philadelphia: Jewish Publication Society, 1982).

BACON, G. "Da'at tora ve-hevlei mashiah" ("Da'at Tora" and Pre-messianic Tribulations), **Tarbiz**, vol. 52, no. 3 (1983), pp. 499-501.

BAECK, L. **This People Israel** (A.H. Friedlander, transl.) (New York: Holt & Winston, 1964; Philadelphia: Jewish Publication Society, 1965).

BANKIER, D. "Hitler and the Policy-Making Process on the Jewish Question," **Holocaust and Genocide Studies**, vol. 3, no. 1 (1988), pp. 1-20.

BARON, S.W. "The Jews of Europe Between the World Wars," in GUTMAN, Y. & L. ROTHKIRCHEN (eds.), **The Catastrophe of European Jewry: Antecedents, History, Reflections: Selected Papers** (Jerusalem: Yad Vashem, 1976).

——————. "European Jewry Before and After Hitler," **American Jewish Yearbook** 63 (1962), pp. 3-49.

BARRETT, S.R. **Is God a Racist? The Right Wing in Canada** (Toronto: University of Toronto Press, 1987).

BARTHES, R. **Aula** (Sao Paulo: Cultrix, 1971).

BAUER, Y. "Jewish Foreign Policy During the Holocaust," **Midstream** (December 1984), pp. 22-25.

———. "Jewish Survivors in DP Camps and Sh'erith Hapletah," in GUTMAN, Y. & A. SAF (eds.), **The Nazi Concentration Camps** (Jerusalem: Yad Vashem, 1984).

———. "The Place of the Holocaust in Contemporary History," **Studies in Contemporary Jewry** I (1984), pp. 201-224.

———. "The Death Marches, January-May 1945" **Modern Judaism** 3 (1983), pp. 1-23.

———. **American Jewry and the Holocaust: The American Jewish Joint Distribution Committee 1939-1945** (Detroit: Wayne State University Press, 1981).

———. "Genocide: Was It the Nazis' Original Plan?" **Annals of the American Academy of Political and Social Science** 45 (1980), pp. 35-45.

———. "Whose Holocaust?" **Midstream** (November 1980), pp. 42-46.

———. **The Jewish Emergence from Powerlessness** (Toronto: University of Toronto Press, 1979).

———. **The Holocaust in Historical Perspective** (Seattle: University of Washington Press, 1978).

———. "Tguvoteha shel ha-manhigut ha-yehudit li-mediniyut ha-natzim" (Reactions of the Jewish Leadership to Nazi Policies), **Yalkut Moreshet** 20 (December 1975), pp. 109-125.

———. **They Choose Life: Jewish Resistance in the Holocaust** (New York: American Jewish Committee, Institute of Human Relations, 1973).

———. "When Did They Know?" **Midstream** (April 1968), pp. 51-58.

——— et al (eds.). **Remembering for the Future**, 3 vols. (Oxford: Pergamon Press, 1989).

——— & N. KEREN. **A History of the Holocaust** (New York & London: Franklin Watts, 1982).

——— & N. ROTENSTREICH (eds.). **The Holocaust as Historical Experience** (New York: Holmes & Meier, 1981).

BAUM, G. **Christian Theology After Auschwitz** (London: Council of Christians and Jews, 1976).

BAUM, R.C. **The Holocaust and the German Elite: Genocide and National Suicide in Germany 1871-1945** (Totowa, NJ: Rowman & Littlefield, 1981).

BECKER, C.L. "What is Evidence?" in WINTER, R. (ed.), **The Historian as Detective: Essays on Evidence** (New York: Harper & Row, 1970).

BECKER, J. **Jacob the Liar** (New York: A Helen & Kurt Wolff Book, 1975).

BELOFF, M. (ed.). **On the Track of Tyranny** (London: published for the Wiener Library, by Vallentine, Mitchell, 1960).

BEN YOSEF, I. "Jewish Religious Response to the Holocaust," **The Journal of Religion, Southern Africa** (January 1987).

BENCHLEY, N. **Bright Candles: A Novel of the Danish Resistance** (London: Andre Deutsch, 1976).

BENTLEY, E. (ed.). **The Storm Over "The Deputy"** (New York: Grove Press, 1964).

BENVENUTI, A. **KZ** (Treviso: Trivigiana, 1983).

BERBEN, P. **Histoire du Camp de Concentration de Dachau 1933-1945** (Brussels: Comite Internationale de Dachau, 1976).

BERENBAUM, M. **The Vision of the Void: Theological Reflections on the Works of Elie Wiesel** (Middletown, Conn.: Wesleyan University, 1979).

——————. "Elie Wiesel and Contemporary Jewish Theology," **Conservative Judaism** (Spring 1976), pp. 19-39.

BERG, M. **The Warsaw Ghetto** (S.L. Schneiderman, ed.) (New York: L.B. Fisher, 1945).

BERGER, A.L. **Crisis and Covenant: The Holocaust in American Jewish Fiction** (Albany: State University of New York Press, 1985).

BERKOVITS, E. **With God in Hell: Judaism in the Ghettos and Death Camps** (New York: Sanhedrin Press, 1979).

——————. "Approaching the Holocaust," **Judaism** (Winter 1973), pp. 18-20.

——————. **Faith After the Holocaust** (New York: Ktav Publishing House, 1973).

BERNSTEIN, S. **Le Nazisme** (Paris: MA Ed., 1985).

BETCHERMAN, L.-R. **The Swastika and the Maple Leaf: Fascist Movements in Canada in the Thirties** (Toronto: Fitzhenry & Whiteside, 1975).

BETTELHEIM, B. **Surviving and Other Essays** (London: Thames & Hudson, 1979).

——————. **The Informed Heart: Autonomy in a Mass Age** (New York: Avon, 1971).

——————. "Individual and Mass Behavior in Extreme Situations," **Journal of Abnormal and Social Psychology** (October 1943).

BEYERCHEIN, A.D. **Scientists Under Hitler** (New Haven: Yale University Press, 1977).

A Biblia de Jerusalem (Sao Paulo: Ed. Paulinas, 1985).

Bilder sind nicht verboten (Dusseldorf: Staedtische Kunsthalle, 1984).

BLATTER, J. & S. MILTON. **Art of the Holocaust** (New York: Routledge, 1981).

BLEEKER, C. & G. WIDENGREN (eds.). **Historia Religionum** (Leiden: E.J. Brill, 1971).

BLIKSTEIN, I. **Kaspar Hauser ou a Fabricacao da Realidade** (Sao Paulo: Cultrix, 1985).

BLOOM, S. "Dictator of the Lodz Ghetto: The Strange History of Mordechai Chaim Rumkowski," **Commentary** 7 (1949), pp. 111-122.

BLUMENTHAL, D.R. **Understanding Jewish Mysticism: The Merkabah Tradition and the Zoharic Tradition** (New York: Ktav Publishing House, 1978. The Library of Jewish Learning; v. 2 2,4).

BLUMENTHAL, N. **Conduct and Actions of a Judenrat: Documents from the Bialystok Ghetto** (Jerusalem: Yad Vashem, 1962).

BOAS, J. "Germany or Diaspora? German Jewry's Shifting Perceptions in the Nazi Era 1933-1938," **Leo Baeck Institute Yearbook** 27 (1982), pp. 109-126.

BOLKOVSKY, S.M. **Distorted Image: German Jewish Perceptions of Germans and Germany 1918-1935** (Amsterdam: Elsevier, 1975).

BORGES, J.L. "Deutsches Requium," in YATES, D.A. & J.E. IRBY (eds.), **Labyrinths, Selected Stories and Other Writings** (New York: New Directions, 1964).

BORKIN, J. **The Crime and Punishment of I.G. Farben** (London: Andre Deutsch, 1979).

BOROWSKI, T. **This Way to the Gas, Ladies and Gentlemen** (New York: Penguin, 1976).

BORZYKOWSKI, T. **Between Tumbling Walls** (M. Kottansky, transl.) (Tel Aviv: Kibbutz Lohamei Hagettaot [Ghetto Fighters' House], 1972).

BOWER, T. **The Pledge Betrayed (Blind Eye to Murder)** (Garden City, New York: Doubleday, 1982).

BRACHER, K.D. **German Dictatorship: The Origins, Structure and Effects of National Socialism** (New York: Praeger, 1970).

BRAHAM, R.L. (ed.). **Jewish Leadership During the Nazi Era** (New York: Social Science Monographs, 1985).

—————————. "What Did They Know and When?" in BAUER, Y. & N. ROTENSTREICH (eds.), **The Holocaust as Historical Experience** (New York: Holmes & Meier, 1981).

—————————. **The Politics of Genocide: The Holocaust in Hungary** (2 vols.) (New York: Columbia University Press, 1980).

—————————. "The Jewish Question in German-Hungarian Relations During the Kallay Era," **Jewish Social Studies** 39 (1977), pp. 183-208.

BRAND, J. **Desperate Mission** (As told by A. Weissberg) (New York: Criterion Books, 1958).

BRAND, S. **Between Two Worlds** (New York: Shengold, 1983).

BRENNER, R.R. **The Faith and Doubt of Holocaust Survivors** (New York: Free Press, 1980).

BROSZAT, M. "Hitler and the Genesis of the 'Final Solution': An Assessment of David Irvin's Theses," **Yad Vashem Studies** XIII (1979), pp. 73-125.

—————————. "The Concentration Camps 1933-1945," in KRAUSNICK, H. et al. (eds.), **Anatomy of the S.S. State** (New York: Walker, 1968).

BROWDER, G.C. "Die Anfang des SD. Dokumente aus der Organisations berichte des Reichsfuehrer SS," **Vierteljahreshefte fuer Zeitgeschichte**, vol. 27, no. 2 (1979), pp. [299]-324.

BROWN, R.M. **Eli Wiesel: Messenger to All Humanity** (Notre Dame: University of Notre Dame Press, 1983).

BROWNING, C.R. "Nazi Resettlement Policy and the Search for a Solution to the Jewish Question 1939-1941," **German Studies Review** IX (1986), pp. 497-517.

———————. **Fateful Months: Essays on the Emergence of the Final Solution** (New York: Holmes & Meier, 1985).

———————. **The Final Solution and the German Foreign Office: A Study of Referat DIII of Abteilung Deutschland 1940-1943** (New York: Holmes & Meier, 1978).

BRUGIONI, D. & R. POIRER. "The Holocaust Revisited," U.S. Central Intelligence Agency Report (Washington, D.C.: Central Intelligence Agency, 1979).

BUBER, M. **I and Thou** (R.G. Smith, transl.) (Edinburgh: T & T Clark, 1971).

———————. **Eclipse of God: Studies in the Relation Between Religion and Philosophy** (Brighton: Harvester Press, 1979).

BUCHHEIM, H. **Totalitarian Rule** (R. Hein, transl.) (Middletown: Wesleyan University Press, 1983).

BULLOCK, A. **Hitler: A Study in Tyranny** (London: Pelican Books, 1969).

VAN BUREN, P.M. "Ecclesia Semper Reformanda: The Challenge of Israel," in LIBOWITZ, R. (ed.), **Faith and Freedom: A Tribute to Franklin H. Littell** (Oxford: Pergamon Press, 1987).

———————. **Discerning the Way: A Theology of the Jewish-Christian Reality** (New York: Seabury Press, 1980).

BUYSSENS, E. **Semiologia e Comunicacao Linguistica** (Sao Paulo: Cultrix, 1982).

CAIN, S. "The Holocaust and Christian Responsibility," **Midstream** (April 1982), pp. 20-27.

CAPLAN, N. **Like One That Dreamed: A Portrait of A.M. Klein** (Toronto: McGraw-Hill, Ryerson, 1982).

CARGAS, H.J. **A Christian Response to the Holocaust** (Denver: Stongehenge Books, 1981).

CARPI, D. "The Rescue of Jews in the Italian Zone of Occupied Croatia," in GUTMAN, Y. & C. HAFT (eds.), **Patterns of Jewish Leadership in Nazi Europe 1933-1945** (Jerusalem: Yad Vashem, 1979).

———————. "The Catholic Church and Italian Jewry under the Fascists," **Yad Vashem Studies** IV (1960), pp. 43-54.

CARSTEN, F.L. **Revolution in Central Europe 1918-1919** (London: Temple Smith, 1972).

CHADWICK, O. **Britain and the Vatican during the Second World War** (Cambridge: Cambridge University Press, 1986).

——————. "Weizsaecker, the Vatican, and the Jews of Rome," **Journal of Ecclesiastical History** 28 (1977), pp. 179-199.

CHARY, F.B. **The Bulgarian Jews and the Final Solution 1940-1944** (Pittsburgh: Pittsburgh University Press, 1972).

CHASE, A. **The Legacy of Malthus** (Chicago: University of Illinois Press, 1980).

CHAZAN, R. **European Jewry and the First Crusade** (Berkeley: University of California Press, 1987).

—————— & M.L. RAPHAEL. **Modern Jewish History: A Source Reader** (New York: Schocken, 1975).

CIMENT, M. "Joy to the World! An Interview with Marcel Ophuls," **American Film** (September 1988).

COHEN, A.A. **The Myth of the Judeo-Christian Tradition** (New York: Schocken, 1969).

COHEN, L. **Flowers for Hitler** (London: J. Cape, 1973).

——————. **Let Us Compare Mythologies** (Toronto: Contact Press, 1956).

COHEN, R. **Burden of Conscience: French Jewry's Response to the Holocaust** (Bloomington: Indiana University Press, 1987).

—————— "The Jewish Community of France in the Face of Vichy-German Persecution 1940-1944," in MALINO, F. & B. WASSERSTEIN (eds.), **The Jews in Modern France** (Hanover [NH]: Published for Brandeis University by: University Press of New England, Tauber Institute Series 4, 1985).

——————. "A Jewish Leader in Vichy France 1940-1943: The Diary of Raymond-Raoul Lambert," **Jewish Social Studies** 43 (1981), pp. 291-310.

COHEN, Y. "Dat u-moledet: le-darka shel ha-konsistoriya ha-merkazit be-tzarfat bi-tkufat milhemet ha-olam ha-sheniya" (Religion and Fatherland: The Central Consistory in France during the Second World War), in ALMOG, S. et al (eds.), **Bein Yisrael La-umot** (Israel and the Nations: Essays Presented in Honor of Shmuel Ettinger) (Jerusalem: Mercaz Zalman Shazar, 1987).

COHN, N. **Warrant for Genocide: The Myth of the Jewish World Conspiracy and the Protocols of the Elders of Zion** (New York: Harper & Row, 1969).

COLLINS, R.G. (ed.). **From an Ancient to a Modern Theatre** (Winnipeg: University of Manitoba Press, 1972).

CONOT, R. **Justice at Nuremberg** (London: Weidenfeld & Nicolson, 1983).

CONSERIU, E. **El Hombre y su Lenguaje** (Madrid: Gredos, 1977).

CONSTANZA, M.S. **The Living Witness: Art in the Concentration Camps and Ghettos** (New York: Free Press, 1982).

Control Council Law No. 10, 24 January 1946. History of the United Nations War Crimes Commission and the Development of the Laws of War (London: Published for the United Nations War Crimes Commission, 1948), p. 576.

CONWAY, J. "Records and Documents of the Holy See Relating to the Second World War," Yad Vashem XV (1983), pp. 327-345.

——————. "Between Apprehension and Indifference: Allied Attitudes to the Destruction of Hungarian Jewry," Wiener Library Bulletin XXVII (1973/74), pp. 37-48.

COWETT, A.J. "Casework Elements in Dealing with Job Refusals by Newcomers," Jewish Social Service Quarterly (June 1952), pp. 428-433.

CRANKSHAW, E. The Gestapo (London: Putnam, 1956).

CRYSTAL, D. The Displaced Person and the Social Agency (New York: United HIAS Service, 1958).

CZERNIAKOW, A. The Warsaw Diary of Adam Czerniakow: Prelude to Doom (R. Hilberg et al., eds.) (New York: Stein & Day, 1979).

DANIELI, Y. "On the Achievement of Integration in Aging Survivors of the Holocaust," Journal of Geriatric Psychiatry, vol. 14, no. 2 (1982), pp. 191-210.

DAVID, C. Hitler et le Nazisme (Paris: PUF, 1979).

DAVID, J. A Square of Sky and a Touch of Earth (New York: Penguin, 1981).

DAVIE, M.R. "Immigration and Refugee Aid," American Jewish Yearbook 50 (1948/49), pp. 223-236.

DAVIES, A.J. Anti-Semitism and the Foundations of Christianity (New York: Paulist Press, 1979).

DAWIDOWICZ, L. The Holocaust and the Historians (Cambridge, Mass.: Harvard University Press, 1986).

——————. A Holocaust Reader (New York: Behrman House, 1976).

——————. The War Against the Jews 1933-1945 (New York: Holt, Rinehart & Winston, 1975).

—————— (ed.). The Golden Tradition: Jewish Life and Thought in Eastern Europe (New York: Holt, Rinehart & Winston, 1967).

——————. "Visualizing the Warsaw Ghetto: Nazi Images of the Jews Refiltered by the BBC," Shoah: A Review of Holocaust Studies and Commemorations, vol. I, no. 1 (1978), p. 6.

DE JONG, L. "Jews and Non-Jews in Occupied Holland," in BELOFF, M. (ed.), On the Track of Tyranny (London: published for Wiener Library, by Vallentine, Mitchell, 1960).

DEKEMJIAN, R.H., in HOVANNISIAN, R. (ed.), The Armenian Genocide in Perspective (New Brunswick: Transaction Books, 1986).

DELARBRE, L. **Dora, Auschwitz, Buchenwald, Bergen-Belsen, Croquis Clandestins** (Paris: Michel de Romilly, 1945).

DERSHOWITZ, A. "The Verdict," **American Film** (December 1987).

DES PRES, T. "The Bettelheim Problem," **Social Research** (Winter 1979), pp. 619-647.

——————. **The Survivor: Anatomy of Life in the Death Camps** (New York: Pocket Books, 1976).

DICKS, H.V. **Licensed Mass Murder** (London: Chatto-Heinemann for Sussex University Press, 1972).

DINNERSTEIN, L. **America and the Survivors of the Holocaust** (New York: Columbia University Press, 1982).

DISTEL, B. **Le Camp de Concentration de Dachau** (Brussels: Comite Internationale de Dachau, 1972).

—————— & R. JAKUSCH (eds.). **Concentration Camp Dachau 1933-1945** (Brussels: Comite Internationale de Dachau, 1978).

DOBKOWSKI, Y.N. & I. WALLIMANN. **Towards the Holocaust: The Social and Economic Collapse of the Weimar Republic** (Westpoint, CT: Greenwood Press, 1983).

DOBROSZYCKI, L. (ed.). **The Chronicle of the Lodz Ghetto** (New Haven: Yale University Press, 1984).

DONAT, A. (ed.). **The Death Camp at Treblinka** (New York: Holocaust Library, 1979, 1980).

——————. **The Holocaust Kingdom: A Memoir** (New York: Holt, Reinhart & Winston, 1965; Holocaust Library, 1982).

DONESON, J.E. **The Holocaust in American Film** (Philadelphia: Jewish Publication Society of America, 1987).

DRUKS, H. (ed.). **Jewish Resistance during the Holocaust** (Jerusalem: 1971).

DUBNOW, S. **History of the Jews in Russia and Poland**, 5 vols. (New York: A.S. Barnes, 1967-73).

——————. **Nationalism and History** (Philadelphia: Jewish Publication Society, 1958).

DVORKJETSKI, M. "The Day to Day Stand of the Jews," in DRUKS, H. (ed.), **Jewish Resistance during the Holocaust** (Jerusalem: Yad Vashem, 1971).

ECKARDT, A.L. "The Holocaust, the Church Struggle and Some Christian Reflections," in LIBOWITZ, R. (ed.), **Faith and Freedom: A Tribute to Franklin H. Littell** (Oxford: Pergamon Press, 1987).

——————. "Post-Holocaust Theology: A Journey Out of the Kingdom of Night," **Holocaust and Genocide Studies**, vol. 1, no. 2 (1986), pp. 229-240.

—————— & A.R. ECKHARDT. "Studying the Holocaust's Impact Today: Some Dilemmas of Language and Method," **Judaism** (Spring 1978), pp. 502-505.

ECKARDT, A.R. **For Righteousness Sake: Contemporary Moral Philosophies** (Bloomington: Indiana University Press, 1987).

—————— & A.L. ECKHARDT. **Long Night's Journey into Day** (Detroit: Wayne State University Press, 1982).

ECO, U. **Tratado de Semiotica General** (Barcelona: Lumen, 1977).

ELEY, G. "Holocaust History," **London Review of Books** (3-16 March 1983).

ELIACH, Y. **Hasidic Tales of the Holocaust: The First Original Hasidic Tales in a Century** (New York: Oxford University Press, 1982).

ELON, A. **Timetable** (London: Hutchinson, 1981).

Encyclopedia Judaica, 16 vols. (Jerusalem: Keter, 1972).

Encyclopedia of the Holocaust, Y. GUTMAN (ed.-in-chief) (Jerusalem: Yad Vashem, 1990).

ENGEL, D. **In the Shadow of Auschwitz: The Polish Government-in-Exile and the Jews** (Chapel Hill: University of North Carolina Press, 1987).

——————. "The Western Allies and the Holocaust," **Polin** I (1986), pp. 300-315.

ENGLEMANN, B. **In Hitler's Germany** (New York: Pantheon Books, 1986).

Entziklopedia lemada-ei ha-hevra (Encyclopedia of the Social Sciences) (Merhavia: Sifriat Hapoalim, 1962; Tel Aviv, 1967).

EPSTEIN, H. **Children of the Holocaust** (New York: Putnam, 1979).

——————. "A Study in American Pluralism Through Oral Histories of Holocaust Survivors," (New York: Wiener Oral History Library of the American Jewish Committee, 1975).

ESH, S. "The Dignity of the Destroyed: Towards a Definition of the Period of the Holocaust," in GUTMAN, Y. & L. ROTHKIRCHEN (eds.), **The Catastrophe of European Jewry: Antecedents, History, Reflections: Selected Papers** (Jerusalem: Yad Vashem, 1976).

——————. "Holiness of Life in the Destruction," in GUTMAN, Y. & L. ROTHKIRCHEN (eds.), **The Catastrophe of European Jewry: Antecedents, History, Reflections: Selected papers** (Jerusalem: Yad Vashem, 1976).

ETTINGER, S. "Jew-Hatred in Its Historical Context," **Immanuel** (Fall 1980).

——————. "The Origins of Modern Anti-Semitism," in GUTMAN, Y. & L. ROTHKIRCHEN (eds.), **The Catastrophe of European Jewry: Antecedents, History, Reflections: Selected Papers** (Jerusalem: Yad Vashem, 1976).

EZRAHI, S. **Not By Words Alone: The Holocaust in Literature** (Chicago: University of Chicago Press, 1980).

FACKENHEIM, E.L. "Holocaust and Weltanschauung: Philosophical Reflections on Why They Did It," **Holocaust and Genocide Studies**, vol. 3, no. 2 (1988), pp. 191-208.

—————. "Foreword," in BAUER, Y., **The Jewish Emergence from Powerlessness** (London: Macmillan, 1980).

—————. **The Jewish Return into History: Reflections in the Age of Auschwitz and a New Jerusalem** (New York: Schocken, 1978).

—————. **God's Presence in History: Jewish Affirmations and Philosophical Reflections** (New York: Harper & Row, 1972).

—————. "Jewish Faith and the Holocaust," **Commentary** (August 1968), pp. 30-36.

FARGION, L.P. "The Anti-Jewish Policy of the Italian Social Republic," **Yad Vashem Studies XVII** (1986), pp. 17-49.

FAVIER, A. & P. MANIA. **Buchenwald, Scenes Pris sur le Vif des Horreurs Nazis** (Lyon: Imprimerie Artistique en Couleur, 1946).

FEIG, K.G. **Hitler's Death Camps: The Sanity of Madness** (New York: Holmes & Meier, 1981).

FEIN, H. **Accounting for Genocide: National Responses and Jewish Victimization during the Holocaust** (New York: Free Press, 1984).

—————. "Socio-Political Responses during the Holocaust," in SHERWIN, B. & S. AMENT (eds.), **Encountering the Holocaust: An Interdisciplinary Survey** (Chicago: Impact Press, 1979).

FEINBERG, N. "Jewish Political Activities Against the Nazi Regime in the Years 1933-1939," in DRUKS, H. (ed.), **Jewish Resistance during the Holocaust** (Jerusalem: Yad Vashem, 1971).

FEINGOLD, H.L. **Did American Jewry Do Enough during the Holocaust?** (New York: Syracuse University Press, 1985).

—————. **The Politics of Rescue: The Roosevelt Administration and the Holocaust** (New Brunswick: Rutgers University Press, 1970).

FENSTER, M. "The Nitra Rav," **Present Tense** (Summer 1985), pp. 26-29.

FENYO, M. **Hitler, Horthy, and Hungary: German-Hungarian Relations 1941-1944** (New Haven: Yale University Press, 1972).

FERENCZ, B. **Less Than Slaves: Jewish Forced Labor and the Quest for Compensation** (Cambridge, Mass.: Harvard University Press, 1979).

FERRO, M. **Cinema et Histoire** (Paris: Denoel/Gontier, 1977).

FIORENZA, E. & D. TRACEY. **The Holocaust as Interruption** (Edinburgh: T & T Clark, 1984).

FISHER, E. "Theological Education and Christian-Jewish Relations," in GARBER, Z. (ed.), **Methodology in the Academic Teaching of Judaism** (Lanham: University Press of America, 1988).

FISHMAN, J.A. (ed.). **Studies in Modern Jewish Social History** (New York: Ktav Publishing House, YIVO Institute for Jewish Research, 1972).

FLEISCHNER, E. (ed.). **Auschwitz: Beginning of a New Era?** (New York: Ktav Publishing House, 1977).

FLEMING, G. **Hitler and the Final Solution** (Berkeley: University of California Press, 1982).

FLENDER, H. **Rescue in Denmark** (New York: MacFadden, 1964).

FLINKER, M. **Young Moshe's Diary: The Spiritual Torment of a Jewish Boy in Nazi Europe** (Jerusalem & New York: Board of Jewish Education, 1965).

FORSTER, J. "The Wehrmacht and the War of Extermination Against the Soviet Union," **Yad Vashem Studies XIV** (1981), pp. 7-34 and in HIRSCHFELD, G. (ed.), **The Policies of Genocide: Jews and Soviet Prisoners of War in Nazi Germany** (London: Allen & Unwin, 1986).

FOUCAULT, M. **Discipline and Punish: Birth of the Prison** (A. Sheridan, transl.) (Harmondsworth: Penguin, 1979).

FOX, J. "The Holocaust: A Non-Unique Event for All Humanity," in BAUER, Y. et al. (eds.), **Remembering for the Future**, Vol. 2 (Oxford: Pergamon Press, 1989).

FRANK, A. **The Diary of a Young Girl** (New York: Pocket Books, 1965).

FRANKL, V.E. **Man's Search for Meaning** (Boston: Beacon Books, 1968).

FRANKLE, H. "The Survivor as a Parent," **Journal of Jewish Communal Service** (Spring 1978), pp. 241-246.

FREUD, S. **Group Psychology and the Analysis of the Ego** (New York & London: W.W. Norton & Co., 1959).

FRIEDLANDER, A. **Out of the Whirlwind: A Reader of Holocaust Literature** (New York: Schocken, 1976).

FRIEDLANDER, H. "The Trials of the Nazi Criminals: Law, Justice and History," **Dimensions: A Journal of Holocaust Studies**, vol. 2, no. 1 (1986), pp. 4-10.

——————. "The Deportation of the German Jews: Postwar Trials of Nazi Criminals," **Leo Baeck Institute Yearbook XXIX** (1984), pp. 201-226.

——————. "The Judiciary and Nazi Crimes in Postwar Germany," **Simon Wiesenthal Center Annual** 1 (1984), pp. 27-44.

—————— & E. MCCARRICK. "The Extradition of Nazi Criminals: Ryan, Artukovic, Demjanjuk," **Simon Wiesenthal Center Annual** 4 (1987), pp. 65-98.

—————— & E. MCCARRICK. "Nazi Criminals in the United States: Denaturalization after Fedorenko," **Simon Wiesenthal Center Annual** 3 (1986), pp. 47-85.

—————— & E. MCCARRICK. "Nazi Criminals in the United States: The Fedorenko Case," **Simon Wiesenthal Center Annual** 2 (1985), pp. 63-93.

——————— & S. MILTON (eds.). **The Holocaust: Ideology, Bureaucracy, and Genocide: The San Jose Papers** (New York: Kraus, 1980).

FRIEDLANDER, S. "From Antisemitism to Extermination: A Historiographical Study of Nazi Policies toward the Jews and an Essay in Interpretation," **Yad Vashem Studies** XVI (1984), pp. 1-50.

———————. **When Memory Comes** (New York: Farrar, Straus & Giroux, 1979).

———————. "Some Aspects of the Historical Significance of the Holocaust," **The Jerusalem Quarterly** (Fall 1976), pp. 36-59.

———————. "The Historical Meaning of the Holocaust," **Molad** 1 (1975), pp. 33-34.

———————. **Pius XII and the Third Reich** (New York: Jewish Publication Society, 1966).

FRIEDMAN, P. **Roads to Extermination: Essays on the Holocaust** (Philadelphia: Jewish Publication Society, 1980).

———————. **Their Brother's Keepers** (New York: Crown Publishers, 1957).

———————. "The Road Back for the DPs: Healing the Psychological Scars of Nazism," **Commentary** (December 1948), pp. 502-510.

———————. "Jewish Resistance during the Holocaust: Forms and Aspects," in GUTMAN, Y. & L. ROTHKIRCHEN (eds.), **The Catastrophe of European Jewry: Antecedents, History, Reflections: Selected Papers** (Jerusalem: Yad Vashem, 1976).

———————. "Two 'Saviors' Who Failed: Moses Merin of Sosnowiec and Jacob Gens of Vilna," **Commentary** 26 (1958), pp. 479-491.

FRIEDMAN, S. **No Haven for the Oppressed** (Detroit: Wayne State University Press, 1973).

FRIEDRICH, O. "The Kingdom of Auschwitz," **The Atlantic** (September 1981), pp. 30-60.

FROMM, E. **The Anatomy of Human Destructiveness** (Greenwich: Fawcett, 1973).

FROMMHOLD, E. **Kunst im Widerstand** (Dresden: VEB, 1968).

GARBER, Z. "Auschwitz: The Real Problem," **Israel Today** (April 1988).

———————. "Blood and Thunder: Israel under Siege," **Israel Today** (March 1988).

———————. "Triumph on the Gallows," **Israel Today** (August 1987).

——————— (ed.). **Methodology in the Academic Teaching of Judaism** (Lanham: University Press of America, 1986/87).

———————. "Sinai and not Cyanide: Witness and not Survivor," remarks given at the Utah State Capitol Rotunda on 19 April 1985, in conjunction with the Governor's proclamation of Holocaust Memorial Week 1985.

———————, A.L. BERGER & R. LIBOWITZ (eds.). **Methodology in the Academic Teaching of the Holocaust** (Lanham: University Press of America, 1988).

——————— & B. ZUCKERMAN. "Why Do We Call the Holocaust 'the Holocaust'? An Inquiry into the Psychology of Labels," in BAUER, Y. et al (eds.), **Remembering for the Future**, Vol. 2 (Oxford: Pergamon Press, 1989).

GARLINSKI, J. **Fighting Auschwitz** (New York: Fawcett, 1971).

GASCAR, P. **Le Temps des Morts** (Paris: Gallimard, 1953).

GAY, P. **Freud, Jews and Other Germans: Masters and Victims in Modernist Culture** (New York: Oxford University Press, 1978).

———————. "German Jews in Wilhelmian Culture," **Midstream** (February 1975).

———————. **The Berlin Jewish Spirit** (New York: Leo Baeck Institute, 1972).

———————. **Weimar Culture: The Outsider as Insider** (Harmondsworth: Penguin, 1974).

GIBB, C.A. "Leadership," in LINDZEY, G. & E. ARONSON (eds.), **The Handbook of Social Psychology**, Vol. 4 (London: Addison-Wesley, 1969).

GILBERT, M. **Atlas of the Holocaust** (Oxford: Pergamon Press, 1988).

———————. **Auschwitz and the Allies** (New York: Holt, Rinehart & Winston, 1981).

———————. **Final Journey: The Fate of the Jews in Nazi Europe** (London: G. Allen & Unwin, 1979).

———————. **The Holocaust** (New York: Hill & Wang, 1978).

———————. "The Question of Bombing Auschwitz," in GUTMAN, Y. & A. SAF (eds.), **The Nazi Concentration Camps** (Jerusalem: Yad Vashem, 1974, 1984).

GILBOA, Y. **The Black Years of Soviet Jewry** (Y. Shachter & D. Ben-Abba, transl.) (Boston: Little, Brown, 1971).

GLATSTEIN, J. (ed.). **Anthology of Holocaust Literature** (Philadelphia: Jewish Publication Society of America, 1977).

GLICK, I.O., R.S. WEISS & C.M. PARKES. **The First Year of Bereavement** (New York: Wiley, 1974).

GLICKSMAN, W. "Social Differentiation in the German Concentration Camps," in FISHMAN, J.A. (ed.), **Studies in Modern Jewish Social History** (New York: Ktav Publishing House; YIVO Institute for Jewish Research, 1972).

GOBINEAU, Count A. de. **The Inequality of the Races** (1854) (transl. from French) (Brighton: Historical Review Press, 1980).

GOLDHAFT, A. **The Golden Egg** (New York: Horizon Press, 1957).

GOLDSTEIN, B. **The Stars Bear Witness** (New York: Viking, 1949).

GOPNIK, A. "Comics and Catastrophe," **The New Republic** (22 June 1987).

GORDON, S. **Hitler, Germans, and the "Jewish Question"** (Princeton: Princeton University Press, 1984).

GRAUBART, J. "The Vatican and the Jews: Cynicism and Indifference," **Judaism** 24 (Spring 1975), pp. 168-180.

GRAY, M. **For Those I Loved** (A. White, transl.) (London: The Bodley Head, 1973).

GREEN, G. **The Artists of Terezin** (New York: Hawthorn, 1969).

GREENBERG, I. "Religious Values After the Holocaust," in PECK, A.J. (ed.), **Jews and Christians After the Holocaust** (Philadelphia: Fortress, 1982).

——————. "Cloud of Smoke, Pillar of Fire: Judaism, Christianity and Modernity After the Holocaust," in FLEISCHNER, E. (ed.), **Auschwitz: Beginning of a New Era?** (New York: Ktav Publishing House, 1977).

GREENE, B. **The Summer of My German Soldier** (London: Hamish Hamilton, 1974).

GREIMAS, A.J. **Semantique Structurale** (Paris: Larousse, 1977).

GROBMAN, A. "What Did They Know? The American Jewish Press and the Holocaust," **American Jewish History** LXVIII (1979), pp. 327-352.

—————— & LANDES, D. (eds.). **Genocide** (Los Angeles & New York: 1983).

GROPPER, W. **Your Brother's Blood Cries Out** (New York: New Masses, 1943).

GROSSMAN, M. **With a Camera in the Ghetto** (New York: Schocken, 1978).

GRUBER, S. **I Chose Life** (G. HIRSCHLER, ed.) (New York: Shengold, 1978).

GUTFERSTEIN, J. "The Indestructible Dignity of Man," **Judaism**, vol. 19, no. 3 (1970), pp. 262-263.

GUTMAN, Y. **Fighters Among the Ruins: The Story of Jewish Heroism During World War II** (Washington: B'nai B'rith Books, 1988).

—————— (ed.). **Jewish Leadership Under Nazi Occupation** (Jerusalem: Yad Vashem, 1980).

——————. **The Jews of Warsaw 1939-1943: Ghetto, Underground, Revolt** (Bloomington: Indiana University Press, 1982).

——————. "Polish Responses to the Liquidation of Warsaw Jewry," **Jerusalem Quarterly** 17 (Fall 1980), pp. 40-55.

—————— & G. GREIFF (eds.). **Ha-shoa ba-historiografia** (The Historiography of the Holocaust Period) (Jerusalem: Yad Vashem, 1987, 1989).

—————— & C.J. HAFT (eds.). **Patterns of Jewish Leadership in Nazi Europe 1933-1945** (Jerusalem: Yad Vashem, 1979).

—————— & L. ROTHKIRCHEN (eds.). **The Catastrophe of European Jewry: Antecedents, History, Reflections: Selected Papers** (Jerusalem: Yad Vashem, 1976).

—————— & A. SAF (eds.). **The Nazi Concentration Camps** (Jerusalem: Yad Vashem, 1974, 1984).

—————— & E. ZUROFF (eds.). **Rescue Attempts during the Holocaust** (Jerusalem: Yad Vashem, 1977).

GUTTERIDGE, R. **Open Thy Mouth for the Dumb: The German Evangelical Church and the Jews 1879-1950** (Oxford: Basil Blackwell, 1976).

GUYOT, A. & P. RESTELLINI. L'Art Nazi (Brussels: Ed. Complexe, 1988).

Ha-entziklopedia ha-ivrit (Encyclopedia Hebraica) (Tel Aviv & Jerusalem: 1953).

HAFTMANN, W. Banned and Persecuted (Cologne: Dumont, 1986).

HALL, E. The Silent Language (New York: Anchor Books, 1973).

HALLIE, P.P. Lest Innocent Blood Be Shed: The Story of the Village of Le Chambon and How Goodness Happened There (London: Michael Joseph, 1979).

HALPERIN, I. "Teaching the Holocaust by Indirection," Judaism 140, vol. 35 (Fall 1986), pp. 441-446.

HALPERN, B. "Antisemitism in the Perspective of Jewish History, in STEMBER, C. et al. (eds.), Jews in the Mind of America (New York: Basic Books, 1966).

——————. "Reactions to Antisemitism in Modern Jewish History," in REINHARZ, J. (ed.), Living with Antisemitism: The Jewish Response in the Modern Period (Hanover & London: University Press of New England, 1987).

——————. "What is Anti-Semitism?" Modern Judaism, vol. 1, no. 3 (1981), pp. 251-262.

HANDLER, A. (ed.). The Holocaust in Hungary (Alabama: University of Alabama Press, 1982).

HANDLIN, O. "Jewish Resistance to the Nazis," Commentary 34 (1962), pp. 398-405.

HARTMAN, D. & A. HALKIN (eds.). Crisis and Leadership: Epistles of Maimonides (Philadelphia: Jewish Publication Society of America, 1985).

HAUSNER, G. Justice in Jerusalem (New York: Shocken, 1970).

HAUTZIG, E. The Endless Steppe (London: Heinemann Education, 1973).

HAYES, J. The Art of Graham Sutherland (New York: Alpine Fine Arts, 1980).

HAYES, P. Industry and Ideology: I.G. Farben in the Nazi Era (Cambridge: Cambridge University Press, 1987).

HEIMLER, E. Concentration Camp (London: Corgi, 1979).

HELLER, C.S. On the Edge of Destruction: Jews of Poland Between the Two World Wars (New York: Columbia University Press, 1977).

HELLIG, J. "Richard L. Rubinstein: Theologian of the Holocaust," Proceedings of the Seventh Judaica Conference, University of the Witwatersrand, 1984.

HELLMAN, P. (ed.). The Auschwitz Album (New York: Holocaust Publications, 1987).

HELMREICH, W.B. "The Impact of Holocaust Survivors on American Society: A Socio-Cultural Portrait," in BAUER, Y. et al, Remembering for the Future, vol. 1 (Oxford: Pergamon Press, 1989).

——————. "Postwar Adaptation of Holocaust Survivors in the United States," Holocaust and Genocide Studies, vol. 2, no. 2 (1987), pp. 307-315.

HELPRIN, M. "Tamar," in Ellis Island and Other Stories (New York: Dell, 1981).

HERSEY, J. **The Wall** (St. Albans: Panther, 1979).

HIDDEN, J. & J. FARQUHARSON (eds.). **Explaining Hitler's Germany: Historians and the Third Reich** (London: Batsford Academic & Educational, 1983).

HILBERG, R. "Is It History or is It Drama?" **New York Times** (13 December 1987).

——————— (ed.). **Documents of Destruction: Germany and Jewry 1933-1945** (Chicago: Quadrangle Books, 1971).

———————. "The Ghetto as a Form of Government: An Analysis of Isaiah Trunk's **Judenrat**," in BAUER, Y. & N. ROTENSTREICH (eds.), **The Holocaust as Historical Experience** (New York: Holmes & Meier, 1981); in Hebrew, **Yalkut Moreshet** 20 (December 1975), pp. 89-103.

———————. **The Destruction of European Jews**, 3 vols., rev. edn. (New York: Holmes & Meier, 1985).

HILL, L. "History and Rolf Hochhuth's **The Deputy**," in COLLINS, R.G. (ed.), **From an Ancient to a Modern Theatre** (Winnipeg: University of Manitoba Press, 1972).

HILLESUM, E. **An Interrupted Life** (New York: Pantheon Books, 1981, 1984).

HIRSCHFELD, G. (ed.). **The Politics of Genocide: Jews and Soviet Prisoners of War in Nazi Germany** (London: Allen & Unwin, 1986).

HIRSCHMANN, I. **Lifeline to a Promised Land** (New York: The Vanguard Press, 1946).

HITLER, A. **Mein Kampf** (R. Manheim, transl.) (London: Hutchinson, 1972).

HOCHHUTH, R. **The Deputy** (New York: Grove Press, 1964).

HOEHNE, H. **The Order of the Death's Head** (New York: Ballantine, 1977).

HOESS, R. **Commandant of Auschwitz** (transl. from German) (London: Pan Books, 1975).

HOLM, A. **I Am David** (also published under the title **Passage North**) (L.W. Kingsland, transl.) (London: Methuen Children's Books, 1980).

HOLTZ, B.W. (ed.). **Back to the Sources: Reading the Classic Jewish Texts** (New York: Summit Books, 1984).

HOROWITZ, I.L. "Many Genocides, One Holocaust?" **Modern Judaism**, vol. 1, no. 1 (1981), pp. 74-89.

———————. **Taking Lives: Genocide and State Power** (New Brunswick: Transaction Books, 1980).

HOVANNISIAN, R. (ed.). **The American Genocide in Perspective** (New Brunswick: Transaction Books, 1986).

———————. **The Armenian Holocaust: A Bibliography Relating to the Deportations, Massacres, and Dispersion of the Armenian People 1915-1923** (Cambridge, Mass.: National Association for Armenian Studies and Research, 1978).

HUGHES, W. "The Evaluation of Film as Evidence," in SMITH, P. (ed.), **The Historian and Film** (Cambridge: Cambridge University Press, 1976).

HULL, D.S. **Film in the Third Reich: A Study of the German Cinema 1933-1945** (Berkeley: University of California Press, 1969).

HUNT, R.N. **Germany's Social Democracy 1918-1933** (New Haven: Yale University Press, 1964).

HUPPERT, S. "King of the Ghetto - Mordechai Haim Rumkowski, the Elder of the Lodz Ghetto," **Yad Vashem Studies** XV (1983), pp. 125-157.

INSDORF, A. **Indelible Shadows: Film and the Holocaust**, 2nd edn. (Cambridge: Cambridge University Press, 1989).

"Interdisciplinarity. A Report by the Group for Research and Innovation in Higher Education" (London: The Nuffield Foundation, July 1975).

International Encyclopedia of the Social Sciences (New York: Macmillan, 1971).

IRVIN, D. **Hitler's War** (London: Hodder & Stoughton, 1977).

ISAAC, J. **The Teaching of Contempt: Christian Roots of Anti-Semitism** (New York: Holt, Rinehart & Winston, 1962, 1964).

JACOT, M. **The Last Butterfly** (Toronto: McClelland & Stewart, 1973).

JAECKEL, E. **Hitler in History** (Hanover & London: University Press of New England for Brandeis University Press, 1984).

—————. **Hitler's Weltanschauung** (Tubingen: R. Wunderlich, 1969). (Eng. edn.: **Hitler's Weltanschauung: A Blueprint for Power** [H. Arnold, transl.] [Middletown, Conn.: Wesleyan University Press, 1972].)

JAHODA, M. & N.W. ACKERMAN. **Disturbios Emocionais e Anti-Semitismo** (Sao Paulo: Perspectiva, 1969).

Jewish Themes: Contemporary American Artists II (New York: Jewish Museum, 1986).

JICK, L.A. A Study of Betrayal (M.A., Hebrew Union College, 1954).

JOFFO, J. **A Bag of Marbles** (M. Sokolinsky, transl.) (Boston: Houghton Mifflin, 1974).

JORADO, F. **Dossie Herzog** (Sao Paulo: Global Ed., 1979).

"Kahan Commission Report," **Jerusalem Post** (9 November 1983).

KANTOR, A. **The Book of Alfred Kantor: An Artist's Journal of the Holocaust** (New York: Schocken, 1987).

KAPLAN, C. **The Scroll of Agony** (A. Kutsch & C. Kaplan eds.) (New York: Macmillan, 1965) (published in paperback under the title **The Warsaw Diary of Chaim Kaplan** [New York: Collier, 1981]).

KARMEL, I. **An Estate of Memory** (Boston: Houghton Mifflin, 1969).

KATER, M. "Everyday Anti-Semitism in Pre-War Nazi Germany: The Popular Basis," **Yad Vashem Studies** XVI (1984), pp. 129-159.

—————. **The Nazi Party** (Cambridge, Mass.: Harvard University Press, 1983).

KATZ, F. "Implementation of the Holocaust: The Behavior of Nazi Officials," **Comparative Studies in Society and History** 24 (1982), pp. 510-529.

KATZ, J. "Was the Holocaust Predictable?" **Commentary** (May 1975), pp. 41-48.

—————. **From Prejudice to Destruction: Antisemitism 1700-1933** (Cambridge, Mass.: Harvard University Press, 1980, 1983). (Hebrew edn.: **Mi-Sin'at Israel Le-Shlilat Ha-Geza** [Tel Aviv: Am Oved, 1979]).

—————. **Exclusiveness and Tolerance** (London: Oxford University Press, 1961).

KATZ, S. **Post-Holocaust Dialogues** (New York: New York University Press, 1983).

—————. "The Unique Intentionality of the Holocaust," **Modern Judaism**, vol. 1, no. 1 (1981), pp. 161-183.

KATZ, Y. **Goy Shel Shabbat** (The Sabbath Gentile) (Philadelphia: Jewish Publication Society, 1989).

—————. **Massoret U-Mashber** (Tradition and Crisis: Jewish Society at the End of the Middle Ages) (Jerusalem: Mosad Bialik, 1959).

KAUFMAN, E. "A Social, Educational, and Recreational Program in the Adjustment of Adult Newcomers," **Jewish Social Service Quarterly** (March 1950), pp. 404-409.

KAZIN, A. "The Heart of the World," in FLEISCHNER, E. (ed.), **Auschwitz: Beginning of a New Era?** (New York: Ktav Publishing House, 1974).

KENEALLY, T. **Schindler's Ark** (London: Hodder & Stoughton, 1981).

KERMISZ, J. **To Live with Honor and Die with Honor: Selected Documents from the Warsaw Ghetto Underground Archives 'O.S.' (Oneg Shabbat)** (Jerusalem: Yad Vashem, 1986).

————— & S. KRAKOWSKI. **Polish-Jewish Relations during the Second World War** (Jerusalem: Yad Vashem, 1974; New York: H. Fertig, 1976).

KERR, J. **A Small Person Far Away** (London: Collins, 1978).

—————. **When Hitler Stole Pink Rabbit** (London: Collins, 1974).

KERSHAW, I. **The Nazi Dictatorship: Problems and Perspectives of Interpretation** (London: Edward Arnold, 1985).

—————. **Popular Opinion and Political Dissent in the Third Reich** (Oxford: Clarendon Press, 1983).

—————. "The Persecution of the Jews and German Popular Opinion in the Third Reich," **Leo Baeck Institute Yearbook** XXVI (1981), pp. 261-289.

KESTENBERG, J. "Psychoanalytic Contributions to the Problem of Children of Survivors from Nazi Persecution," **Israel Annals of Psychiatry and Related Disciplines**, vol. 10, no. 4 (1972), pp. 311-325.

KETTENACKER, L. "Hitler's Final Solution and Its Rationalization," in HIRSCHFELD, G. (ed.), **The Policies of Genocide: Jews and Soviet Prisoners of War in Nazi Germany** (London: Allen & Unwin, 1986).

KINTNER, E.W. (ed.). **The Hadamar Trial**, in FYFE, D.W. (ed.), **War Crime Trials**, vol. 4 (London: W. Hodge, 1949).

KIRSCHMANN, D. & S. SAVIN. "Refugee Adjustment - Five Years Later," **Jewish Social Service Quarterly** (Winter 1953), pp. 197-201.

R.B. Kitaj (London: Marlborough Fine Art, 1985).

KLEIN, A.M. **Beyond the Sambation** (Toronto: University of Toronto Press, 1982).

——————. **The Second Scroll** (New York: A.A. Knopf, 1952).

KLEIN, C. **Anti-Judaism in Christian Theology** (Philadelphia: Fortress Press, 1979).

KLEIN, G. **All But My Life** (New York: Hill & Wang, 1971).

KLEINER, J. "The Attitudes of Martin Bucer and Langrave Philipp Toward the Jews of Hesse (1538-1539)," in LIBOWITZ, R. (ed.), **Faith and Freedom: A Tribute to Franklin H. Littell** (Oxford: Pergamon Press, 1987).

KLIGER, H. "Traditions of Grass-Roots Organization and Leadership: The Continuity of Landsmanshaften in New York," **American Jewish History**, vol. 76, no. 1 (September 1986), pp. 25-39.

KOEHL, R. **The Black Corps: The Structure and Power Struggles of the Nazi SS** (Madison: University of Wisconsin Press, 1983).

——————. **RKFDV: German Resettlement and Population Policy** (Cambridge, Mass.: Harvard University Press, 1957).

KOGON, E. **The Theory and Practice of Hell** (H. Norden, transl.) (New York: Berkley Publishing Corp., 1960).

KOHN, N. & H. ROITER. **A Voice From the Forest** (New York: Holocaust Library, 1980).

KORCZAK, J. **Ghetto Diary** (New York: Holocaust Library, 1978, 1981).

KORZEC, P. **Juifs en Pologne** (Paris: Presses de la Fondation National des Sciences Politiques, 1980).

KOSINSKI, J. **The Painted Bird** (London: Corgi, 1972).

KOVNER, A. "The Mission of the Survivor," in GUTMAN, Y. & L. ROTHKIRCHEN (eds.), **The Catastrophe of European Jewry: Antecedents, History, Reflections: Selected Papers** (Jerusalem: Yad Vashem, 1976).

——————. **My Little Sister** (S. Kaufman, transl.) (Oberlin: Oberlin College, 1986).

KRACAUER, S. **From Caligari to Hitler** (transl. from French) (Princeton: Princeton University Press, 1947).

KRAKOWSKI, S. **The War of the Doomed: Jewish Armed Resistance in Poland 1942-1944** (New York: Holmes & Meier, 1984). (Hebrew edn.: **Lehima Yehudit Be-Polin Neged Ha-Natzim** [Tel Aviv: Sifriat Poalim, 1977]).

KRAUSNICK, H. et al (eds.). **Anatomy of the SS State** (New York: Walker, 1968).

KRAUT, B. "Faith and the Holocaust," **Judaism** (Spring 1982), pp. 185-201.

KREISEL, H. **The Betrayal** (Toronto: McClelland & Stewart, 1979).

——————. **The Rich Man** (Toronto: McClelland & Stewart, 1961).

KREMERS, H. "The Contribution of the New Testament to a Christology within the Jewish-Christian Dialogue," in LIBOWITZ, R. (ed.), **Faith and Freedom: A Tribute to Franklin H. Littell** (Oxford: Pergamon Press, 1987).

KREN, G. & L. RAPPAPORT. **The Holocaust and the Crisis of Human Behavior** (New York: Homes & Meier, 1980).

KULKA, O.D. "'Public Opinion' in Nazi Germany and the 'Jewish Question'," **Jerusalem Quarterly** 25 (1982), pp. 121-144, 26 (1983), pp. 34-45.

——————. "Ha-hitahdut ha-artzit shel ha-yehudim be-germania 1938/39-1943" (The Reich Association of the Jews in Germany 1939/39-1943), in GUTMAN, Y. & C.J. HAFT (eds.), **Patterns of Jewish Leadership in Nazi Europe 1933-1945** (Jerusalem: Yad Vashem, 1979).

——————. **Ha-Megamot Be-Fitron Ha-Ba'aya Ha-Yehudit Ba-Reich Ha-Shlishi** (Diverse Trends in the Attempt to Solve the "Jewish Problem" in the Third Reich) (Jerusalem: The Hebrew University Collection of Sources, 1972).

—————— & P.R. MENDES-FLOHR (eds.). **Judaism and Christianity under the Impact of National Socialism 1919-1945** (Jerusalem: Historical Society of Israel, 1987).

KUPER, L. **The Prevention of Genocide** (New Haven: Yale University Press, 1985).

KVAM, R. "Among Two Hundred Survivors from Auschwitz" (O. Reinert, transl.), **Judaism** (Summer 1979), pp. 283-292.

LANG, D. & C. WALKER. **The Armenians**, Report No. 32, rev. edn. (London: Minority Rights Group, 1987).

VON LANG, J. & C. SIBYLL (eds.). **Eichmann Interrogated: Transcripts from the Archives of the Israeli Police** (R. Mannheim, transl.) (New York: Farrar, Straus & Giroux, 1983).

LANGER, L.L. **The Holocaust and the Literary Imagination** (New Haven: Yale University Press, 1977).

LANZMANN, C. **Shoah** (New York: Pantheon Books, 1985).

LAQUEUR, W. "Hitler's Holocaust: Who Knew What, When and How?" **Encounter** 55 (1980), pp. 6-25.

——————. **The Terrible Secret: Suppression of the Truth about Hitler's 'Final Solution'** (London: Weidenfeld & Nicholson, 1980).

——————. "Jewish Daniel and the Holocaust," **Commentary** (December 1979), pp. 44-55.

LAYTON, I. **Fortunate Exiles** (Toronto: McClelland & Stewart, 1987).

——————. "Waiting for the Messiah," **Canadian Literature** 101 (1984), pp. 7-14.

——————. **Taking Sides** (Oakville, Ont.: Mosaic Press, 1977).

LEISER, E. **Nazi Cinema** (New York: Collier Books, 1975).

LEON, J.R. et al. "Survivors of the Holocaust and their Children: Current Status and Adjustment," **Journal of Personality and Social Psychology** 41 (1981), pp. 468-478.

LEVI, P. **If This is a Man** (S. Woolf, transl.) (Harmondsworth: Penguin, 1979).

——————. **Survival in Auschwitz: The Nazi Assault on Humanity** (New York: Summit Books, 1987).

——————. **If Not Now, When?** (New York: Summit Books, 1985).

——————. **Moments of Reprieve** (New York: Summit Books, 1986).

LEVIN, D. **Fighting Back: Lithuanian Jewry's Armed Resistance to the Nazis 1941-1945** (New York: Holmes & Meier, 1985).

LEVIN, I.H. "Vineland - A Haven for Refugees," **The Jewish Poultry Farmers Association of South Jersey, Tenth Anniversary Journal** (1962).

LEVIN, N. **The Holocaust** (Melbourne, Fla.: Kreiger Publishing Co., 1990).

LEVINE, H.J. & B. MILLER. **The American Farmer in Changing Times** (New York: Jewish Agricultural Society, 1966).

LEVOY, M. **Alan and Naomi** (London: Bodley Head, 1979).

LEVY, R.S. **The Downfall of the Anti-Semitic Political Parties in Imperial Germany** (New Haven: Yale University Press, 1975).

LEWIS, J.R. (comp.). **Uncertain Judgment: A Bibliography of War Crime Trials** (Santa Barbara: ABC-Clio, 1979).

LEWIS, S. **Art Out of Agony: The Holocaust Theme in Literature, Sculpture and Film** (Toronto: CBC Enterprises, 1984).

LEWY, G. **The Catholic Church and Nazi Germany** (New York: McGraw-Hill, 1964).

LEYDA, J. **Films Beget Film** (New York: Hill & Wang, 1971).

LIBOWITZ, R. (ed.). **Faith and Freedom: A Tribute to Franklin H. Littell** (Oxford: Pergamon Press, 1987).

LIFTON, R.J. **The Nazi Doctors: Medical Killing and the Psychology of Genocide** (New York: Basic Books, 1986).

LINDZEY, G. & E. ARONSON (eds.). **The Handbook of Social Psychology** (London: Addison-Wesley, 1969).

LIONEL, R. **Le Nazisme et la Culture** (Nazism and Culture) (Brussels: Ed. Complexe, 1988).

LIPSTADT, D. **Beyond Belief: The American Press and the Coming of the Holocaust 1933-1945** (New York: Free Press, 1986).

LITTELL, F.H. **The Crucifixion of the Jews: The Failure of the Christians to Understand the Jewish Experience** (New York: Harper & Row, 1975).

LIVINGSTONE, M. **R.B. Kitaj** (New York: Rizzoli, 1985).

LOCKE, H. "Church Struggle and the Holocaust: Reflections of a By-Stander," in **The London Agreement**, in **History of the United Nations War Crimes Commission and the Development of the Laws of War** (London: Published for the United Nations War Crimes Commission, 1948), p. 457; also in DAVIDSON, E. **The Trials of the Germans** (New York: McMillan, 1966), pp. 9-10.

LOZOWICK, L. **William Gropper** (Philadelphia: Art Alliance, 1983).

LUBETKIN, Z. **In the Days of Destruction and Revolt** (S. Tubin, transl.; Yanui, Y., ed.) (Tel Aviv: Hakibbutz Hameuchad Publishing House and Ghetto Fighter's House in cooperation with Am Oved Publishers, 1981).

LUCHTERHAND, E.G. "Early and Late Effects of Imprisonment in Nazi Concentration Camps," **Social Psychology** 5 (1970), pp. 102-109.

LUKAS, R. **Forgotten Holocaust: The Poles under German Occupation 1939-1944** (Lexington: University of Kentucky Press, 1986).

LUSTIG, A. **A Prayer for Katerina Horovitzova** (New York: Avon, 1973).

MAGURSHAK, D. "The 'Incomprehensibility' of the Holocaust: Tightening Up Some Loose Usage," **Judaism** (Spring 1980), pp. 233-242.

MAIMONIDES. **Guide to the Perplexed**, 2 vols. (S. Pines, transl.) (Chicago: University of Chicago Press, 1975).

MALINO, F. & B. WASSERSTEIN (eds.). **The Jews in Modern France** (Hanover, NH: University Press of New England, 1985).

MANN, C.C. "Hitler: A Clue to History," **Judaism** (Winter 1988), pp. 9-21.

MANVELL, A.R. & H. FRAENKEL. **The Incomparable Crime** (London: Heinemann, 1967).
——————. **Heinrich Himmler** (London: Heinemann, 1965).

MARGALIOT, A. "The Reaction of German Jewry to the Nuremberg Laws," **Yad Vashem Studies** XII (1978), pp. 75-107.
——————. "The Reasons for the Late Emigration of German Jews," in GUTMAN, Y. & E. ZUROFF (eds.), **Rescue Attempts During the Holocaust** (Jerusalem: Yad Vashem, 1978).
——————. "The Dispute over the Leadership of German Jewry," **Yad Vashem Studies** X (1974), pp. 129-148.

—————————. "The Struggle for Survival of the Jewish Community in Germany in the Face of Oppression," in DRUKS, H. (ed.), **Jewish Resistance During the Holocaust** (Jerusalem: Yad Vashem, 1971).

—————————. "The Jews of Germany in the Last One Hundred Years Before the Destruction," **Molad** (April-May 1968), pp. 731-738.

MARK, B. **Uprising in the Warsaw Ghetto** (G. Freidlin, transl.) (New York: Schocken, 1976).

MARRUS, M. "The History of the Holocaust: A Survey of Recent Literature," **Journal of Modern History** 59 (1987), pp. 114-160.

—————————. **The Holocaust in History** (Hanover & London: University Press of New England, 1987).

—————————. **The Unwanted: European Refugees in the Twentieth Century** (Oxford: Oxford University Press, 1985).

—————————. "The Theory and Practice of Antisemitism," **Commentary**, vol. 74, no. 2 (1982), pp. 38-42.

—————————. **The Politics of Assimilation: The French Jewish Community at the Time of the Dreyfus Affair** (Oxford: Oxford University Press, 1980).

————————— & R.O. PAXTON. "The Nazis and the Jews in Occupied Western Europe," **Journal of Modern History** 54 (1982), pp. 687-714.

————————— & R.O. PAXTON. **Vichy France and the Jews** (New York: Schocken, 1983).

MARRUS, V. (transl.). **The Protocols of the Learned Elders of Zion: World Conquest Through World Government** (Chulmleigh: Britons, 1972).

MASER, W. **Nuremberg: A Nation on Trial** (R. Barry, transl.) (London: Allen Lane, 1979).

MASSING, P. **Rehearsal for Destruction** (New York: Harper, 1949; H. Fertig, 1967).

MAYBAUM, I. **The Face of God After Auschwitz** (Amsterdam: Polak & Van Gennep, 1965).

MEED, V. **On Both Sides of the Wall: Memoirs from the Warsaw Ghetto** (New York: Holocaust Library, 1979).

MELAMED, M.M. (transl.). **A Lei de Moises** (Rio de Janeiro: Grafica Americana, S.A., 1962).

MELTZER, M. **Never to Forget: The Jews of the Holocaust** (New York: Harper & Row, 1976).

MENDELSOHN, E. "Jewish Reactions to Antisemitism in East Central Europe," in REINHARZ, J. (ed.), **Living with Antisemitism: The Jewish Response in the Modern Period** (Hanover & London: University Press of New England, 1987).

——————. "Interwar Poland: Good for the Jews or Bad for the Jews?" in ABRAMSKY, C., M. JACHIMCZYK & A. POLONSKY (eds.), **The Jews in Poland** (Oxford: Basil Blackwell, 1986).

——————. **The Jews of East Central Europe Between the World Wars** (Bloomington: Indiana University Press, 1983).

——————. "Ha-hanhaga ha-yehudit be-mizrah europea ba-tkufa she-bein shtei milhamot ha-olam" (Jewish Leadership in Eastern Europe Between the Two World Wars), in GUTMAN, Y. & C. HAFT (eds.), **Patterns of Jewish Leadership in Nazi Europe 1933-1945** (Jerusalem: Yad Vashem, 1979).

MENDES-FLOHR, P. & J. REINHARZ (eds.), **The Jew in the Modern World: A Documentary History** (New York: Oxford University Press, 1980).

MERKL, P. **Political Violence under the Swastika** (Princeton: Princeton University Press, 1975).

METZ, J. **The Emergent Church** (New York: Crossroad, 1981).

MICHAELIS, M. **Mussolini and the Jews: German-Italian Relations and the Jewish Question 1922-1945** (New York: Oxford University Press, 1978).

MICHEL, H. **Les Fascismes** (Fascisms) (Paris: PUF, 1977).

——————. "Jewish Resistance and the European Resistance Movement," **Yad Vashem Studies** VII (1968), pp. 7-16.

MICHMAN, D. **Bi-Mei Shoah u-Fkuda** (In Days of Holocaust and Reckoning) (Tel Aviv: Everyman's University, 1987).

——————. **El Holocausto, Un Estudio Historico** (Tel Aviv: Universidad Abierta de Israel, 1987).

MILGRAM, S. **Obedience to Authority: An Experimental View** (New York: Harper & Row, 1975).

MILLER, B.E. **Teaching the Art of Literature** (Urbana, Ill.: National Council of Teachers of English, 1980).

MILLER, J. "Erasing the Past: Europe's Amnesia about the Holocaust," **New York Times Magazine** (16 November 1986).

MILZA, P. **Le Fascisme** (Paris: MA Ed., 1986).

—————— & S. BERNSTEIN. **Le Fascisme Italien 1919-1945** (Paris: Seuil, 1980).

MINTZ, A. **Hurban: Responses to Catastrophe in Hebrew Literature** (New York: Columbia University Press, 1984).

MOCZANSKI, K. "Conversations with a Hangman," **Midstream** (November 1980), pp. 31-41.

MODRAS, R. "Jews and Poles: A Relationship Reconsidered," **America** 146 (January 2-9, 1982), pp. 5-8.

MOLTMANN, J. **The Crucified God** (R.A. Wilson & J. Bowden, transl.) (London: SCM Press, 1976).

MOMMSEN, H. "The Realization of the Unthinkable: The 'Final Solution of the Jewish Question' in the Third Reich," in HIRSCHFELD, G. (ed.), **The Policies of Genocide: Jews and Soviet Prisoners of War in Nazi Germany** (London: Allen & Unwin, 1986).

MORLEY, J.F. **Vatican Diplomacy and the Jews During the Holocaust 1939-1943** (New York: Ktav Publishing House, 1980).

MORROW, L. "The History-Devouring Machine," **Horizon** (July 1978), pp. 18-23.

MORSE, A. **While Six Million Died: A Chronicle of American Apathy** (New York: Random House, 1968).

The Moscow Declaration (1943), in **History of the United Nations War Crimes Commission and the Development of the Laws of War** (London: Published for the United Nations War Crimes Commission 1948), p. 583; also in DAVIDSON, E. **The Trials of the Germans** (New York: Macmillan, 1966), p. 5.

MOSKIN, M. **I am Rosemarie** (New York: Day, 1972).

MOSKOVITZ, S. **Love Despite Hate** (New York: Schocken Books, 1983).

MOSSE, G.L. **German Jews Beyond Judaism** (Bloomington: Indiana University Press, 1980; Cincinnati: Hebrew Union College Press, 1985).

——————. **Towards the Final Solution: A History of European Racism** (London: J.M. Dent, 1978).

——————. **Nazism - An Historical and Comparative Analysis of National Socialism** (Oxford: Basil Blackwell, 1979).

——————. **The Nationalization of the Masses** (New York: H. Fertig, 1975).

——————. "European History: The Seedbed of the Holocaust," **Midstream** (May 1973), pp. 3-25.

——————. **Germans and Jews: The Right and the Left in the Search for a "Third Force" in Pre-Nazi Germany** (New York: Howard Fertig, 1970).

——————. **The Crisis of German Ideology: Intellectual Origins of the Third Reich** (New York: Grosset & Dunlap, 1964).

——————. **Nazi Culture: Intellectual, Cultural and Social Life in the Third Reich** (New York: Schocken, 1981).

MUELLER-HILL, B. **Murderous Science: Elimination by Scientific Selection of Jews, Gypsies, and Others: Germany 1933-1945** (Oxford: Oxford University Press, 1988).

MURPHEY, J. & R. GROSS. **Learning by Television** (New York: The Fund for the Advancement of Education, 1966).

Music: Nous ne sommes pas les derniers (Paris: Galerie de France, 1970/71).

Music: L'oeuvre graphique (Paris: Centre Georges Pompidou, 1988).

Music: Opere 1946-1985 (Milan: Electa, 1985).

NAGY-TALAVERA, N. The Green Shirts and Others (Stanford: Hoover Institution Press, 1970).

Nazi Conspiracy and Aggression [Red Series], 8 vols. & 2 suppl. (Washington: Government Printing Office, 1946-48).

NELSON, F.B. "The Holocaust and the Oikumene: An Episode for Rememberance,: in LIBOWITZ, R. (ed.), Faith and Freedom: A Tribute to Franklin H. Littell (Oxford: Pergamon Press, 1987).

NEUMAN, S. (ed.). Henry Kreisel: Another Country (Edmonton: Newest Press, 1985).

NEUSNER, J. "Wanted: A New Myth," Moment Magazine (March 1980).

——————. Stranger at Home (Chicago: University of Chicago Press, 1981).

NICHOLLS, A.J. Weimar and the Rise of Hitler (London: Macmillan, 1968).

NIEWYK, D.L. The Jews in Weimar Germany (Baton Rouge: Louisiana University Press, 1980).

——————. Socialist, Anti-Semite and Jew (Baton Rouge: Louisiana University Press, 1971).

NILSEN, A. & K. DONELSON. Literature for Today's Young Adults (Glenview, Ill.: Scott, Foresman, 1985).

NOAKES, J. The Nazi Party in Lower Saxony 1921-1933 (Oxford: Oxford University Press, 1972).

NOLTE, E. Three Faces of Fascism: Action Francaise, Italian Fascism, National Socialism (New York: New American Library, 1970).

NOVITCH, M. Sobibor: Martyrdom and Revolt: Documents and Testimonies (New York: Holocaust Library, 1980).

——————. Resistenza Spirituale 1940-1945 (Milan: Commune of Milan, 1979).

——————, L. DAWIDOWICZ & T.L. FREUDENHEIM. Spiritual Resistance: Art from the Concentration Camps 1940-1945 (Philadelphia: Jewish Publication Society of America, 1982).

NSDAP's Twenty-Five Point Programme of 1920 in ARAD, Y., Y. GUTMAN & A. MARGALIOT (eds.), Documents on the Holocaust (Jerusalem: Yad Vashem, 1981; also New York: Pergamon Press), pp. 15-18.

NYISZLI, M. Auschwitz: A Doctor's Eyewitness Account (London: Mayflower, 1973).

OBERMAN, S. & E. NEWTON (eds.). Mirror of the People: Canadian Jewish Experience in Poetry and Prose (Winnipeg: Jewish Educational Publishers of Canada, 1985).

OREN, N. "The Bulgarian Exception: A Reassessment of the Salvation of the Jewish Community," Yad Vashem Studies VII (1968), pp. 83-106.

OSTOW, M. (ed.). **Judaism and Psychoanalysis** (New York: Ktav Publishing House, 1982). "An Overall Plan for Anti-Jewish Legislation in the 3rd Reich," **Yad Vashem Studies** XI (1976), Appendix: Draft Law, pp. 42-55.

PALDIEL, M. "Sparks of Light," in LIBOWITZ, R. (ed.), **Faith and Freedom: A Tribute to Franklin H. Littell** (Oxford: Pergamon Press, 1987).

PARIS, E. **Jews: An Account of Their Experience in Canada** (Toronto: MacMillan of Canada, 1980).

PARKES, J. **Antisemitism** (Chicago: Quadrangle Books, 1969).

PAWELZYNSKA, A. **Values and Violence in Auschwitz: A Sociological Analysis** (C.S. Leach, transl.) (Los Angeles: University of California Press, 1979).

PAWLIKOWSKI, J. **Christ in the Light of the Christian-Jewish Dialogue** (New York: Paulist Press, 1982).

PECK, A.J. (ed.). **Jews and Christians After the Holocaust** (Philadelphia: Fortress, 1982).

PENKOWER, M. **The Jews were Expendable: Free World Diplomacy and the Holocaust** (Urbana: University of Illinois Press, 1983).

PETITFILS, J.-Ch. **Le Droite en France (De 1789 a Nos Jours)** (Paris: PUF, 1973).

PETUCHOWSKI, J.J. (ed.). **When Jews and Christians Meet** (Albany: State University of New York Press, 1988).

PEUKERT, D. **Inside Nazi Germany: Conformity, Opposition, and Racism in Everyday Life** (R. Deveson, transl.) (New Haven: Yale University Press, 1987).

PHILLIPS, B. **Swastika, Cinema of Oppression** (New York: Warner Books, 1976).

PHILLIPS, R. (ed.). **The Belsen Trial**, in **War Crimes Trials**, vol. 2, FYFE, D.M. (ed.) (London: W. Hodge, 1949).

PINGEL, F. "Resistance and Resignation in Nazi Concentration Camps," in HIRSCHFELD, G. (ed.), **The Policies of Genocide: Jews and Soviet Prisoners of War in Nazi Germany** (London: Allen & Unwin, 1986).

PINSKY, J. **Origens do Nacionalismo Judaico** (Sao Paulo: Hucitec, 1978).

POLIAKOV, L. **The History of Antisemitism**, 3 vols. (Oxford: Oxford University Press, 1985).

——————————. **O Mito Ariano**, trans. from French **Le Mythe Aryen** (Sao Paulo: Perspectiva, Edusp., 1974).

——————————. **Harvest of Hate: The Nazi Program for the Destruction of the Jews of Europe**, rev. edn. (New York: Holocaust Library, 1959).

POPPEL, S. **Zionism in Germany 1897-1933** (Philadelphia: Jewish Publication Society, 1977).

PORTELA, A. **Salazarismo e Artes Plasticas em Portugal** (Lisbon: Instituto de Cultura Portuguesa, 1982).

PORTNOY, D.S. "The Adolescent Immigrant," **Jewish Social Service Quarterly** (December 1948), pp. 268-273.

PRESSER, J. **The Destruction of the Dutch Jews** (New York: E.P. Dutton, 1969).

PULZER, P. "Why Was There a Jewish Question in Imperial Germany?" **Leo Baeck Institute Yearbook** 25 (1980), pp. 133-146.

——————. **The Rise of Political Antisemitism in Germany and Austria 1870-1914** (New York: J. Wiley, 1964).

RABINOWITZ, D. **New Lives: Survivors of the Holocaust Living in America** (New York: Avon, 1976).

Raphael Mandelzweig (Buenos Aires: Comite de Homenaje a R. Mandelzweig, 1950).

RAGINS, S. **Jewish Responses to German Anti-Semitism 1870-1914** (Cincinnati: Hebrew Union College Press, 1980).

RAVITCH, N. "The Problems of Christian Anti-Semitism," **Commentary**, vol. 73, no. 4 (1982), pp. 41-52.

REINHARZ, J. (ed.). **Living with Antisemitism: The Jewish Response in the Modern Period** (Hanover & London: University Press of New England, 1987).

——————. **Fatherland or Promised Land? The Dilemma of the German Jews 1893-1914** (Ann Arbor: University of Michigan Press, 1975).

REISS, J. **The Upstairs Room** (Harmondsworth: Penguin, 1979).

REITLINGER, G. **The Final Solution: The Attempt to Exterminate the Jews of Europe 1939-1945**, 2nd rev. and augmented edn. (New York: Thomas Yoseloff, 1968).

——————. **S.S.: Alibi of the Nation 1922-1945** (New York: Viking, 1968).

RHODES, A. **The Vatican in the Age of the Dictators 1922-1945** (London: Hodder & Stoughton, 1973).

RHUE, M. **The Wave** (New York: Delacorte Press, 1981).

RICH, N. **Hitler's War Aims**, 2 vols. (New York: Norton, 1973/74).

RICHLER, M. **Joshua Then and Now** (London: Macmillan, 1980).

——————. **The Street** (Harmondsworth: Penguin, 1977).

——————. **Shovelling Trouble** (London: Quartet Books, 1973).

——————. **St. Urbain's Horseman** (London: Panther, 1973).

——————. "This Year in Jerusalem: An Israeli Journal, March 31, 1962," in **Hunting Tigers Under Glass** (Toronto: McClelland & Stewart, 1968).

RICHTER, H.P. **Friedrich** (London: Heinemann Educational, 1978).

RICHTER, L. "Notes on Newsreels," Appendix 2 (25 April 1945), in SHORT, K.R.M. & S. DOLEZEL (eds.), **American Newsreels and the Collapase of Nazi Germany** (London: Croom Helm, 1988), p. 23.

RINGELBLUM, E. **Notes from the Warsaw Ghetto** (Slan, J. ed.) (New York: McGraw-Hill, 1958; Schocken pb., 1974).

ROBINSON, J. "The Holocaust," in GUTMAN, Y. & L. ROTHKIRCHEN (eds.), **The Catastrophe of European Jewry: Antecedents, History, Reflections: Selected Papers** (Jerusalem: Yad Vashem, 1976).

——————. **And the Crooked Shall Be Made Straight** (Philadelphia: Jewish Publication Society, 1965).

ROSENBAUM, I.J. **The Holocaust and Halakhah** (New York: Ktav Publishing House, 1976).

ROSENFELD, A. **A Double Dying: Reflections on Holocaust Literature** (Bloomington & London: Indiana University Press, 1980).

—————— & I. GREENBERG (eds.). **Confronting the Holocaust: The Impact of Elie Wiesel** (Bloomington & London: Indiana University Press, 1978).

ROSENKRANZ, H. "Yahadut ostria bein hagira kefuya le-vein geirush" (Austrian Jewry Between Forced Emigration and Deportation), in GUTMAN, Y. & C. HAFT (eds.), **Patterns of Jewish Leadership in Nazi Europe 1933-1945** (Jerusalem: Yad Vashem, 1979).

ROSKIES, D.G. (ed.). **The Literature of Destruction: Jewish Responses to Catastrophe** (Philadelphia: Jewish Publication Society, 1989).

——————. **Against the Apocalypse: Responses to Catastrophe in Modern Jewish Culture** (Cambridge, Mass. & London: Harvard University Press, 1984).

ROTH, C. **Histoire du Peuple Juif** (Paris: Stock, 1980).

ROTH, J.K. **A Consuming Fire: Encounters with Elie Wiesel and the Holocaust** (Atlanta: John Knox Press, 1979).

ROTHBERG, A. "The Animal Trainer," in NADEL, M. (ed.), **Portraits of the American Jew** (Woodbury, N.Y.: Barron's Educational Series, 1977).

RUBENSTEIN, R. **The Cunning of History: Mass Death and the American Future** (New York: Harper & Row, 1975).

——————. **After Auschwitz: Radical Theology and Contemporary Judaism** (Indianapolis: Bobbs-Merrill, 1966).

—————— & J. ROTH. **Approaches to Auschwitz: The Holocaust and Its Legacy** (Atlanta: John Knox Press, 1987).

RUBIN, W. (ed.). **Pablo Picasso: A Retrospective** (New York: Museum of Modern Art, 1980).

RUDMAN, M.K. **Children's Literature: An Issues Approach** (New York: D.C. Heath, 1976).

RUECKERL, A. **The Investigation of Nazi Crimes** (Heidelberg & Karlsruhe: C.F. Muller, 1979).

RUETER-EHLERMANN, A. & C.F. RUETER (eds.). **Justiz und NS-verbrechen; sammlung deutscher strafurteile wegen nationalsozialistischer toetungs-verbrechen** (22 vols.) (Amsterdam: Amsterdam University Press, 1968-1981).

RUETHER, R.R. **To Change the World** (New York: Crossroads, 1983).

—————. "Anti-Semitism and Christian Theology," in FLEISCHNER, E. (ed.), **Auschwitz: Beginning of a New Era?** (New York: Ktav Publishing House, 1974).

—————. **Faith and Fratricide: The Theological Roots of Antisemitism** (New York: Seabury, 1974).

RUPPIN, A. **Jews in the Modern World** (New York: Arno Press, 1973).

RUSSAK, M. "Helping the New Immigrant Achieve His Own Beginning in the U.S.," **Journal of Jewish Communal Service** (December 1949), pp. 239-254.

RYAN, M. "Religious Affirmation After Auschwitz," in LIBOWITZ, R. (ed.), **Faith and Freedom: A Tribute to Franklin H. Littell** (Oxford: Pergamon Press, 1987).

————— (ed.). **Human Responses to the Holocaust** (New York: Edwin Mellen Press, 1981).

SACHER, H.M. **The Course of Modern Jewish History** (New York: Dell, 1977).

SACHS, M. **A Pocket Full of Seeds** (London: Macdonald, 1978).

SAMUEL, M. "Prejudice and the Chosen People," **The Recontructionist** (6 April 1962), pp. 9-14.

SAMUELS, G. **Mottele** (London: Harper & Row, 1977).

SARTRE, J.-P. **Anti-Semite and Jew** (G. Becker, transl.) (New York: Schocken, 1968).

SCHAFF, A. **Language et Connaissance** (Paris: Anthropos, 1974).

SCHEFFLER, W. "The Forgotten Part of the 'Final Solution': The Liquidation of the Ghettos," **Simon Wiesenthal Center Annual** 2 (1985), pp. 31-51.

SCHLEUNES, K. **The Twisted Road to Auschwitz** (Urbana: University of Chicago Press, 1970).

SCHOCHET, S. **Feldafing** (Vancouver: November House, 1983).

SCHOENBERNER, G. **Yellow Star: The Persecution of the Jews in Europe 1933-1945** (S. Sweet, transl.) (London: Corgi, 1969).

SCHOLEM, G. **The Messianic Idea in Judaism and Other Essays on Jewish Spirituality** (New York: Schocken, 1971).

—————. "Jews and Germans," in DANNHAUSER, W.J. (ed.), **Jews and Judaism in Crisis** (New York: Schocken Books, 1978).

SCHORSCH, I. **Jewish Reactions to German Anti-Semitism 1870-1914** (New York & London: Columbia University Press, 1972).

——————. "German Antisemitism in the Light of Post-War Historiography," **Leo Baeck Institute Yearbook** XIX (1974), pp. 257-271.

SCHWARTZ, L. **Great Ages and Ideas of the Jewish People** (New York: Modern Library, 1956).

——————. **The Redeemers** (New York: Farrar, Straus, 1953).

—————— (ed.). **The Root and the Bough** (New York: Rinehart & Co., 1949).

SCHWARZ-BART, A. **The Last of the Just** (S. Becker, transl.) (New York: Bantam, 1977).

SCHWEITZER, A. **Big Business in the Third Reich** (Bloomington: Indiana University Press, 1965).

SEGAL, L. **In Other People's Houses** (New York: New American Library, 1973).

SELZER, M. **Deliverance Day: The Last Hours at Dachau** (London: Sphere, 1980).

—————— & F. MIALE. **The Nuremberg Mind** (New York: Quadrangle New York Times Books, 1975).

SEMPRUN, J. **The Long Voyage** (Paris: Gallimard, 1963).

SENESH, H. **Hannah Senesh: Her Life and Diary** (New York: Schocken, 1972).

SERENY, G. **Into That Darkness: From Mercy Killing to Mass Murder** (London: Andre Deutsch, 1974).

SETON-WATSON, H. "Government Policies Towards the Jews in Pre-Communist Eastern Europe," **Soviet Jewish Affairs** (December 1969), pp. 20-25.

SHEEHY, G. **Spirit of Survival** (New York: Morrow & Co., 1986).

SHERMAN, A.J. **Island Refuge: Britain and Refugees from the Third Reich 1933-1939** (London: P. Elek, 1973).

SHERWIN, B. & S. AMENT (eds.). **Encountering the Holocaust: An Interdisciplinary Survey** (Chicago: Impact Press, 1979).

SHIRER, W.L. **The Rise and Fall of the Third Reich** (London: Secker & Warburg, 1960).

SHORT, K.R.M. (ed.). **Feature Films as History** (Knoxville: University of Tennessee Press, 1981).

—————— (ed.). **Film and Radio Propaganda in World War II** (Knoxville: University of Tennessee Press, 1981).

—————— & S. DOLEZEL (eds.). **Hitler's Fall: The Newsreel Witness** (London: Croom Helm, 1988).

SIJES, B.A. "Several Observations Concerning the Position of the Jews in Occupied Holland during World War II," in GUTMAN, Y. & E. ZUROFF (eds.), **Rescue Attempts during the Holocaust** (Jerusalem: Yad Vashem, 1977).

SINGER, I.B. **Un Amigo de Kafka** (Porto Alegre: L & PM Ed., 1987).

——————. **A Crown of Feathers and Other Stories** (New York: Penguin Books, 1980).

SLOMAN, A. "Notes on the 'Cognitive Studies' Programme in the School of Social Science, University of Sussex," quoted in **Interdisciplinarity: A Report by the Group for Research and Innovation in Higher Education** (London: The Nuffield Foundation, July 1975).

SMITH, B.F. **Reaching Judgment at Nuremberg** (London: Andre Deutsch, 1977).

SMITH, P. **The Historian and Film** (Cambridge: Cambridge University Press, 1976).

SNELL, J.L. (ed.). **The Nazi Revolution: Hitler's Dictatorship and the German Nation** (New York: D.C. Heath, 1974).

SNYDER, C.W. "The Selling of Adolf Hitler," **Central European History** XII (1979).

SNYDER, L. **The Weimar Republic** (Princeton, NJ: D. Van Nostrand, 1966).

SORLIN, P. **L'Antisemitisme Allemand** (Paris: Flammarion, 1969).

SPEER, A. **Infiltration** (New York: Macmillan, 1981).

——————. **Inside the Third Reich** (R. & C. Winston, transl.) (New York: Macmillan, 1970).

——————. **Spandau: The Secret Diaries** (transl. from German, R. & C. Winston) (New York: Macmillan, 1976).

SPIEGEL, I. "A Ghetto Dog," in BELLOW, S. (ed.), **Great Jewish Short Stories** (New York: Dell Publishing Co., 1963).

SPIEGEL, S. **The Last Trial** (J. Goldin, transl.) (New York: Schocken, 1969).

——————. "Perur me'agadot ha'akedah," (Fragment of Tales of the Sacrifice) in **The Abraham Weiss Jubilee Volume** (New York: Shulsinger Brothers, 1964).

SPIEGELMAN, A. **Maus: A Survivor's Tale** (Harmondsworth: Penguin, 1986).

VON STADEN, W. **Darkness Over the Valley** (M.C. Peters, transl.) (New Haven: Ticknor & Fields, 1981).

STADTLER, B. **The Holocaust: A History of Courage and Resistance** (New York: Behrman House, 1974).

The Statutory Criminal Law of Germany with Comments (Library of Congress, Washington, D.C., 1947).

STEINBERG, M.W. & U. CAPLAN (eds.). **A.M. Klein: Beyond the Sambation: Selected Essays and Editorials 1928-1955** (Toronto: University of Toronto Press, 1982).

STEINER, G. **In Bluebeard's Castle** (New Haven: Yale University Press, 1971).

STEMBER, C. et al (eds.). **Jews in the Mind of America** (New York: Basic Books, 1966).

STERN, F. **Dreams and Delusions: The Drama of German History** (New York: A.A. Knopf, 1987).

STOEHR, M. "Anti-Semitism as an Ideology," in LIBOWITZ, R. (ed.), **Faith and Freedom: A Tribute to Franklin H. Littell** (Oxford: Pergamon Press, 1987).

STOKES, L. "The German People and the Destruction of the European Jews," **Central European History** 6 (1973), pp. 167-191.

STONE, I.W. **Underground to Palestine** (New York: Boni & Gaer, 1946).

STRAUSS, H.A. "Jewish Emigration from Germany: Nazi Policies and Jewish Response," **Leo Baeck Institute Yearbook** 25 (1980), pp. 313-363; 26 (1981), pp. 343-409.

STROM, M. & W. PARSONS. **Facing History and Ourselves: Holocaust and Human Behavior** (Watertown: International Educations, 1982).

STYRON, W. **Sophie's Choice** (London: Jonathan Cape, 1979).

SUHL, Y. (ed.). **They Fought Back: The Story of Jewish Resistance in Nazi Europe** (New York: Schocken, 1976).

—————. **Uncle Misha's Partisans** (London: Hamish Hamilton, 1975).

SWIDLER, L. "Can One Gain Salvation Only Through Yeshua the Christ?" in LIBOWITZ, R. (ed.), **Faith and Freedom: A Tribute to Franklin H. Littell** (Oxford: Pergamon Press, 1987).

SYRKIN, M. **Blessed is the Match** (Philadelphia: Jewish Publication Society, 1947).

SZONYI, D.M. **The Holocaust: An Annotated Bibliography and Resource Guide** (New York: Ktav Publishing House, 1985).

TAL, U. "On the Study of the Holocaust and Genocide," **Yad Vashem Studies** XIII (1982), pp. 7-52.

—————. **Christians and Jews in Germany: Religion, Politics and Ideology in the Second Reich 1870-1914** (Ithaca: Cornell University Press, 1975).

TALMON, J. "Mission and Testimony: The Universal Significance of Modern Anti-Semitism," in GUTMAN, Y. & L. ROTHKIRCHEN (eds.), **The Catastrophe of European Jewry: Antecedents, History, Reflections: Selected Papers** (Jerusalem: Yad Vashem, 1976).

—————. "European History as the Seedbed of the Holocaust," **Midstream** XIX (May 1973), pp. 3-25.

TAMIR, V. **Bulgaria and Her Jews** (New York: Sepher-Hermon Press, 1979).

TAMMAROFF, T. **Dapim Min ha-Dleka** (Pages from the Fire) (Tel Aviv: Kibbutz Hameuchad, 1947).

TASLITZKY, B. **111 dessins faits a Buchenwald 1944-1945** (Paris: Bibliotheque Francaise, 1945).

TAYLOR, R. **Film Propaganda: Soviet Russia and Nazi Germany** (London: Croom Helm, 1979).

TAYLOR, T. **Final Report to the Secretary of the Army on the Nuremberg War Crimes Trials under Control Council Law 10** (Washington: U.S. Government Printing Office, 1949).

TEC, N. **When Light Pierced the Darkness: Christian Rescue of Jews in Nazi-Occupied Poland** (New York: Oxford University Press, 1986).

——————. **Dry Tears** (New York: Oxford University Press, 1984).

THOMAS, D.M. **The White Hotel** (London: Gollancz, 1981).

THOMPSON, V.A. **A Mission in Art: Recent Holocaust Works in America** (Ann Arbor: UMI, 1983).

TIMERMAN, J. **The Longest War: Israel in Lebanon** (New York: Vintage Books, 1982).

TOLAND, J. **Adolf Hitler** (New York: Ballantine Books, 1978).

TOURY, J. "Defence Activities of the Osterreichisch - Israelitische Union before 1914," in REINHARZ, J. (ed.), **Living with Antisemitism: The Jewish Response in the Modern Period** (Hanover & London: University Press of New England, 1987).

——————. "From Forced Emigration to Expulsion - The Jewish Exodus over the Non-Slavic Borders of the Reich as a Prelude to the 'Final Solution'," **Yad Vashem Studies** XVII (1986), pp. 51-91.

——————. "Irgunim yehudiyim ve-hanhagoteihem be-artzot ha-emantzipatziya" (Jewish Organizations and Their Leadership in the Countries of the Emancipation) **Yalkut Moreshet** 4 (1965), pp. 118-129.

TRACHTENBERG, J. **The Devil and the Jews: The Medieval Conception of the Jews and Its Relation to Modern Antisemitism** (New York: Harper & Row, 1966).

TRACY, D. **The Analogical Imagination** (New York: Crossroad, 1981).

TRAININ, I. **In My People's Service, Vol. 3: Communal Diary** (New York: Commission on Synagogue Relations, 1981).

Trial of the Major War Criminals Before the International Military Tribunal: Official Text [Blue Series], 42 vols. (Nuremberg, 1947/49).

Trial of War Criminals Before the Nuremberg Military Tribunals under Control Council Law No. 10 [Green Series], 15 vols. (Washington, 1949/53).

TRUNK, I. "Note: Why was There No Armed Resistance Against the Nazis in the Lodz Ghetto?" **Jewish Social Studies** 43 (1981), pp. 329-334.

——————. **Jewish Responses to Nazi Persecution** (New York: Stein & Day, 1979, 1980, 1982).

——————. "The Typology of the Judenraete in Nazi Europe," in GUTMAN, Y. & C.J. HAFT (eds.), **Patterns of Jewish Leadership in Nazi Europe 1933-1945** (Jerusalem: Yad Vashem, 1979).

——————. "The Attitude of the Judenrats to the Problems of Armed Resistance Against the Nazis," in GUTMAN, Y. & L. ROTHKIRCHEN (eds.), **The Catastrophe of European Jewry: Antecedents, History, Reflections: Selected Papers** (Jerusalem: Yad Vashem, 1976).

——————. Judenrat: The Jewish Councils in Eastern Europe under Nazi Occupation (New York: Stein & Day, 1977).

TUCCI, C.M.L. O Anti-Semitismo na era de Vargas 1930-1945 (Sao Paulo: Ed. Brasiliense, 1988).

TUSHNET, L. Pavement of Hell (New York: St. Martin's Press, 1972).

TUTOROW, N.E. (comp.). War Crimes, War Criminals and War Crimes Trials: An Annotated Bibliography and Source Book (New York, Westport & London: Greenwood Press, 1986).

Ueberleben und Widerstehen: Zeichnungen von Haeftlingen des Konzentrationslagers Auschwitz 1940-1946 (Cologne: Pahl-Rugenstein, 1980).

UNESCO. Vida e Valores do Povo Judeu (1969) (Sao Paulo: Perspectiva, 1972).

VAGO, B. "Some Aspects of the Yishuv Leadership Activities during the Holocaust," in BRAHAM, R. (ed.), Jewish Leadership during the Nazi Era (New York: Social Science Monographs, and Institute for Holocaust Studies of the City University of New York, 1985).

——————— & G.L. MOSSE. Jews and Non-Jews in Eastern Europe 1918-1945 (New York: Transaction Books, 1974).

VALENTIN, H. "Rescue and Relief Activities on Behalf of Jewish Victims of Nazism in Scandinavia," YIVO Annual of Jewish Social Science VIII (1953), pp. 224-251.

VATICAN COUNCIL II. Nostra Aetate, 28 October 1965, in AUSTIN FLEMING, O.P. (ed.), Vatican Council II, The Conciliar and Post-Conciliar Documents (Wilmington, Del.: Scholarly Resources), pp. 738-742; also in WIGODER, J. Jewish-Christian Relations Since the Second World War (Manchester: Manchester University Press, 1988), Appendix, p. 143.

VOLKOV, S. "Antisemitism as a Cultural Code - Reflections on the History and Historiography of Antisemitism in Imperial Germany," Leo Baeck Institute Yearbook XXIII (1978), pp. 25-46.

——————. The Rise of Popular Anti-Modernism in Germany (Princeton: Princeton University Press, 1978).

VRBA, R. & A. BESTIC. I Cannot Forgive (London: Sidgwick & Jackson, 1963).

WADDINGTON, M. (ed.). The Collected Poems of A.M. Klein (Toronto: McGraw-Hill Ryerson, 1974).

WALK, J. "Ha-hanhaga ha-datit bi-tkufat ha-shoa" (Religious Leadership during the Holocaust Period), in GUTMAN, Y. & C. HAFT (eds.), Patterns of Jewish Leadership in Nazi Europe 1933-1945 (Jerusalem: Yad Vashem, 1979).

WALLIMANN, B. & M. DOBKOWSKI (eds.). Genocide and the Modern Age: Etiology and Case Studies in Mass Death (New York: Greenwood Press, 1987).

WASSERSTEIN, B. **Britain and the Jews of Europe 1939-1945** (Oxford: Oxford University Press, 1988).

WEINBERG, M. **Because They Were Jews: A History of Antisemitism** (New York: Greenwood Press, 1986).

WEINFELD, M., W. SHAFFIR & I. COTTLER (eds.).**The Canadian Jewish Mosaic** (Toronto: J. Wiley, 1981).

WEINSTEIN, F. **The Dynamics of Nazism: Leadership, Ideology, and the Holocaust** (New York: Academic Press, 1980).

WEISBORD, M. **The Strangest Dream: Canadian Communists, the Spy Trials and the Cold War** (Toronto: L. & D. Dennys, 1983).

WEISMAN, A. **Crackpot** (Toronto: McClelland & Stewart, 1982).

——————. **The Sacrifice** (Toronto: McClelland & Stewart, 1972).

WEISS, A. "Ha-mahloket ba-historiografia al dmutam shel ha-yudenratim ve-tafkideihem" (The Historiographical Controversy on the Jewish Councils and Their Role), in GUTMAN, Y. & G. GREIFF (eds.), **Ha-Shoa ba-Historiografia** (The Historiography of the Holocaust Period) (Jerusalem: Yad Vashem, 1987).

——————. "Categories of Camps - Their Character and Role in the Execution of the 'Final Solution of the Jewish Question'," in GUTMAN, Y. & A. SAF (eds.), **The Nazi Concentration Camps** (Jerusalem: Yad Vashem, 1984).

——————. "Beirurim bi-sheilat ma'amada ve-emdoteha shel ha-hanhaga ha-yehudit be-polin ha-kevusha" (Some Considerations Concerning the Status and Policies of the Jewish Leadership in Occupied Poland) **Kovetz Yad Vashem** XII (1978), pp. 243-266.

——————. "Le-ha'arakhatam shel ha-yudenratim" (Evaluating the Judenraete), **Yalkut Moreshet** 11 (1969), pp. 108-111.

WEISS, P. **The Investigation** (A. Gross, transl.) (London: John Calder, 1966).

WELCH, D. **Propaganda and the German Cinema 1933-1945** (London: Oxford University Press, 1983).

WELLS, L.W. **The Death Brigade** (New York: Holocaust Library, 1978) (first edition entitled **The Janowska Road** [New York: Macmillan, 1963]).

WELTSCH, R. "The Yellow Badge, Wear It With Pride," transl. from **Juedische Rundschau** (4 April 1933).

WERBLOWSKY, Z. "Judaism," in BLEEKER, C. & G. WIDENGREN (eds.), **Historia Religionum**, vol. II (Leiden: E.J. Brill, 1971).

WERFEL, F. **Forty Days of Musa Dagh** (New York: Viking, 1934).

WERNER, A. "The New Refugees," **Jewish Frontier** (July 1946), pp. 21-23.

Widerstand statt anpassung (Berlin: Elefauten, 1980).

WHITE, A.M. (ed.). **Interdisciplinary Teaching** (San Francisco, Washington & London: Jossey-Bass, 1981).

WIESEL, E. "And Rabbi Ishmael Did Not Weep," in LIBOWITZ, R. (ed.), **Faith and Freedom: A Tribute to Franklin H. Littell** (Oxford: Pergamon Press, 1987).

——————. **Dawn** (F. Frenaye, transl.) (Toronto: Bantam Books, 1982).

——————. "Why I Write," in ROSENFELD, A. & I. GREENBERG (eds.), **Confronting the Holocaust: The Impact of Eli Wiesel** (Bloomington & London: Indiana University Press, 1978).

——————. **Messengers of God** (New York: Summit Books, 1976).

——————. **Night** (S. Rodway, transl.) (New York: Avon, 1970).

——————. **The Gates of the Forest** (New York: Avon, 1966).

WIESENTHAL, S. **The Sunflower** (New York: Schocken, 1978).

WILHELM, H.-H. "The Holocaust in National-Socialist Rhetoric and Writings: Some evidence against the thesis that before 1945 nothing was known about the 'Final Solution'," **Yad Vashem Studies** XVI (1984), pp. 95-127.

WINCKLER, L. **A Funcao Social da Linguagem Fascista** (Lisbon: Estampa, 1969).

WINTER, R. (ed.). **The Historian as Detective: Essays on Evidence** (New York: Harper & Row, 1970).

WIRTH, A. (ed.). **The Stroop Report: "The Warsaw Ghetto is No More"** (London: Secker & Warburg, 1980).

WISTRICH, R. **Hitler's Apocalypse: Jews and the Nazi Legacy** (London: Weidenfeld & Nicolson, 1985).

——————. "The Anti-Zionist Masquerade," **Midstream** (August/September 1983), pp. 8-18.

WYMAN, D. **The Abandonment of the Jews: America and the Holocaust 1941-1945** (New York: Pantheon, 1984).

——————. "The American Jewish Leadership and the Holocaust," in BRAHAM, R. (ed.), **Jewish Leadership during the Nazi Era** (New York: Social Science Monographs, 1985).

——————. **Paper Walls: America and the Refugee Crisis 1938-1941** (Amherst: University of Massachusetts Press, 1968).

YAHIL, L. "The Jewish Leadership of France," in GUTMAN, Y. & C. HAFT (eds.), **Patterns of Jewish Leadership in Nazi Europe 1933-1945** (Jerusalem: Yad Vashem, 1979).

——————. "The Holocaust in Jewish Historiography," in GUTMAN, Y. & L. ROTHKIRCHEN (eds.), **The Catastrophe of European Jewry: Antecedents, History, Reflections: Selected Papers** (Jerusalem: Yad Vashem, 1976).

————————. "Methods of Persecution: A Comparison of the 'Final Solution' in Holland and Denmark," **Scripta Hierosolymitana** 23 (1972), pp. 279-300.

————————. "Jewish Resistance - An Examination of Active and Passive Forms of Jewish Survival in the Holocaust Period," in DRUKS, H. (ed.), **Jewish Resistance during the Holocaust** (Jerusalem: Yad Vashem, 1971).

————————. **The Rescue of Danish Jewry** (Philadelphia: Jewish Publication Society of America, 1969).

YERUSHALMI, Y.H. **Zakhor: Jewish History and Jewish Memory** (Seattle: University of Washington Press, 1982).

ZERNER, S. "Men of Faith: 'Hearing the Music'," in LIBOWITZ, R. (ed.), **Faith and Freedom: A Tribute to Franklin H. Littell** (Oxford: Pergamon Press, 1987).

ZIMMERMAN, M. "From Radicalism to Antisemitism," in ALMOG, S. (ed.), **Antisemitism Through the Ages** (Oxford: Pergamon Press, 1988).

ZUCCOTTI, S. **The Italians and the Holocaust: Persecution, Rescue, Survival** (New York: Basic Books, 1987).

Zwischen widerstand und anpassung, Kunst in Deutschland 1933-1945 (Berlin: Akademia der Kuenste, 1978).

ABOUT THE EDITOR

DR. GIDEON SHIMONI is on the faculty of the Institute of Contemporary Jewry of The Hebrew University, Jerusalem, and is incumbent of the Argov Chair in Israel-Diaspora Relations. He has been Director of the Continuing Workshop on Contemporary Jewish Civilization of the International Center for University Teaching of Jewish Civilization since its inception in 1981.

Dr. Shimoni has written various studies in English and Hebrew on the history of Zionism and on Jewish communities in the Western world. He is the author of *Jews and Zionism: The South African Experience* (Oxford: Oxford University Press, 1980), and the editor of *Contemporary Jewish Civilization, Selected Syllabi* (New York: Markus Wiener, 1985).